I0834868

SPEECHES, ADDRESSES,

AND

OCCASIONAL SERMONS,

BY

THEODORE PARKER,
MINISTER OF THE TWENTY-EIGHTH CONGREGATIONAL CHURCH IN BOSTON.

IN THREE VOLUMES.
VOL. II.

BOSTON:
HORACE B. FULLER,
(SUCCESSOR TO WALKER, FULLER, AND COMPANY,)
245, WASHINGTON STREET.
1867.

CONTENTS OF VOLUME II.

A SERMON OF THE SPIRITUAL CONDITION OF BOSTON.—PREACHED AT THE MELODEON, ON SUNDAY, FEBRUARY 18, 1849.

MATTHEW VIII. 20.

By their fruits ye shall know them.

LAST Sunday I said something of the moral condition of Boston; to-day I ask your attention to a Sermon of the Spiritual Condition of Boston. I use the word spiritual in its narrower sense, and speak of the condition of this town in respect to piety. A little while since, in a sermon of piety, I tried to show that love of God lay at the foundation of all manly excellence, and was the condition of all noble, manly development; that love of truth, love of justice, love of love, were respectively the condition of intellectual, moral, and affectional development, and that they were also respectively the intellectual, moral, and affectional forms of piety; that the love of God as the Infinite Father, the totality of truth, justice, and love was the general condition of the total development of man's spiritual powers. But I showed, that sometimes this piety, intellectual, moral, affectional or total, did not arrive at self-consciousness; the man only unconsciously loving the Infinite in one or all these modes, and in such cases the man was a loser by frustrating his piety, and allowing it to stop in the truncated form of unconsciousness.

Now what is in you will appear out of you; if piety be there in any of these forms, in either mode, it will come out; if not there, its fruits cannot appear. You may reason forward or backward: if you know piety exists, you may foretell its appearance; if you find fruits thereof, you may reason back and be sure of its existence. Piety is love of God as God, and as we only love what we are like, and in that degree, so it is also a likeness to God. Now it is a general doctrine in Christendom that divinity must manifest itself; and, in assuming the highest form of manifestation known to us, divinity becomes humanity. However, that doctrine is commonly taught in the specific and not generic form, and is enforced by an historical and concrete example, but not by way of a universal thesis. It appears thus: The Christ was God; as such He must manifest himself; the form of manifestation was that of a complete and perfect man. I reject the concrete example, but accept the universal doctrine on which the special dogma of the Trinity is erected. From that I deduce this as a general rule: If you follow the law of your nature, and are simple and true to that, as much of godhead as there is in you, so much of manhood will come out of you, and, as much of manhood comes out of you, so much of godhead was there within you; as much subjective divinity, so much objective humanity.

Such being the case, the demands you can make on a man for manliness must depend for their answer on the amount of piety on deposit in his character; so it becomes important to know the condition of this town in respect of piety, for if this be not right in the above sense, nothing else is right; or, to speak more clerically, "Unless the Lord keep the city, the watchman waketh but in vain," and unless piety be developed or a-developing in men, it is vain for the minister to sit up late of a Saturday night to concoct his sermon, and to rise up early of a Sunday morning to preach the same; he fights but as one that beateth the air, and spends his strength for that which is nought. They are in the right, therefore, who first of all things demand piety: so let us see what signs or proof we have, and of what amount of piety in Boston.

To determine this, we must have some test by which to judge of the quality, distinguishing piety from impiety, and some standard whereby to measure the quantity thereof; for though you may know what piety is in you, I what is in me, and God what is in both and in all the rest of us, it is plain that we can only judge of the existence of piety in other men, and measure its quantity by an outward manifestation thereof, in some form which shall serve at once as a trial test and a standard measure.

Now, then, as I mentioned in that former sermon, it is on various sides alleged that there are two outward manifestations of piety, a good deal unlike: each is claimed by some men as the exclusive trial test and standard measure. Let me say a word of each.

I. Some contend for what I call the conventional standard; that is, the manifestation of piety by means of certain prescribed forms. Of these forms there are three modes or degrees: namely, first, the form of bodily attendance on public worship; second, the belief in certain doctrines, not barely because they are proven true, or known without proof, but because they are taught with authority; and third, a passive acquiescence in certain forms and ceremonies, or an active performance thereof.

II. The other I call the natural standard; that is, the manifestation of piety in the natural form of morality in its various degrees and modes of action.

It is plain, that the amount of piety in a man or a town, will appear very different when tested by one or the other of these standards. It may be that very little water runs through the wooden trough which feeds the saw-mill at Niagara, and yet a good deal, blue and bounding, may leap over the rock, adown its natural channel. In a matter of this importance, when taking account of a stock so precious as piety, it is but fair to try it by both standards.

Let us begin with the conventional standard, and examine piety by its manifestation in the ecclesiastical forms. Here is a difficulty at the outset, in determining upon the measure, for there is no one and general ecclesiastical standard, common to all parties of Christians, from the Catholic to the Quaker; each measures by its own standard, but denies the correctness of all the others. It is as if a foot were declared the unit of long measure, and then the actual foot of the chief justice of a State, were taken as the rule by which to correct all measurements; then the foot would vary as you went from North Carolina to South, and, in any one State, would vary with the health of the judge. However, to do what can be done with a measure thus uncertain, it is plain, that, estimated by any ecclesiastical standard, the amount of piety is small. There is, as men often say, "A general decline of piety;" that is a common complaint, recorded and registered. But what makes the matter worse to the ecclesiastical philosopher, and more appalling to the complainers, is this: it is a decline of long standing. The disease which is thus lamented is said to be acute, but is proved to be chronic also; only it would seem, from the lamentations of some modern Jeremiahs, that the decline went on with accelerated velocity, and, the more chronic the disease was, the acuter it also became.

Tried by this standard, things seem discouraging. To get a clearer view, let us look a little beyond our own borders, at first, and then come nearer home. The Catholic church complains of a general defection. The majority of the Christian church confesses that the Protestant Reformation was not a revival of religion, not a " Great awakening," but a great falling to sleep; the faith of Luther and Calvin was a great decline of religion — a decline of piety in the ecclesiastical form; that modern philosophy, the physics of Galileo and Newton, the metaphysics of Descartes and of Kant, mark another decline of religion — a decline of piety in the philosophical form; that all the modern democracy of the eighteenth and nineteenth centuries, marks a yet further decline of religion — a decline of piety in the political form; that all the modern secular societies, for removing the evils of men and their sins, mark a yet fourth decline of religion — a decline of piety in the philanthropic form. Certainly, when measured by the mediæval standard of Catholicism, these mark four great declensions of piety, for, in all four, the old principle of subordination to an external and personal authority is set aside.

All over Europe this decline is still going on; ecclesiastical establishments are breaking down; other establishments are a-building up. Pius the Ninth seems likely to fulfil his own prophecy, and be the last of the Popes; I mean the last with temporal power. There is a great schism in the north of Europe; the Germans will be Catholics, but no longer Roman. The old forms of piety, such as service in Latin, the withholding of the Bible from the people, compulsory confession, the ungrateful celibacy of a reluctant priesthood—all these are protested against. It is of no avail that the holy coat of Jesus, at Treves, works greater miracles than the apostolical napkins and aprons; of no avail that the Virgin Mary appeared on the nineteenth of September, 1846, to two shepherd-children, at La Salette, in France. What are such things to Ronge and Wessenberg? Neither the miraculous coat, nor the miraculous mother, avails aught against this untoward generation, charm they never so wisely. The decline of piety goes on. By the new Constitution of France, all forms of religion are equal; the Catholic and the Protestant, the Mahometan and the Jew, are equally sheltered under the broad shield of the law. Even Spain, the fortress walled and moated about, whither the spirit of the middle ages retired and shut herself up long since, womanning her walls with unmanly priests and kings, with unfeminine queens and nuns—even Spain fails with the general failure. British capitalists buy up her convents and nunneries, to turn them into woollen mills. Monks and nuns forget their beads in some new handicraft; sister Mary, who sat still in the house, is now also busy with serving, careful, indeed, about more things than formerly, but not cumbered nor troubled as before. Meditative Rachels, and Hannahs, long unblest, who sat in solitude, have now become like practical Dorcas, making garments for the poor; the Bank is become more important than the Inquisition. The order of St. Francis d'Assisi, of St. Benedict, even of St. Dominic himself, is giving way before the new order of Arkwright, Watt, and Fulton, — the order of the spinning jenny and the power-loom. It is no longer books on the miraculous conception, or meditations on the five wounds of the Saviour, or commentaries on the song of songs which is Solomon's, that get printed there: but fiery novels of Eugene Sue, and George Sand; and so extremes meet.

Protestant establishments share the same peril. A new sect of Protestants rises up in Germany, who dissent as much from the letter and spirit of Protestantism, as the Protestants from Catholicism; men that will not believe the infallibility of the Bible, the doctrine of the Trinity, the depravity of man, the eternity of future punishment, nor justification by faith — a justification before God, for mere belief before men. The new spirit gets possession of new men, who cannot be written down, nor even howled down. Excommunication or abuse does no good on such men as Bauer, Strauss, and Schwegler; and it answers none of their questions. It seems pretty clear, that in all the north of Germany, within twenty years, there will be entire freedom of worship, for all sects, Protestant and Catholic.

In England, Protestantism has done its work less faithfully than in Germany. The Protestant spirit of England came here two hundred years ago, so that new and Protestant England is on the west of the ocean; in England, an established church lies there still, an iceberg in the national garden. But even there, the decline of the ecclesiastical form of piety is apparent: the new bishops must not sit in the House of Lords, till the old ones die out, for the number of lords spiritual must not increase, though the temporal may; the new attempt, at Oxford and elsewhere, to restore the Middle Ages, will not prosper. Bring back all the old rites and forms into Leeds and Manchester; teach men the theology of Thomas Aquinas, or of St. Bernard; bid them adore the uplifted wafer, as the very God, men who toil all day with iron mills, who ride in steam-drawn coaches, and talk by lightning in a whisper, from the Irk to the Thames,—they will not consent to the philosophy or the theology of the Middle Ages, nor be satisfied with the old forms of piety, which, though too elevated for their fathers in the time of Elizabeth, are yet too low for them, at least too antiquated. Dissenters have got into the House of Commons;

the test-act is repealed, and a man can be a captain in the army, or a postmaster in a village, without first taking the Lord's Supper, after the fashion of the Church of England. Some men demand the abandonment of tithes, the entire separation of Church and State, the return to "The voluntary principle" in religion. "The battering ram which levelled old Sarum," and other boroughs as corrupt, now beats on the church, and the "Church is in danger." Men complain of the decline of piety in England. An intelligent and very serious writer, not long ago, lamenting this decline, in proof thereof, relates, that formerly men began their last wills, "In the name of God, Amen;" and headed bills of lading with, "Shipped in good order, by the grace of God;" that indictments for capital crimes charged the culprit with committing felony, "At the instigation of the devil," and now, he complains, these forms have gone out of use.

In America, in New England, in Boston, when measured by that standard, the same decline of piety is apparent. It is often said that our material condition is better than our moral; that in advance of our spiritual condition. There is a common clerical complaint of a certain thinness in the churches; men do not give their bodily attendance, as once they did; they are ready enough to attend lectures, two or three in a week, no matter how scientific and abstract, or how little connected with their daily work, yet they cannot come to the church without teasing beforehand, nor keep awake while there. It is said the minister is not respected as formerly. True, a man of power is respected, heard, sought, and followed, but it is for his power, for his words of grace and truth, not for his place in a pulpit; he may have more influence as a man, but less as a clergyman. Ministers lament a prevalent disbelief of their venerable doctrines; that there is a concealed skepticism in regard to them, often not concealed. This, also, is a well-founded complaint; the well-known dogmas of theology were never in worse repute; there was never so large a portion of the community in New England who were doubtful of the Trinity, of eternal damnation, of total depravity, of the atonement, of the Godhead of Jesus, of the miracles of the New Testament, and of the truth of every word of the Bible. A complaint is made, that the rites and forms which are sometimes called "the ordinances of religion," are neglected; that few men join the church, and though the old hedge is broken down before the altar, yet the number of communicants diminishes, and it is no longer able-headed men, the leaders of society, who come; that the ordinances seem haggard and ghastly to young men, who cannot feed their hungry souls on such a thin pittance of spiritual aliment as these afford; that the children are not baptized. These things are so; so in Europe, Catholic and Protestant; so in America, so in Boston. Notwithstanding the well-founded complaint that our modern churches are too costly for the times, we do not build temples which bear so high a proportion to our wealth as the early churches of Boston; the attendance at meeting does not increase as the population; the ministers are not prominent, as in the days of Wilson, of Cotton, and of Norton; their education is not now in the same proportion to the general culture of the times. Harvard College, dedicated to "Christ and the Church," designed at first chiefly for the education of the clergy, graduates few ministers; theological literature no longer overawes all other. The number of church members was never so small in proportion to the voters as now; the number of Protestant births never so much exceeded the number of Protestant baptisms. Young men of superior ability and superior education have little affection for the ministry; take little interest in the welfare of the church. Nay, youths descended from a wealthy family seldom look that way. It is poor men's sons, men of obscure family, who fill the pulpits; often, likewise, men of slender ability, eked out with an education proportionately scant. The most active members of the churches are similar in position, ability, and culture. These are undeniable facts. They are not peculiar to New England. You find them wherever the voluntary principle is resorted to. In England, in Catholic countries. you find the old historic names in the Established Church; there is no lack of aristocratic blood in clerical veins; but there and everywhere the church seems falling astern of all other craft which can keep the sea.

Since these things are so, men who have only the conventional standard wherewith to measure the amount of piety, only that test to prove its existence by, think we are rapidly going to decay; that the tabernacle is fallen down, and no man rises to set it up. They complain that Zion is in distress; theological newspapers lament that there are no revivals to report; that "The Lord has withheld His arm," and does not "pour out His Spirit upon the churches." Ghastly meetings are held by men with sincere and noble heart, but saddened face; speeches are made which seem a groan of linked wailings long drawn out. Men mourn at the infidelity of the times, at the coldness of some, at the deadness of others. All the sects complain of this, yet each loves to attribute the deadness of the rival sects to their special theology; it is Unitarianism which is choking the Unitarians, say their foes, and the Unitarians know how to retort after the same fashion. The less enlightened put the blame of this misfortune on the good God who has somehow "withheld His hand," or omitted to "pour out His Spirit,"—the people perishing for want of the open vision. Others put the blame on mankind; some on "poor human nature," which is not what might have been expected, not perceiving that if the fault be there it is not for us to remedy, and if God made man a bramble-bush, that no wailing will make him bear figs. Yet others refer this condition to the use made of human nature, which certainly is a more philosophical way of looking at the matter.

Now there is one sect which has done great service in former days, which is, I think, still doing something to enlighten and liberalize the land, and, I trust, will yet do more, more even than it consciously intends. The name of Unitarian is deservedly dear to many of us, who yet will not be shackled by any denominational fetters. This sect has always been remarkable for a certain gentlemanly reserve about all that pertained to the inward part of religion; other faults it might have, but it did not incur the reproach of excessive enthusiasm, or a spirituality too sublimated and transcendental for daily use. This sect has long been a speckled bird among the denominations, each of which has pecked at her, or at least cawed with most unmelodious croak against this new-fledged sect. It was said the Unitarians had "denied the Lord that bought them;" that theirs was the church of unbelief — not the church of Christ, but of No-Christ; that they had a Bible of their own, and a thin, poor Bible, too; that their ways were ways of destruction; "Touch not, taste not, handle not," was to be written on their doctrines; that they had not even the grace of lukewarmness, but were moral and stone-cold; that they looked fair on the side turned towards man, but on the Godward side it was a blank wall with no gate, nor window, nor loop-hole, nor eyelet for the Holy Ghost to come through; that their prayers were only a show of devotion to cover up the hard rock of the flinty heart, or the frozen ground of morality. Their faith, it was said, was only a conviction after the case was proven by unimpeachable evidence, and good for nothing; while belief without evidence, or against proof, seems to be the right ecclesiastical talisman.

For a long time the Unitarian sect did not grumble unduly, but set itself to promote the cultivation of reason and apply that to religion; to cultivate morality and apply it to life; and to demand the most entire personal freedom for all men in all matters pertaining to religion. Hence came its merits; they were very great merits, too, and not at all the merits of the times, held in common with the other sects. I need not dwell on this, and the good works of Unitarianism, in this the most Unitarian city in the world; but as a general thing the Unitarians, it seems to me, did neglect the culture of piety; and of course their morality, while it lasted, would be unsatisfactory, and in time would wither and dry up because it had no deepness of earth to grow out of. The Unitarians, as a general thing, began outside, and sought to work inward, proceeding from the special to the general, by what might be called the inductive mode of religious culture; that was the form adopted in pulpits, and in families so far as there was any religious education attempted in private. That is not the method of nature, where all growth is the development of a living germ, which by an inward power appropriates the outward things it needs, and grows thereby. Hence came the defects of Unitarianism, and they were certainly very great defects; but they came almost unavoidably from the circumstances of the times. The sensational philosophy was the only philosophy that prevailed; the Orthodox sects had always rejected a part of that philosophy, not in the name of science, but of piety, and they supplied its place not with a better philosophy, but with tradition, speaking with an authority which claimed to be above human nature. It was not in the name of reason that they rejected a false philosophy, but in the name of religion often denounced all philosophy and the reason which demanded it. The Unitarians rejected that portion of Orthodoxy, became more consistent sensationalists, and arrived at results which we know. Now it is easy to see their error; not difficult to avoid it; but forty or fifty years ago it was almost impossible not to fall into this mistake. Sometimes it seems as if the Unitarians were half conscious of this defect, and so dared not be original, but borrowed Orthodox weapons, or continued to use Trinitarian phrases long after they had blunted those weapons of their point, and emptied the phrases of their former sense. In the controversy between the Orthodox and Unitarians, neither party was wholly right: the Unitarians had reason to charge the Orthodox with debasing man's nature, and representing God as not only unworthy, but unjust, and somewhat odious; the Trinitarians were mainly right in charging us with want of conscious piety, with beginning to work at the wrong end; but at the same time it must be remembered, that, in proportion to their numbers, the Unitarians have furnished far more philanthropists and reformers than any of the other sects. It is time to confess this on both sides.

For a long time the Unitarian sect did not complain much of the decline of piety; it did not care to have an organization, loving personal freedom too well for that, and it had not much denominational feeling; indeed, its members were kept together, not so much by an agreement and unity of opinion among themselves, as by a unity of opposition from without; it was not the hooks on their shields that held the legion together with even front, but the pressure of hostile shields crowded upon them from all sides. They did not believe in spasmodic action; if a body was dead, they gave it burial, without trying to galvanize it into momentary life, not worth the spark it cost; they knew that a small cloud may make a good many flashes in the dark, but that many lightnings cannot make light. They stood apart from the violent efforts of other churches to get converts. The converts they got commonly adhered to their faith, and in this respect differed a good deal from those whom "Revivals" brought into other churches; with whom Christianity sprung up in a night, and in a night also perished. Some years ago, when this city was visited and ravaged by Revivals, the Unitarians kept within doors, gave warning of the danger, and suffered less harm and loss from that tornado than any of the sects. Unitarianism seems, in this city, to have done its original work; so the company is breaking up by degrees, and the men are going off, to engage in other business, to weed other old fields, or to break up new land, each man following his own sense of duty, and for himself determining whether to go or stay. But at the same time, an attempt is made to keep the company together; to cultivate a denominational feeling; to put hooks and staples on the shields which no longer offer that formidable and even front; to teach all trumpets to give the same sectarian bray, all voices to utter the same war-cry. The attempt does not succeed; the ranks are disordered, the trumpets give an uncertain sound, and the soldiers do not prepare themselves for denominational battle; nay, it often happens that the camp lacks the two sinews of war — both money, and men. Hence the denominational view of religious affairs has undergone a change; I make no doubt a real and sincere change, though I know this has been denied, and the change thought only official. The men I refer to are sincere and devout men; some of them quite above the suspicion of mere official conduct. This sect is now the loudest in its wailing; these Christian Jeremiahs tell us that we do not realize spiritual things, that we are all dead men, that there is no health in us. These cold Unitarian Thomases crowd unwontedly together in public to bewail the spiritual weather, the dearth of piety in Boston, the "General decline of religion" in New England. Church unto church raises the Macedonian cry, "Come over and help us!" The opinion seems general that piety is in a poor way, and must have watchers, the strongest medicine, and nursing quite unusual, or it will soon be all over, and Unitarianism will give up the ghost. Various causes have I heard assigned for the malady; some think that there has been over-much preaching of philosophy, though perhaps there is not evidence to convict any one man in particular of the offence; that philosophy is the dog in the manger, who keeps the hungry Unitarian flock from their spiritual hay, and cut-straw, which are yet of not the smallest use to him. But look never so sharp, and you do not find this dangerous beast in the neighborhood of the fold. Others think that there has been also an excess of moral preaching, against the prevalent sins of the nation, I suppose — but few individuals seem liable to conviction on that charge. Yet others think this decline comes from the fact that the terrors have not been duly and sufficiently administered from the pulpit; that while Catholics and Methodists thrive under such influences, the Unitarian widows are neglected in the weekly ministration of terror and of threat; that there has not been so much an excess of lightning in the form of philosophy or morality, but only a lack of thunder.

This temporary movement among the Unitarians of Boston is natural; in some respects it is what our fathers would have called "judicial." The Unitarians have been cold, have looked more at the outward manifestations of goodness than at the inward spirit of piety which was to make the manifestations; they have not had an excess of philosophy, or of morality, but a defect of piety. They have been more respectable than pious. They have not always quite rightly appreciated the enthusiasm of sterner and more austere sects; not always done justice to the inwardness of religion those sects sought to promote. When their churches get a little thin, and their denominational affairs a little disturbed, it is quite natural these Unitarians should look after the cause and pass over to lamentations at the present state of things; while looking at the community from the new point of view, it is quite natural that they should suppose piety on the decline, and religion dying out. Yes, in general it is plain that, if men have no eyes but conventional eyes, no spirit but that of the ecclesiastical order they serve in, and of the denomination they belong to, it is natural for them to think that because piety does not flow in the old ecclesiastical channel, it does not flow anywhere, and there is none at all to run. Thus it is easy to explain the complaint of the Catholics at the great defection of the most enlightened nations of Europe; the lamentation of the Protestants at the heresy of the most enlightened portion of their sect; and the Unitarian wail over the general decline of piety in the city of Boston. Some men can only judge the present age by the conventional standard of the past, and as the old form of piety does not appear, they must conclude there is no piety.

Let us now recur to the other or natural standard, and look at the manifestation of piety in the form of morality. Last Sunday I spoke of our moral condition; and it appeared that morals were in a low state here when compared with the ideal morals of Christianity. Now as the outward deed is but the manifestation of the inward life, and objective humanity the index of subjective divinity, so the low state of morals proves a low state of piety; if the heart of this town was right towards God, then would its hand also be right towards man. I am one of those who for long years have lamented the want of vital piety in this people. We not only do not realize spiritual things, but we do not make them our ideals. I see proofs of this want of piety in the low morals of trade, of the public press; in poverty, intemperance, and crime; in the vices and social wrongs touched on the last Sunday. I judge the tree by its fruit. But it is not on this ground that the ecclesiastical complaint is based. Men who make so much ado about the absence of piety, do not appeal for proof thereof to the great vices and prominent sins of the times; they see no sign of that in our trade and our politics; in the misery that festers in putrid lanes, one day to breed a pestilence, which it were even cheaper to hinder now, than cure at a later time; nobody mentions as proof the Mexican War, the political dishonesty of officers, the rapacity of office-seekers, the servility of men who will tamely suffer the most sacred rights of three millions of men to be trodden into the dust. Matters which concern millions of men came up before your Congress; the great Senator of Massachusetts loitered away the time of the session here in Boston, managing a lawsuit for a few thousand dollars, and no fault was publicly found with such neglect of public duty; but men see no lack of piety indicated by this fact, and others like it; they find signs of that lack in empty pews, in a deserted communion-table, in the fact that children, though brought up to reverence truth and justice, to love man and to love God, are not baptized with water; or in the fact that Unitarianism or Trinitarianism is on the decline! How many wailings have we all heard or read, because the Puritan churches of Boston have not kept the faith of their grim founders; what lamentations at the rising up of a sect which refuses the doctrine of the Trinity, or at the appearance of a few men who, neglecting the common props of Christianity, rest it, for its basis, on the nature of man and the nature of God: though almost all the eminent philanthropy of the day is connected with these men, yet they are still called "Infidel," and reviled on all hands!

The state of things mentioned in the last sermon does indicate a want of piety, a deep and a great want. I do not see signs of that in the debt and decay of churches, in absence from meetings, in doubt of theological dogmas, in neglect of forms and ceremonies which once were of great value; but I do see it in the low morals of trade, of the press; in the popular vices. On a national scale I see it in the depravity of political parties, in the wicked war we have just fought, in the slavery we still tolerate and support. Yes, as I look on the churches of this city, I see a want of piety in the midst of us. If eminent piety were in them, and allowed to follow its natural bent, it would come out of them in the form of eminent humanity; they would lead in the philanthropies of this day, where they hardly follow. In this condition of the churches I see a most signal proof of the low estate of piety; they do not manifest a love of truth, which is the piety of the intellect; nor a love of justice, which is the piety of the moral sense; nor a love of love, which is the piety of the affections; nor a love of God as the Infinite Father of all men, which is the total piety of the whole soul. For lack of this internal divinity there is a lack of external humanity. Who can bring a clean thing out of an unclean? This is what I complain of, what I mourn over.

The clergymen of this city are most of them sincere men, I doubt not; some of them men of a superior culture; many of them laborious men; most, perhaps all of them, deeply interested in the welfare of the churches, and the promotion of piety. But how many of them are marked and known for their philanthropy, distinguished for their zeal in putting down any of the major sins of our day, zealous in any work of reform? I fear I can count them all on the fingers of a single hand; yet there are enough to bewail the departure of monastic forms, and of the theology which led men in the dimness of a darker age, but cannot shine in the rising light of this. I find no fault with these men; I blame them not; it is their profession which so blinds their eyes. They are as wise and as valiant as the churches let them be. What sect in all this land ever cared about temperance, education, peace betwixt nations, or even the freedom of all men in our own, so much as this sect cares for the baptizing of children with water, and that for the baptizing of men; this for the doctrine of the Trinity, and all for the infallibility of the Bible? Do you ask the sects to engage in the work of extirpating concrete wrong? It is in vain; each reformer tries it — the mild sects answer, "I pray thee have me excused;" the sterner sects reply with awful speech. A distinguished theological journal of another city thinks the philanthropies of this day are hostile to piety, and declares that true spiritual Christianity never prevails where men think slavery is a sin. A distinguished minister of a highly respectable sect declares the temperance societies unchristian, and even atheistical. He reasons thus: The church is an instrument appointed by God and Christ, to overcome all forms of wrong, intemperance among the rest; to neglect this instrument and devise another, a temperance society, to wit, is to abandon the institutions of God and Christ, and so it is unchristian and atheistical. In other words, here is intemperance, a stone of stumbling, and a rock of offence, in our way; there is an old wooden beetle, which has done great service of old time, and is said to have been made by God's own hand; men smite therewith the stone or smite it not; still it lies there a stone of stumbling and a stone of shame; other men approach, and with a sledge-hammer of well-tempered steel smite the rock, and break off piece after piece, smoothing the rough impracticable way; they call on men to come to their aid, with such weapons as they will. But our minister bids them beware; the beetle is "of the Lord," the iron which breaks the rock in pieces is an unchristian and atheistical instrument. Yet was this minister an earnest, a pious, and a self-denying man, who sincerely sought the good of men. He had been taught to know no piety but in the church's form. I would not do dishonor to the churches; they have done great service, they still do much; I would only ask them to be worthy of their Christian name. They educate men a little, and allow them to approach emancipation, but never to be free and go alone.

I see much to complain of in the condition of piety; yet nothing to be alarmed at. When I look back, it seems worse still, far worse. There has not been "A decline of piety" in Boston of late years. Religion is not sick. Last Sunday, I spoke of the great progress made in morality within fifty years; I said it was an immense progress within two hundred years. Now, there cannot be such a progress in the outward manifestation without a corresponding and previous development of the inward principle. Morality cannot grow without piety more than an oak without water, earth, sun, and air. Let me go back one hundred years; see what a difference between the religious aspect of things then and now! certainly there has been a great growth in spirituality since that day. I am not to judge men's hearts; I may take their outward lives as the test and measure of their inward piety. Will you say the outward life never completely comes up to that? It does so as completely now as then. Compare the toleration of these times with those; compare the intelligence of the community; the temperance, sobriety, chastity, virtue in general. Look at what is now done in a municipal way by towns and States for mankind; see the better provision made for the poor, for the deaf, the dumb, the blind, for the insane, even for the idiot; see what is done for the education of the people — in schools, academies, colleges, and by public lectures; what is done for the criminal to prevent the growth of crime. See what an amelioration of the penal laws; how men are saved and restored to society, who had once been wholly lost. See what is done by philanthropy still more eminent, which the town and State have not yet overtaken and enacted into law; by the various societies for reform — those for temperance, for peace, for the discipline of prisons, for the discharged convicts, for freeing the slave. See this Anti-slavery party, which, in twenty years, has become so powerful throughout all the Northern States, so strong that it cannot be howled down, and men begin to find it hardly safe to howl over it; a party which only waits the time to lift up its million arms, and hurl the hateful institution of slavery out of the land! All these humane movements come from a divine piety in the soul of man. A tree which bears such fruits is not a dead tree; is not wholly to be despaired of; is not yet in a "decline," and past all hope of recovery. Is the age wanting in piety, which makes such efforts as these? Yes, you will say, because it does no more. I agree to this, but it is rich in piety compared to other times. Ours is an age of faith; not of mere belief in the commandments of men, but of faith in the nature of man and the commandments of God.

This prevailing and contagious complaint about the decline of religion is not one of the new things of our time. In the beginning of the last century, Dr. Colman, first minister of the church in Brattle street, lamented in small capitals over the general decline of piety:—"The venerable name of religion and of the church is made a sham pretence for the worst of villanies, for uncharitableness and unnatural oppression of the pious and the peaceable;" "the perilous times are come, wherein men are lovers only of their own selves." "Ah, calamitous day," says he, "into which we are fallen, and into which the sins of our infatuated age have brought us!" He looks back to the founders of New England; they "were rich in faith, and heirs of a better world," "men of whom the world was not worthy;" "they laid in a stock of prayers for us which have brought down many blessings on us already." Samuel Willard bewailed "the checkered state of the gospel church;" it was "in every respect a gloomy day, and covered with thick clouds."

We retire yet further back, to the end of the seventeenth century; a hundred and sixty or seventy years ago, Dr. Increase Mather, not only in his own pulpit, but also at "the great and Thursday lecture," lamented over "the degeneracy and departing glory of New England." He complained that there was a neglect of the Sabbath, of the ordinances, and of family worship; he groaned at the lax discipline of the churches, and looked, says another, "as fearfully on the growing charity as on the growing vices of the age." He called the existing generation "an unconverted generation." "Atheism and profaneness," says he, "have come to a prodigious height;" "God will visit" for these things; "God is about to open the windows of heaven, and pour down the cataracts of His wrath ere this generation . . . is passed away." If a comet appeared in the sky, it was to admonish men of the visitation, and make "the haughty daughters of Zion reform their pride of apparel." "The world is full of unbelief" (that is, in the malignant aspect and disastrous influence of comets), "but there is an awful Scripture for them that do profanely condemn such signal works!"

One of the present and well-known indications of the decline of piety, that is often thought a modern luxury, and ridiculously denounced in the pulpit, which has done its part in fostering the enjoyment, was practised to an extent that alarmed the prim shepherds of the New England flock in earlier days. The same Dr. Mather preached a series of sermons "tending to promote the power of godliness," and concludes the whole with a discourse "Of sleeping at sermons," and says: "To sleep in the public worship of God is a thing too frequently and easily practised; it is a great and a dangerous evil." "Sleeping at a sermon is a greater sin than speaking an idle word. Therefore, if men must be called to account for idle words, much more for this!" "Gospel sermons are among the most precious talents which any in this world have conferred upon them. But what a sad account will be given concerning those sermons which have been slept away! As light as thou makest of it now, it may be conscience will roar for it upon a death-bed!" "Verily, there is many a soul that will find this to be a dismal thought at the day of judgment, when he shall remember so many sermons I might have heard for my everlasting benefit, but I slighted and slept them all away. Therefore consider, if men allow themselves in this evil their souls are in danger to perish." "It is true that a godly man may be subject unto this as well as unto other infirmities; but he doth not allow himself therein." "The name of the glorious God is greatly prophaned by this inadvertency." "The support of the evangelical ministry is . . . discouraged." He thought the character of the pulpit was not sufficient explanation of this phenomenon, and adds, in his supernatural way, "Satan is the external cause of this evil;" "he had rather have men wakeful at any time than at sermon time." The good man mentions, by way of example, a man who "had not slept a wink at a sermon for more than twenty years together," and also, but by way of warning, the unlucky youth in the Acts who slept at Paul's long sermon, and fell out of the window, and "was taken up dead." Sleeping was "adding something of our own to the worship of God;" "when Nadab and Abihu did so, there went out fire from the Lord and consumed them to death." "The holy God hath not been a little displeased for this sin." "It is not punished by men, but therefore the Lord himself will visit for it." "Tears of blood will trickle down thy dry and damned cheeks forever and ever, because thou mayest not be so happy as to hear one sermon, or to have one offer of grace more throughout the never-ending dayes of eternity." Other men denounced their "Wo to sleepy sinners," and issued their "Proposals for the revival of dying religion."

Dr. Mather thought there was "A deluge of prophaneness," and bid men "be much in mourning and humiliation that God's bottle may be filled with tears." He thought piety was going out because surplices were coming in; it was wicked to "consecrate a church;" keeping Christmas was "like the idolatry of the calf." The common-prayer, an organ, a musical instrument in a church, was "not of God." Such things were to our worthy fathers in the ministry what temperance and anti-slavery societies are to many of their sons — an "abomination," "unchristian and atheistic!" The introduction of "regular singing" was an indication to some that "all religion is to cease;" "we might as well go over to Popery at once." Inoculation for the smallpox was as vehemently and ably opposed as the modern attempt to abolish the gallows; it was "a trusting more to the machinations of men than to the all-wise providence of God."

"When the enchantments of this world," says the ecclesiastical historian, "caused the rising generation more sensibly to neglect the primitive designs and interests of religion propounded by their fathers; a change in the tenor of the divine dispensation towards this country was quickly the matter of every one's observation." "Our wheat and our pease fell under an unaccountable blast." "We were visited with multiplied shipwrecks;" "pestilential sicknesses did sometimes become epidemic among us." "Indians cruelly butchered many hundreds of our inhabitants, and scattered whole towns with miserable ruins." "The serious people throughout the land were awakened by these intimations of divine displeasure to inquire into the causes and matters of the controversie." Accordingly, 1679, a synod was convened at Boston, to "inquire into the causes of the Lord's controversie with his New England people," who determined the matter.*

---

* The Synod declared: "That God hath a controversie with his New England people is undeniable." "There are visible manifest evils, which without doubt the Lord is provoked by." 1. "A great and visible decay of the power of Godliness amongst many professors in these churches." 2. "Pride doth abound in New England. Many have offended God by strange apparel." 3. "Church fellowship and other divine institutions are grossly neglected." "Quakers are false worshippers," "and Anabaptists . . . do no better than set up an Altar against the Lord's Altar." 4. "The holy and glorious name of God hath been polluted;" "because of swearing the land mourns." "It is a frequent thing for men to sit in prayer-time . . . and to give way to their own sloth and sleepiness." "We read of but one man in Scripture that slept at a sermon, and that sin had like to have cost him his life." 5. "There is much Sabbath-breaking; since there are multitudes that do profanely absent themselves from the public worship of God, . . . walking abroad and travelling . . . being a common practice on the Sabbath Day." "Worldly unsuitable discourses are very common upon the Lord's Day." "This brings wrath, fires, and other judgments upon a professing people." 6. "As to what concerns families and Government thereof, there is much amiss." "Children and servants . . . are not kept in due subjection." "This is a sin which brings great judgments, as we see in Eli's and David's family." 7. "Inordinate passions, sinful heats and hatreds, and that amongst church members." 8. "There is much intemperance:" "it is a common practice for

A little later, in 1690, the General Court considered the subject anew, and declared, that " A corruption of manners, attended with inexcusable degeneracies and apostacies . . . is the cause of the controversie." We "are now arriving at such an extremity, that the axe is laid to the root of the trees, and we are in eminent danger of perishing, if a speedy reformation of our provoking evils prevent it not." In 1702, Cotton Mather complains that " Our manifold indispositions to recover the dying power of

---

town-dwellers, yea, and church members, to frequent public houses, and there to misspend precious time." 9. " There is much want of truth amongst men." " The Lord is not wont to suffer such an iniquity to pass unpunished." 10. " Inordinate affection unto the world." " There hath been in many professors an insatiable desire after land and worldly accommodations; yea, so as to forsake churches and ordinances, and to live like heathen, only so that they might have elbow-room in the world. Farms and merchandisings have been preferred before the things of God." " Such iniquity causeth war to be in the gate, and cities to be burned up." " When Lot did forsake the land of Canaan and the church which was in Abraham's family, that so he might have better worldly accommodations in Sodom, God fired him out of all." " There are some traders that sell their goods at excessive rates; day-laborers and mechanics are unreasonable in their demands." 11. " There hath been opposition to the work of reformation." 12. " A public spirit is greatly wanting in the most of men." 13. " There are sins against the gospel, whereby the Lord has been provoked." " Christ is not prized and embraced in all his offices and ordinances as ought to be."

Godliness, were successive calamities, under all of which, our apostacies from that Godliness, have rather proceeded than abated." "The old spirit of New England has been sensibly going out of the world, as the old saints in whom it was have gone; and, instead thereof, the spirit of the world, with a lamentable neglect of strict piety, has crept in upon the rising generation."

You go back to the time of the founders and fathers of the colony, and it is no better. In 1667, Mr. Wilson, who had "A singular gift in the practice of discipline," on his death-bed declared, that "God would judge the people for their rebellion and self-willed spirit, for their contempt of civil and ecclesiastical rulers, and for their luxury and sloth," and before that he said, "People rise up as Corah, against their ministers." "And for our neglect of baptizing the children of the church, . . . I think God is provoked by it. Another sin I take to be the making light . . . of the authority of the Synods." John Norton, whose piety was said to be "Grace, grafted on a crab-stock," in 1660, growled, after his wont, on account of the "Heart of New England, rent with the blasphemies of this generation." John Cotton, the ablest man in New England, who "Liked to sweeten his mouth with a piece of Calvin, before he went to sleep," and was so pious that another could not swear while he was under the roof, mourned at "The condition of the churches;" and, in 1652, on his death-bed, after bestowing his blessing on the President of Harvard College, who had begged it of him, exhorted the elders to "Increase their watch against those declensions, which he saw the professors of religion falling into."* In 1641, such was the condition of piety in Boston, that it was thought necessary to banish a man, because he did not believe in original sin. In 1639, a fast was appointed, "To deplore the prevalence of the small-pox, the want of zeal in the professors of religion, and the general decay of piety." "The church of God had not been long in this wilderness," thus complains a minister, one hundred and fifty years

---

* In 1646, Mr. Samuel Symonds wrote to Governor Winthrop, as follows: "I will also mention the text preached upon at our last fast, and the propositions raised thereupon, because it was so seasonable to New England's condition. Jeremiah 30:17; For I will restore health to thee, and heal thee of thy wounds, saith the Lord; because they called thee an outcast, saying, This is Zion, whom noe man careth for.

"1. Prop. That sick tymes doe passe over Zion.

"2. That sad and bitter neglect is the portion, aggravation and affliction of Zion in the tyme of his sicknesse and wounds, but especially in the neglect of those that doe neglect it, and yet, notwithstanding, doe acknowledge it to be Zion.

"3. That the season of penitent Zion's passion, is the season of God's compassion.

"This sermon tended much to the settling of Godly minds here in God's way, and to raise their spirits, and, as I conceive, hath suitable effects."

ago, "before the dragon cast forth several floods to devour it; but not the least of these floods was one of the Antinomian and familistical heresies." "It is incredible what alienations of mind, and what a very calenture the devil raised in the country upon this odd occasion." "The sectaries" "began usually to seduce women into their notions, and by these women, like their first mother, they soon hooked in the husbands also." So, in 1637, the Synod of Cambridge was convened, to despatch "The apostate serpent:" one woman was duly convicted of holding "About thirty monstrous opinions," and subsequently, by the civil authorities, banished from the colony. The synod, after much time was "spent in ventilation and emptying of private passions," condemned eighty-two opinions, then prevalent in the colony, as erroneous, and decided to "Refer doubts to be resolved by the great God." Even in 1636, John Wilson lamented "The dark and distracted condition of the churches of New England."

"The good old times," when piety was in a thriving state, and the churches successful and contented, lay as far behind the "Famous Johns," as it now does behind their successors in office and lamentation. Then, as now, the complaint had the same foundation: ministers and other good men could not see that new piety will not be put into the old forms, neither the old forms of thought, nor the old forms of action. In the days of Wilson, Cotton, and Norton, there was a gradual growth of piety; in the days of the Mathers, of Colman, and Willard, and from that time to this, there has been a steady improvement of the community, in intellectual, moral, and religious culture. Some men could not see the progress two hundred years ago, because they believed in no piety, except as it was manifested in their conventional forms. It is so now. Mankind advances by the irresistible law of God, under the guidance of a few men of large discourse, who look before and after, but amid the wailing of many who think each advance is a retreat, and every stride a stumble.

Now-a-days nobody complains at "The ungodly custom of wearing long hair;" no dandy is dealt with by the church, for his dress; the weakest brother is not offended by "Regular singing," — so it be regular, — "by organs and the like;" nobody laments at "The reading of Scripture lessons," or "The use of the Lord's Prayer" in public religious services, or is offended, because a clergyman makes a prayer at a funeral, and solemnizes a marriage, — though these are "prelatical customs," and were detested by our fathers. Yet, other things, now as much dreaded, and thought "of a bad and dangerous tendency," will one day prove themselves as innocent, though now as much mourned over. Many an old doctrine will fade out, and though some think a star has fallen out of heaven, a new truth will rise up and take its place. It is to be expected that ministers will often complain of "The general decay of religion." The position of a clergyman, fortunate in many things, is unhappy in this: he seldom sees the result of his labors, except in the conventional form mentioned above. The lawyer, the doctor, the merchant and mechanic, the statesman and the farmer, all have visible and palpable results of their work, while the minister can only see that he has baptized men, and admitted them to his church; the visible and quotable tokens of his success, are a large audience, respectable and attentive, a thriving Sunday school, or a considerable body of communicants. If these signs fail, or become less than formerly, he thinks he has labored in vain; that piety is on the decline, for it is only by this form that he commonly tests and measures piety itself. Hence, a sincere and earnest minister, with the limitations which he so easily gets from his profession and social position, is always prone to think ill of the times, to undervalue the new wine which refuses to be kept in the old bottles, but rends them asunder; hence he bewails the decline of religion, and looks longingly back to the days of his fathers.

But you will ask, Why does not a minister demand piety in its natural form? Blame him not; unconsciously he fulfils his contract, and does what he is taught, ordained, and paid for doing. It is safe for a minister to demand piety of his parish, in the conventional form; not safe to demand it in the form of morality — eminent piety, in the form of philanthropy: it would be an innovation; it would "Hurt men's feelings;" it might disturb some branches of business; at the North, it would interfere with the liquor-trade; at the South, with the slave-trade; everywhere it would demand what many men do not like to give. If a man asks piety in the form of bodily attendance at church, on the only idle day in the week, when business and amusement must be refrained from; in the form of belief in doctrines which are commonly accepted by the denomination, and compliance with its forms, — that is customary; it hurts nobody's feelings; it does not disturb the liquor-trade, nor the slave-trade; it interferes with nothing, not even with respectable sleep in a comfortable pew. A minister, like others loves to be surrounded by able and respectable men; he seeks, therefore, a congregation of such. If he is himself an able man, it is well; but there are few in any calling, whom we designate as able. Our weak man cannot instruct his parishioners; he soon learns this, and ceases to give them counsel on matters of importance. They would not suffer it, for the larger includes the less, not the less the larger. He is not strong by nature; their position overlooks and commands his. He must speak and give some counsel; he wisely limits himself to things of but little practical interest, and his parishioners are not offended: "That is my sentiment exactly," says the most worldly man in the church, " Religion is too pure to be mixed up with the practical business of the street." The original and effectual preaching in such cases, is not from the pulpit down upon the pews, but from the pews up to the pulpit, which only echoes, consciously or otherwise, but does not speak.

In a solar system, the central sun, not barely powerful from its position, is the most weighty body; heavier than all the rest put together; so with even swing they all revolve about it. Our little ministerial sun was ambitious of being amongst large satellites; he is there, but the law of gravitation amongst men is as certain as in matter; he cannot poise and swing the system; he is not the sun thereof, not even a primary planet, only a little satellite revolving with many nutations round some primary, in an orbit that is oblique, complicated, and difficult to calculate; now waxing in a " Revival," now waning in a " Decline of piety," now totally eclipsed by his primary that comes between him and the light which lighteth every man. Put one of the cold thin moons of Saturn into the centre of the solar system, — would the universe revolve about that little dot? Loyal matter with irresistible fealty gravitates towards the sun, and wheels around the balance-point of the world's weight, be it where it may, called by whatever name.

While ministers insist unduly on the conventional manifestation of piety, it is not a thing unheard of for a layman to resolve to go to heaven by the ecclesiastical road, yet omit resolving to be a good man before he gets there. Such a man finds the ordinary forms of piety very convenient, and not at all burdensome; they do not interfere with his daily practice of injustice and meanness of soul; they seem a substitute for real and manly goodness; they offer a royal road to saintship here and heaven hereafter. Is the man in arrears with virtue, having long practised wickedness and become insolvent? This form is a new bankrupt law of the spirit, he pays off his old debts in the ecclesiastical currency — a pennyworth of form for a pound of substantial goodness. This bankrupt sinner, cleared by the ecclesiastical chancery, is a solvent saint; he exhorts at meetings, strains at every gnat, and mourns over "The general decay of piety," and teaches other men the way in which they should go — to the same end.

> "So morning insects that in muck begun,
> Shine, buzz, and fly-blow in the evening sun."

I honor the founders of New England; they were pious men — their lives proved it; but domineered over by false opinions in theology, they put their piety into very unnatural and perverted forms. They had ideas which transcended their age; they came here to make those ideas into institutions. That they had great faults, bigotry, intolerance, and superstition, is now generally conceded. They were picked men, "wheat sifted out of three kingdoms," to plant a new world withal. They have left their mark very deep and very distinct in this town, which was their prayer and their pride. It may seem unjust to ourselves to compare a whole community like our own with such a company as filled Boston in the first half century of its existence, — men selected for their spiritual hardihood; but here and now, in the midst of Boston, are men quite as eminent for piety who as far transcend this age, as the Puritans and the pilgrims surpassed their time. The Puritan put his religion into the ecclesiastical form; not into the form of the Roman or the English Church, but into a new one of his own. His descendant, inheriting his father's faith in God, and stern self-denial, but sometimes without his bigotry, intolerance, and superstition, with little fear but with more love of God, and consequently with more love of man, puts his piety into a new form. It is not the form of the old Church; the Church of the Puritans is to him often what the Church of the Pope and the prelates was to his ungentle sire. He puts his piety into the form of goodness; eminent piety becomes philanthropy, and takes the shape of reform. In such men, in many of their followers, I see the same trust in God, the same scorn of compromising right and truth, the same unfaltering allegiance to the eternal Father, which shone in the pilgrims who founded this new world, which fired the reformers of the Church; yes, which burned in the hearts of Paul and John. Piety has not failed and gone out; each age has its own forms thereof; the old and passing can never understand the new, nor can they consent to decrease with the increase of the new. Once, men put their piety into a church, Catholic or Protestant; they made creeds and believed them; they devised rites and symbols, which helped their faith. It was well; but we cannot believe those creeds, nor be aided by such symbols and such rites. Why pretend to drag a weighty crutch about because it helped your father once, wandering alone and in the dark, sounding on his dim and perilous way? Once earthen roads were the best we knew, and horses' feet had shoes of swiftness; now we need not, out of reverence, refuse the iron road, the chariot and the steed of flame; nor out of irreverence need we spurn the path our fathers trod; sorely bested and hunted after, tear-bedewed and travel-stained, they journeyed there, passing on to their God. If the mother that bore us were never so rude, and to our eyes might seem never so graceless now, still she was our mother, and without her we should not have been born. Wives and children may men have, and manifold; each has but one mother. The great institution we call the Christian Church has been the mother of us all; and though in her own dotage she deny our piety, and call us infidel, far be it from me to withhold the richly earned respect. Behind a decent veil, then, let us hide our mother's weakness, and ourselves pass on. Once piety built up a theocracy, and men say it was divine; now piety, everywhere in Christendom, builds up democracies; it is a diviner work.

The piety of this age must manifest itself in Morality, and appear in a church where the priests are men of active mind and active hand; men of ideas, who commune with God and man through faith and works, finding no truth is hostile to their creed, no goodness foreign to their litany, no piety discordant with their psalm. The man who once would have built a convent and been its rigorous chief, now founds a temperance society, contends against war, toils for the pauper, the criminal, the madman, and the slave, for men bereft of senses and of sense. The synod of Dort and of Cambridge, the assembly of divines at Westminster, did what they could with what piety they had; they put it into decrees and platforms, into catechisms and creeds. But the various conventions for reform put their piety into resolves and then into philanthropic works. I do not believe there has ever been an age when piety bore so large a place in the whole being of New England as at this day, or attendance on church-forms so small a part. The attempts made and making for a better education of the people, the lectures on science and literature abundantly attended in this town, the increased fondness for reading, the better class of books which are read — all these indicate an increased love of truth, the intellectual part of piety; societies for reform and for charity show an increase of the moral and affectional parts of piety; the better, the lovelier idea of God which all sects are embracing, is a sign of increased love of God. Thus all parts of piety are proving their existence by their work. The very absence from the churches, the disbelief of the old sour theologies, the very neglect of outward forms and ceremonies of religion, the decline of the ministry itself, under the present circumstances, shows an increase of piety. The baby-clothes were well and wide for the baby; now, the fact that he cannot get them on, shows plainly that he has outgrown them, is a boy and no longer a baby.

Once Piety fled to the Church as the only sanctuary in the waste wide world, and was fondly welcomed there, fed and fostered. When power fled off from the Church — "Wilt thou also go away?" said she; "Lord," said Piety, "to whom shall we go? Thou only hast the words of everlasting life." Once convents and cathedrals were what the world needed as shelter for this fair child of God; then she dwelt in the grim edifice that our fathers built, and for a time counted herself "lodged in a lodging where good things are." Now is she grown able to wander forth fearless and free, lodging where the night overtakes her, and doing what her hands find to do, not unattended by the Providence which hitherto has watched over and blessed her. I respect piety in the Hebrew saints, prophets, and bards, who spoke the fiery speech, or sung their sweet and soul-inspiring psalm:

> "Out from the heart of Nature rolled
> The burdens of the Bible old."

I honor piety among the saints of Greece, clad in the form of philanthropy and art, speaking still in dramas, in philosophies, and song, and in the temple and the statue too:

> "Not from a vain and shallow thought
> His awful Jove young Phidias brought."

I admire at the piety of the Middle Ages, which founded the monastic tribes of men, which wrote the theologies, scholastic and mystic both, still speaking to the mind of men, or in poetic legends insinuated truth; which built that heroic architecture, overmastering therewith the sense and soul of man:

> "The passive master lent his hand
> To the vast Soul that o'er him planned:
> And the same Power that reared the shrine,
> Bestrode the tribes that knelt therein."

But the piety which I find now, in this age, here in our own land, I respect, honor, and admire yet more; I find it in the form of moral life; that is the piety I love, piety in her own loveliness. Would I could find poetic strains as fit to sing of her — but yet such

> "Loveliness needs not the foreign aid of ornament,
> But is, when unadorned, adorned the most."

Let me do no dishonor to other days, to Hebrew or to Grecian saints. Unlike and hostile though they were, they jointly fed my soul in earliest days. I would not underrate the mediæval saints, whose words and works have been my study in a manlier age; yet I love best the fair and vigorous piety of our own day. It is beautiful, amid the strong, rank life of the nineteenth century, amid the steam-mills and the telegraphs which talk by lightning, amid the far-reaching enterprises of our time, and 'mid the fierce democracies, it is beautiful to find this fragrant piety growing up in unwonted forms, in places where men say no seed of heaven can lodge and germinate. So in a June meadow, when a boy, and looking for the cranberries of another year, faded and tasteless, amid the pale but coarse rank grass, and discontented that I found them not, so I have seen the crimson arethusa or the cymbidium shedding an unexpected loveliness o'er all the watery soil and all the pale and coarse rank grass, a prophecy of summer near at hand. So in October, when the fields are brown with frost, the blue and fringed gentian meets your eye, filling with thankful tears.

There is no decline of piety, but an increase of it;

a good deal has been done in two hundred years, in one hundred years, yes, in fifty years. Let us admit, with thankfulness of heart, that piety is in greater proportion to all our activity now than ever before: but then compare ourselves with the ideal of human nature, our piety with the ideal piety, and we must confess that we are little and very low. Boston is the most active city in the world, the most enterprising. In no place is it so easy to obtain men's ears and their purses for any good word and work. But think of the evils we know of and tolerate; think of an ideal Christian city, then think of Boston; of a Christian man, aye of Christ himself, and then think of you and me, and we are filled with shame. If there were a true, manly piety in this town, in due proportion to our numbers, wealth, and enterprise, how long would the vices of this city last? How long would men complain of a dead body of divinity and a dead church, and a ministry that was dead? How long would intemperance continue, and pauperism, in Boston; how long slavery in this land?

Last Sunday, in the name of the poor, I asked you for your charity. To-day I ask for dearer alms: I ask you to contribute your piety. It will help the town more than the little money all of us can give. Your money will soon be spent; it feeds one man once; we cannot give it twice, though the blessing thereof may linger long in the hand which gave. Few of us can give much money to the poor; some of us none at all. This we can all give: the inspiration of a man with a man's piety in his heart, living it out in a man's life. Your money may be ill spent, your charity misapplied, but your piety never. After all, there is nothing you can give which men will so readily take and so long remember as this. Mothers can give it to their daughters and their sons; men, after spending thereof profusely at home, can coin their inexhausted store into industry, patience, integrity, temperance, justice, humanity, a practical love of man. A thousand years ago, it was easy to excuse men if they chiefly showed religion in the conventional pattern of the church. Forms then were helps, and the nun has been mother to much of the charity of our times. It is easy to excuse our fathers for their superstitious reverence for rites and forms. But now, in an age which has its eyes a little open, a practical and a handy age, we are without excuse if our piety appears not in a manly life, our faith in works. To give this piety to cheer and bless mankind, you must have it first, be cheered and blessed thereby yourself. Have it, then, in your own way; put it into your own form. Do men tell you, "This is a degenerate age," and "Religion is dying out?" tell them that when those stars have faded out of the sky from very age, when other stars have come up to take their place, and they too have grown dim and hollow-eyed and old, that religion will still live in man's heart, the primal, everlasting light of all our being. Do they tell you that you must put piety into their forms; put it there if it be your place; if not, in your place. Let men see the divinity that is in you by the humanity that comes out from you. If they will not see it, cannot, God can and will. Take courage from the past, not its counsel; fear not now to be a man. You may find a new Eden where you go, a river of God in it, and a tree of life, an angel to guard it; not the warning angel to repel, but the guiding angel to welcome and to bless.

It was four years yesterday since I first came here to speak to you; I came hesitatingly, reluctant, with much diffidence as to my power to do what it seemed to me was demanded. I did not come merely to pull down, but to build up, though it is plain much theological error must be demolished before any great reform of man's condition can be brought about. I came not to contend against any man, or sect, or party, but to speak a word for truth and religion in the name of man and God. I was in bondage to no sect; you in bondage to none. When a boy I learned that there is but one religion though many theologies. I have found it in Christians and in Jews, in Quakers and in Catholics. I hope we are all ready to honor what is good in each sect, and in rejecting its evil not to forget our love and wisdom in our zeal.

When I came I certainly did not expect to become a popular man, or acceptable to many. I had done much which in all countries brings odium on a man, though perhaps less in Boston than in any other part of the world. I had rejected the popular theology of Christendom. I had exposed the low morals of society, had complained of the want of piety in its natural form. I had fatally offended the sect, small in numbers, but respectable for intelligence and goodness, in which I was brought up. I came to look at the signs of the times from an independent point of view, and to speak on the most important of all themes. I thought a house much smaller than this would be much too large for us. I knew there would be fit audience; I thought it would be few, and the few would soon have heard enough and go their ways.

I know I have some advantages above most clergymen: I am responsible to no sect; no sect feels responsible for me; I have rejoiced at good things which I have seen in all sects; the doctrines which I try to teach do not rest on tradition, on miracles, or on any man's authority; only on the nature of man. I seek to preach the natural laws of man. I appeal to history for illustration, not for authority. I have no fear of philosophy. I am willing to look a doubt fairly in the face, and think reason is sacred as conscience, affection, or the religious faculty in man. I see a profound piety in modern science. I have aimed to set forth absolute religion, the ideal religion of human nature, free piety, free goodness, free thought. I call that Christianity, after the greatest man of the world, one who himself taught it; but I know that this was never the Christianity of the churches, in any age. I have endeavored to teach this religion and apply it to the needs of this time. These things certainly give me some advantages over most other ministers. Of the disadvantages which are personal to myself, I need not speak in public, but some which come from my position, ought to be noticed with a word. The walls of this house, the associations connected with it, furnish little help to devotion; we must rely on ourselves wholly for that. Other clergymen, by their occasional exchanges, can present their hearers with an agreeable variety in substance and in form. A single man, often heard, becomes wearisome and unprofitable, for " No man can feed us always." This I feel to be a great disadvantage which I labor under. Your kindness and affectionate indulgence make me feel it all the more. But one man cannot be twenty men.

When I came here I knew I should hurt men's feelings. My theology would prove more offensive and radical than men thought; the freedom of speech which men liked at a distance would not be pleasing when near at hand; my doctrines of morality I knew could not be pleasing to all men; not to all good men. I saw by your looks that in my abstractions I did not go too far for your sympathy, or too fast for your following. I soon found that my highest thought and most pious sentiment were most warmly welcomed as such; but when I came to put abstract thought and mystical piety into concrete goodness, and translate what you had accepted as Christian faith into daily life; when I came to apply piety to trade, politics, life in general, I knew that I should hurt men's feelings. It could not be otherwise. Yet I have had a most patient and faithful hearing. One thing I must do in my preaching: I must be in earnest. I cannot stand here before you and before God, attempting to teach piety and goodness, and not feel the fire and show the fire. The greater the wrong, the more popular, the more must I oppose it, and with the clearer, abler speech. It is not necessary for me to be popular, to be acceptable, even to be loved. It is necessary that I should tell the truth. But let that pass. You come hither week after week, it is now year after year that you come, to listen to one humble man. Do you get poor in your souls? Does your religion become poor and low? Are you getting less in the qualities of a man? If so, then leave me, to empty seats, to cold and voiceless walls; go elsewhere, and feed your souls with a wise passiveness, or an activity wiser yet. Such is your duty; let no affection for me hinder you from performing it. The same theology, the same form suits not all men. But if it is not so, if I do you good, if you grow in mind and conscience, heart and soul, then I ask one thing—Let your piety become natural life, your divinity become humanity.

II.

SOME THOUGHTS ON THE MOST CHRISTIAN USE OF THE SUNDAY.—A SERMON PREACHED AT THE MELODEON, ON SUNDAY, JANUARY 30, 1848.

MARK II. 27.

The Sabbath was made for man, and not man for the Sabbath.

From past ages we have received many valuable institutions, that have grown out of the transient wants or the permanent nature of man. Amongst these are two which have done a great service in promoting the civilization of mankind, which still continue amongst us. I speak now of the institution of Sunday, and that of preaching. By the one, a seventh part of the time is separated from the common pursuits of life, in order that it may be devoted to bodily relaxation, and to the culture of the spiritual powers of man; by the other, a large body of men, in most countries the best educated class, are devoted to the cultivation of these spiritual powers. Such at least is the theory of those two institutions, be their effect in practice what it may. This morning, let us look at one of them, and so I invite your attention to some thoughts relative to the Sunday — to the most Christian and profitable use of that day.

There is a stricter party of Christians amongst us, who speak out their opinions concerning the Sunday; this comprises what are commonly called the more "evangelical" sects. There is a party less strict in many particulars, comprising what are commonly called the more "liberal" sects. They have hitherto been comparatively silent on this theme. Their opinions about the Sunday have not usually been so plainly spoken out, but have been made apparent by their actions, by occasional and passing words, rather than by full, distinct, and emphatic declarations. The stricter party, of late years, have been growing a little more strict; the party less strict likewise advance in the opposite direction. Recently, a call has been published by a few men, for a convention to consult and take some steps towards the less rigid course, for the purpose, as I understand it, of making the Sunday even more valuable than it is now. I take it for granted that both parties desire to make the best possible use of the Sunday — the use most conducive to the highest interests of mankind; that they desire this equally. There are good men on both sides, the more and the less strict; pious men, in the best sense of that word, may be found on both sides. There is no need of imputing bad motives to either party in order to explain the difference between the two.

Such is the aspect of the two parties in the field, looking opposite ways, but at one another. It seems likely that there will be a quarrel, and, as is usual in such cases, hard words on each side, hard thoughts and unkind feelings on both sides. Before the quarrel begins, and our eyes are blinded by the dust of controversy; before our blood is fired, and we become wholly incapable of judgment — let us look coolly at the matter, and ask, Do we need any change in respect to the observance of the Sunday? Are the present opinions respecting the origin, nature, and original design of that institution just and true? Is the present mode of observing it the most profitable that can be devised? The inquiry is one of great importance.

To answer these questions, it is necessary to go back a little into the history of the Hebrew Sabbath and the Christian Sunday. However, it is not needful to go much into detail, or consume this precious hour in a learned discussion on antiquarian matters which concern none but scholars.

With the Hebrews the actual observance of Saturday — the Sabbath — as a day rest, seems to be of pretty late origin. The first mention of it in authentic Hebrew history, as actually observed, occurs about two hundred years after Samuel, and about six hundred after Moses — a little less than nine hundred before Christ. The passage is found in 2 Kings 4: 23; a child had died, as the narrative relates — the mother wished to send for Elisha, "the man of God." Her husband objects, saying, "Wherefore wilt thou go to him to-day? it is neither new moon nor Sabbath." This connection with the new moon is significant. In the earlier historical books of Joshua, Judges, the two books of Samuel, and the first of Kings, there is no mention of the Sabbath, not the least allusion to it.

This seems to have been the origin of its observance: — The worship of one God, with the distinctive name Jehovah, gradually got established in the Hebrew nation; for this they seem largely indebted to Moses. Gradually this worship of Jehovah became connected with a body of priests, who were regularly organized at length, and claimed descent from Levi — some of them from Aaron, his celebrated descendant, the elder brother of Moses. The rise of the Levitical priesthood is remarkable, and easily traced in the Old Testament. Some books are entirely destitute of a Levitical spirit, such as Genesis and Judges; others are filled with it, as Leviticus, Deuteronomy, and the books of Chronicles. With the priesthood it seems there came the observance of certain days for religious or festal purposes — New Moon days, Full Moon days, and the like. These seem to have been derived from the nations about them, with whom the moon — deified as Astarte, the Queen and Mother of Heaven, and under other names — was long an object of worship. The observance of those days points back to the period when Fetichism, the worship of Nature, was the prominent form of religion. With the other days of religious observance came the seventh day, called the Sabbath. No one knows its true historical origin. The statement respecting its origin, in the fourth commandment, and elsewhere in the Old Testament, can hardly be accepted as literally true by any one in this century. No scientific man, in the present stage of philosophic inquiry, will believe that God created the universe in six days, and then rested on the seventh. Did other nations observe this day before the Hebrews; was it also connected with some Fetichistic form of worship; what was the historical event which led to the selection of that day in special? This it is easy to ask, but perhaps not possible to answer. These are curious questions; they are of little practical importance to us at this moment.

After the Hebrew institutions of religion got fixed — the worship of Jehovah, the Levitical priesthood, and the peculiar forms of sacrifice — it became common to refer their origin back to the time of Moses, who lived fourteen or fifteen hundred years before Christ. Since few memorials from his age have come down to us, it is plain we can know little of him. But from the impression which his character left on his nation, and through them on the whole world; from the myths so early connected with his name, it seems pretty clear that he was one of the greatest and most extraordinary men that ever lived. Mankind seldom tell great things of little men. It is difficult to say what share he had in making the laws of the Hebrew nation which are commonly referred to him, — and, as it is popularly taught, revealed to him directly by Jehovah. Perhaps we are not safe in referring to him even the whole of the ten commandments; surely not in any one of their present forms.* Was the Sabbath observed as a day of rest before Moses? Was its observance enforced by him? Was it even known to him? These questions are not easily answered. This is only certain: from the time of Moses to that of Jehoram, a period of about six hundred years, there is no historical mention of its observance, not the least allusion to it. Yet we have documents which treat of that period, — the books of Joshua, Judges, Samuel, and the Kings, — some of them historical documents, which go into the minute detail of the national peculiarities, and were evidently writ-

* These celebrated commandments have come down to us in three distinct forms; namely, in Exodus xx., in Exodus xxxiv., and in Deut. v. The differences between these several codes are quite remarkable and significant.

ten with a good deal of concern for strict integrity and truth; they refer to the national rite of circumcision. Now, if the Sabbath had been observed during that period, it is difficult to believe it would have received no passing notice in those historical books. But not only is there no mention of it therein, none even in the times of David and Solomon, who favored the priesthood so strongly; but in the book of Chronicles, the most Levitical book in the Bible, at a date more than two hundred years later than the time of Jehoram, it is distinctly declared that the Sabbath had not been kept for nearly five hundred years.* But even if this statement is true, which is scarcely probable, it is plain from the frequent mention of the Sabbath in the writings of the latter part of that period — Isaiah, Jeremiah, and others — that the institution was one well known and highly regarded by religious men. After the return from the Babylonian exile, it seems to have been kept with considerable rigor; this we learn from the book of Nehemiah.

The Hebrew law, as it is contained in the Pentateuch, is a singular mixture of conflicting statutes, evidently belonging to different ages, many of them wholly unsuitable to the condition of the people when the laws are alleged to have been given. However, they are all referred back to the time of Moses in the Pentateuch itself, and by the popular theology

---

* 2 Chron. 36 : 21.

at the present day. In the law the command is given to keep the seventh day as a day of rest, and that command is referred distinctly to Jehovah himself. The reason is given for choosing that day: — "For in six days the Lord made heaven and earth, and on the seventh day he rested and was refreshed;" the Sabbath, therefore, was to be kept in commemoration of the fact, that after Jehovah had spent the week in creating the world, "he rested and was refreshed." It was to be a day of rest for master and slave, for man and beast. A special sacrifice was offered on that day, in addition to the usual ceremonies, but no provision was made for the religious instruction of the people. The Sabbath was what its Hebrew name implies, a rest from all labor. The law, in general terms, forbade all work; but, not content with that, it descends to minute details, specifically prohibiting by statute the gathering or preparation of food on the Sabbath, even of food to be consumed on that day itself; the lighting of a fire, or the removal from one's place; and, by a decision where the statute did not apply, forbade the gathering of sticks of wood. The punishment for violating the Sabbath in general, or in any one of these particulars, was death: "Whosoever doeth work therein shall be put to death." However, amusement was not prohibited, nor eating and drinking, only work. The command, "Let no man go out of his place on the seventh day," at a later period, was liberally interpreted, and a man was allowed to go two thousand cubits, a Sabbath-day's journey.

Long after the time of Moses, some of the Hebrews returned from exile amongst a more civilized and refined people. It seems probable that only the stricter portion returned and established themselves in the land of their fathers. Nehemiah, their leader, enforced the observance of the Sabbath with a strictness and rigor of which earlier times afford no evidence. But the nation was not content with making it a day of idleness. They established synagogues, where the people freely assembled on the Sabbath and other public days, for religious instruction, and thus founded an excellent institution which has shown itself fruitful of good results. So far as I know, that is the earliest instance on record of provision being made for the regular religious instruction of the whole people. Experience has shown its value, and now all the most highly civilized nations of the earth have established similar institutions. However, in the synagogues the business of religious instruction was not at all in the hands of the priests, but in those of the people, acting in their primary character without regard to Levitical establishments. A priest, as such, is never an instructor of the people; he is to go through his ritual, not beyond it.

It is easy to learn from the New Testament what were the current opinions about the Sabbath in the time of Christ. It was unlawful to gather a head of wheat on the Sabbath, as a man walked through the fields; it was unlawful to cure a sick man, though that cure could be effected by a touch or a word; unlawful for a man to walk home and carry the light cushion on which he had lain. What was unlawful was reckoned wicked also; for what is a crime in the eyes of the priest, he commonly pretends is likewise a sin before the eyes of God. Yet it was not unlawful to eat, drink, and be merry on the Sabbath; nor to lift a sheep out of the ditch; nor to quarrel with a man who came to deliver mankind from their worst enemies. It was lawful to perform the rite of circumcision on the Sabbath, but unlawful to cure a man of any sickness. Jesus once placed these two, the allowing of that ritual mutilation and the prohibition of the humane act of curing the sick on the Sabbath, in ridiculous contrast. In the fourth gospel he goes further, and actually denies the alleged ground for the original institution of the Sabbath; he denies that God had ever ceased from his work, or rested: "My father worketh hitherto." * However, in effecting these cures he committed a capital offence; the Pharisees so regarded it, and took measures to insure his punishment. It does not appear that they were illegal measures. It is probable they took regular and legal

* John 5 : 1–18, and 7 : 19–24.

means to bring him to condign punishment as a Sabbath-breaker. He escaped by flight.

Such was the Sabbath with the Hebrews, such the recorded opinion of Jesus concerning it. There were also other days in which labor was forbidden, but with them we have nothing to do at present. Jesus taught piety and goodness without the Hebrew limitations; of course, then, the new wine of Christianity could not be put into the old bottles of the Jews. Their fast days and Sabbath days, their rites and forms, were not for him.

Now, not long after the death of Christ, his followers became gradually divided into two parties. First, there were the Jewish Christians; that was the oldest portion, the old school of Christians. They are mentioned in ecclesiastical history as the Ebionites, Nazarines, and under yet other names. Peter and James were the great men in that division of the early Christians. Matthew, and the author of the Gospel according to the Hebrews, were their evangelists. The church at Jerusalem was their strong-hold. They kept the whole Hebrew law; all its burdensome ritual, its circumcision and its sacrifices, its new-moon days and its full-moon days, Sabbath, fasts, and feasts; the first fifteen bishops of the church at Jerusalem were circumcised Jews. It seems to me they misunderstood Jesus fatally; counting him nothing but the Messiah of the Old

Testament, and Christianity, therefore, nothing but Judaism brightened up and restored to its original purity.

I have often mentioned how strongly Matthew, taking him for the author of the first gospel, favors this way of thinking. He represents Jesus as commanding his disciples to observe all the Mosaic law, as the Pharisees interpreted that law,* though such a command is utterly inconsistent with the general spirit of Christ's teachings, and even with his plain declaration, as preserved in other parts of the same gospel. It is worthy of note, that this command is peculiar to Matthew. But there is another instance of the same Jewish tendency, though not so obvious at first sight. Matthew represents Jesus as saying, "The Son of man," that is, the Messiah, "is Lord even of the Sabbath day." Accordingly, he is competent to expound the law correctly, and determine what is lawful to do on that day. In Matthew, therefore, Jesus, in his character of Messiah, is represented as giving a judicial opinion, and ruling that it "is lawful to do well on the Sabbath days." Now, Mark and Luke represent it a little different. In Mark, Jesus himself declares that "The Sabbath was made for man, and not man for the Sabbath." Matthew entirely omits that remarkable saying. According to Mark, Jesus declares in general terms,

---

* Matthew 23 : 1–3.

that man is of more consequence than the observance of the Sabbath, while Matthew only considers that the Messiah is "Lord of the Sabbath day." The cause of this diversity is quite plain. Matthew was a Jewish Christian, and thought Christianity was nothing but restored Judaism.

The other party may be called liberal Christians, though they must not be confounded with the party which now bears that name. They were the new school of the early Christians. They rejected the Hebrew law, so far as it did not rest on human nature, and considered that Christianity was a new thing; Christ, not a mere Jew, but a universal man, who had thrown down the wall of partition between Jews and Gentiles. All the old, artificial distinctions, therefore, were done away with at once. Paul was the head of the liberal party among the primitive Christians. He was considered a heretic; and though he was more efficient than any of the other early preachers of Christianity, yet the author of the Apocalypse thought him not worthy of a place in the foundation of the new Jerusalem, which rests on the twelve apostles.* The fourth gospel with peculiarities of its own, is written wholly in the interest of this party; James is not mentioned in it at all, and Peter plays but quite a subordinate part, and is

* Rev. 21: 14.

thrown into the shade by John. The disciples are spoken of as often misunderstanding their great Teacher. These peculiarities cannot be considered as accidental; they are monuments of the controversy then going on between the two parties. Paul stood in direct opposition to the Jewish Christians. This is plain from the epistle to the Galatians, in which the heads of the rival sects appear very unlike the description given of them in the book of Acts. The observance of Jewish sacred days was one of the subjects of controversy. Let us look only at the matter of the Sabbath, as it came in question between the two parties. Paul exalts Christ far above the Messianic predictions of the Old Testament, calling him an image of the invisible God, and declaring that all the fulness of divinity dwells in him, and adds, that he had annulled the old Hebrew law. "Therefore," says Paul, "let no man judge you in meat or in drink, or in respect of a holy day, or of the new moon, or of the Sabbath." * Here he distinctly states the issue between the two Christian sects. Elsewhere he speaks of the Jewish party, as men that "would pervert the gospel of Christ," by teaching that a man was "justified by the works of the law;" that is, by a minute observance of the Hebrew ritual. † Paul rejects the authority of the Old Testament. The law of Moses was but a

* Coloss. 2: 16. † Galat. 1: 5.

schoolmaster's servant, to bring us to Christ; man had come to Christ, and needed that servant no longer; the law was a taskmaster and guardian set over man in his minority, now he had come of age, and was free; the law was a shadow of good things, and they had come; it was a law of sin and death, which no man could bear, and now the law of the spirit of life, as revealed by Jesus Christ, had made men free from the law of sin and death. Such was the work of the glorious gospel of the blessed God. Thus sweeping off the authority of the old law in general, he proceeds to particulars: he rejects circumcision, and the offering of sacrifices; rejects the distinction of nations as Jew and Gentile; the distinction of meats as clean and unclean, and all distinction of days, as holy and not holy. If one man thought one day holier than another day; if another man thought all days equally holy, he would have each man true to his conviction, but not seek to impose that conviction on his brothers. Such was Paul's opinion of "The law of Moses;" such, of the Sabbath; the Christians were not "subject to ordinances."

Let us come now to the common practice of the early Christians. The apostles went about and preached Christianity, as they severally understood it. They spoke as they found opportunity; on the Sabbath to the Jews in the synagogues, and on other days, as they found time and hearers. It does not appear from the New Testament, that they limited themselves to any particular day; they were missionaries, some of them remained but a little while in a place, making the most of their time. It seems that the early Christians, who lived in large towns, met every day for religious purposes. But as that would be found inconvenient, one day came to be regarded as the regular time of their meetings. The Jewish Christians observed the Sabbath with pharisaic rigor, while the liberal Christians neglected it. But both parties of Christians observed, at length, the first day of the week as a peculiar day. No one knows when this observance of the Sunday began; it is difficult to find proof in the New Testament, that the apostles regarded it as a peculiar day; it seems plain that Paul did not. But it is certain that in the second century after Jesus, the Christians in general did so regard it, and perhaps all of them.

Why was the Sunday chosen as the regular day for religious meeting? It was regarded as the day on which Jesus rose from the dead; and, following the mythical account in Genesis, it was the day on which God began the creation, and actually created the light. Here there were two reasons for the selection of that day; both are frequently mentioned by the early Christian writers. Sunday, therefore, was to them a symbol of the new creation, and of the light that had come into the world. The liberal

Christians, in separating from the Jewish Sabbath, would naturally exalt the new religious day. Athanasius, I think, is the first who ascribes a divine origin to the institution of Sunday. He says, " The Lord changed this day from the Sabbath to the Sunday;" but Athanasius lived three centuries after Christ, and seems to have known little about the matter.

The officers and the order of services in the churches on the Sunday seem derived from the usages of the Jewish synagogues. The Sunday was thus observed: the people came together in the morning; the exercises consisted of readings from the Old Testament and such writings of the Christians as the assembly saw fit to have read to them. In respect to these writings there was a wide difference in the different churches, some accepting more and others less. The overseer, or bishop, made an address, perhaps an exposition of the passage of Scripture. Prayers were said and hymns chanted; the Lord's supper was celebrated. The form no doubt differed, and widely, too, in different places. It was not the form of servitude but the spirit of freedom, they observed. But all these things were done, likewise, on other days; the Lord's supper could be celebrated on any day, and is on every day by the Catholic church, even now; for the Catholics have been true to the early practices in more points than the Protestants are willing to admit. In some places it is certain there was a "communion" every day. Sunday was regarded holy by the early Christians, just as certain festivals are regarded holy by the Catholics, the Episcopalians, and the Lutherans, at this day; as the New Englanders regard Thanksgiving day as holy. Other days, likewise, were regarded as holy; were used in the same manner as the Sunday. Such days were observed in honor of particular events in the life of Jesus, or in honor of saints and martyrs, or they were days consecrated by older festivals belonging to the more ancient forms of religion. In the Catholic church such days are still numerous. It is only the Puritans who have completely rejected them, and they have been obliged to substitute new ones in their place. However, there was one peculiarity of the Sunday which distinguished it from most or all other days. It was a day of religious rejoicing. On other days the Christians knelt in prayer; on the Sunday they stood up on joyful feet, for light had come into the world. Sunday was a day of gladness and rejoicing. The early Christians had many fasts; they were commonly held on Wednesdays and Fridays, often on Saturday also, the more completely to get rid of the Jewish superstition which consecrated that day; but on Sunday there must be no fast. He would be a heretic who should fast on Sunday. It is strictly forbidden in the "canons of the apostles;" a clergyman must be degraded and a layman excommunicated, for the offence. Says St. Ignatius, in the second century, if the epistle be genuine, "Every lover of Christ feasts on the Lord's day." "We deem it wicked," says Tertullian in the third century, "to fast on the Sunday, or to pray on our knees." "Oh," says St. Jerome, "that we could fast on the Sunday, as Paul did and they that were with him." St. Ambrose says, the "Manichees were damned for fasting on the Lord's day." At this day the Catholic church allows no fast on Sunday, save the Sunday before the crucifixion; even Lent ceases on that day.

It does not appear that labor ceased on Sunday, in the earliest age of Christianity. But when Sunday became the regular and most important day for holding religious meetings, less labor must of course be performed on that day. At length it became common in some places to abstain from ordinary work on the Sunday. It is not easy to say how early this was brought about. But after Christianity had become "respectable," and found its way to the ranks of the wealthy, cultivated and powerful, laws got enacted in its favor. Now, the Romans, like all other ancient nations, had certain festal days in which it was not thought proper to labor unless work was pressing. It was disreputable to continue common labor on such days without an urgent reason; they were pretty numerous in the Roman calendar. Courts did not sit on those days; no public business was transacted. They were observed as

Christmas and the more important saints' days in Catholic countries; as Thanksgiving day and the Fourth of July with us. In the year three hundred and twenty-one, Constantine, the first Christian emperor of Rome, placed Sunday among their ferial days. This was perhaps the first legislative action concerning the day. The statute forbids labor in towns, but expressly excludes all prohibition of field-labor in the country.* About three hundred and sixty-six or seven, the Council of Laodicea decreed that Christians "ought not to Judaize and be idle on the Sabbath, but to work on that day; especially observing the Lord's day, and if it is possible, as Christians, resting from labor." Afterwards the Emperor Theodosius forbade certain public games on Sunday, Christmas, Epiphany, and the whole time from Easter to Pentecost. Justinian likewise forbade theatrical exhibitions, races in the circus, and the fights of wild beasts, on Sunday, under severe penalties. This was done in order that the religious services of the Christians might not be disturbed. By his laws the Sunday continued to be a day in which public business was not to be transacted. But the Christmas days, the fifteen days of Easter, and numerous other days previously observed by Christians or pagans, were put in the same class by the law. All this it seems was done from no super-

* Justinian, *Cod.* Lib. iii. Tit. xii. l. 3.

stitious notions respecting those days, but for the sake of public utility and convenience. However, the rigor of the Jewish Sabbatical laws was by no means followed. Labors of love, *opera caritatis*, were considered as suitable business for those days. The very statute of Theodosius recommended the emancipation of slaves on Sunday. All impediments to their liberation were removed on that day, and though judicial proceedings in all other matters were forbidden on Sunday, an exception was expressly made in favor of emancipating slaves. This statute was preserved in the code of Justinian.* All these laws go to show that there were similar customs previously established among the Christians, without the aid of legislation.

About the middle of the sixth century the Council of Orleans forbade labor in the fields, though it did not forbid travelling with cattle and oxen, the preparation of food, or any work necessary to the cleanliness of the house or the person — declaring that rigors of that sort belong more to a Jewish than to a Christian observance of the day. That, I think, is the earliest ecclesiastical decree which has come down to us forbidding field-labor in the country; a decree unknown till five hundred and thirty-eight years after Christ. But before that, in the year three hundred and thirteen, the Council of Elvira in Spain

---

* *Cod.*, Lib. iii. Tit. xii. l. 2. See also, l. 3 and 11.

decreed, that if any one in a city absented himself three Sundays consecutively from the church, he should be suspended from communion for a short time. Such a regulation, however, was founded purely on considerations of public utility. Many church establishments have thought it necessary to protect themselves from desertion by similar penal laws.

In Catholic countries, at the present day, the morning of Sunday is appropiated to public worship, the people flocking to church. But the afternoon and evening are devoted to society, to amusement of various kinds. Nothing appears sombre, but every thing has a festive air; even the theatres are open. Sunday is like Christmas, or a Thanksgiving day in Boston, only the festive demonstrations are more public. It is so in the Protestant countries on the continent of Europe. Work is suspended, public and private, except what is necessary for the observance of the day; public lectures are suspended; public libraries closed; but galleries of paintings and statues are thrown open and crowded; the public walks are thronged. In Southern Germany, and, doubtless, elsewhere, young men and women have I seen in summer, of a Sunday afternoon, dancing on the green, the clergyman, Protestant or Catholic, looking on and enjoying the cheerfulness of the young people. Americans think their mode of keeping Sunday is unholy; they, that ours is Jewish and pharisaical. In Paris, sometimes, courses of scientific lectures are delivered after the hours of religious services, to men who are busy during the week with other cares, and who gladly take the hours of their only leisure day to gain a little intellectual instruction.

When England was a Catholic country, Catholic notions of Sunday of course prevailed. Labor was suspended; there was service in the churches, and afterwards there were sports for the people, but they were attended with quarrelling, noise, uproar, and continual drunkenness. It was so after the Reformation. In the time of Elizabeth, the laws forbade labor except in time of harvest, when it was thought right to work, if need were, and "save the thing that God hath sent." Some of the Protestants wished to reform those disorders, and convert the Sunday to a higher use. The government, and sometimes the superior clergy, for a long time interfered to prevent the reform, often to protect the abuse. The "Book of Sports," appointed to be read in churches, is well known to us from the just indignation with which it filled our fathers.

Now, it is plain, that in England, before the Reformation, the Sunday was not appropriated to its highest use; not to the highest interests of mankind; no, not to the highest concerns, which the people, at that time, were capable of appreciating. The attempts, made then and subsequently, by government, to enforce the observance of the day, for purposes not the highest, led to a fearful reaction; that to other and counter reactions. The ill consequences of those movements have not yet ceased on either side of the ocean.

The Puritans represented the spirit of reaction against ecclesiastical and other abuses of their time, and the age before them. Let me do these men no injustice. I honor the heroic virtues of our fathers not less because I see their faults; see the cause of their faults, and the occasion which demanded such masculine and terrible virtues as the Puritans unquestionably possessed. I speak only of their doctrine of the Sunday. They were driven from one extreme to the other, for oppression makes wise men mad. They took mainly the notions of the Sabbath, which belong to the later portions of the Old Testament; they interpreted them with the most pharisaical rigor, and then applied them to the Sunday. Did they find no warrant for that rigor in the New Testament? they found enough in the Old; enough in their own character, and their consequent notions of God. They thus introduced a set of ideas respecting the Sunday, which the Christian church had never known before, and rigidly enforced an observance thereof utterly foreign both to the letter and spirit of the New Testament. They made Sunday a terrible day; a day of fear, and of fasting, and of trembling under the terrors of the Lord. They even called it by the Hebrew name — the Sabbath. The Catholics had said it was not safe to trust the Scriptures in the hands of the people, for an inspired Word needed an expositor also inspired. The abuse which the Puritans made of the Bible by their notions of the Sunday, seemed a fulfilment of the Catholic prophecy. But the Catholics did not see what is plain to all men now — that this very abuse of Sunday and Scripture was only the reaction against other abuses, ancient, venerated, and enforced by the Catholic church itself.

Every sect has some institution which is the symbol of its religious consciousness, though not devised for that purpose. With the early Christians, it was their love-feasts and communion; with the Catholics, it is their gorgeous ritual with its ancient date and divine pretensions — a ritual so imposing to many; with the Quakers, who scorn all that is symbolic, the symbol equally appears in the plain dress and the plain speech, the broad brim, and *thee* and *thou*. With the Puritans, this symbol was the Sabbath, not the Sunday. Their Sabbath was like themselves, austere, inflexible as their "divine decrees;" not human and of man, but Hebrew and of the Jews, stern, cold, and sad.

The Puritans were possessed with the sentiment of fear before God; they had ideas analogous to that sentiment, and wrought out actions akin to those ideas. They brought to America their ideas and sentiments. Behold the effect of their actions. Let us walk reverently backward, with averted eyes to cover up their folly, their shame, and their sin, as they could not walk to conceal the folly of their progenitors. The Puritans are the fathers of New England and her descendant States; the fathers of the American idea; of most things in America that are good; surely, of most that is best. They seem made on purpose for their work of conquering a wilderness and founding a State. It is not with gentle hands, not with the dalliance of effeminate fingers, that such a task is done. The work required energy the most masculine, in heart, head, and hands. None but the Puritans could have done such a work. They could fast as no men; none could work like them; none preach; none pray; none could fight as they fought. They have left a most precious inheritance to men who have the same greatness of soul, but have fallen on happier times. Yet this inheritance is fatal to mere imitators, who will go on planting of vineyards, where the first planter fell intoxicated with the fruit of his own toil. This inheritance is dangerous to men who will be no wiser than their ancestors. Let us honor the good deeds of our fathers; and not eat, but reverently bury their honored bones.

The Puritans represented the natural reaction of mankind against old institutions that were absurd or tyrannical. The Catholic church had multiplied feast days to an extreme, and taken unnecessary pains to promote fun and frolic. The Puritans would have none of the saints' days in their calendar; thought sport was wicked; cut down Maypoles, and punished a man who kept Christmas after the old fashion. The Catholic church had neglected her golden opportunities for giving the people moral and religious instruction; had quite too much neglected public prayer and preaching, but relied mainly on sensuous instruments — architecture, painting, music. In revenge, the Puritan had a meeting-house as plain as boards could make it; tore the pictures to pieces; thought an organ "was not of God," and had sermons long and numerous, and prayers full of earnestness, zeal, piety, and faith, in short, possessed of all desirable things except an end. Did the Catholics forbid the people the Bible, emphatically the book of the people — the Puritan would read no other book; called his children Hebrew names, and reënacted "the laws of God" in the Old Testament, "until we can make better." Did Henry and Elizabeth underrate the people and overvalue the monarchy, nature had her vengeance for that abuse, and the Puritan taught the world that kings, also, had a joint in their necks.

The Puritans went to the extreme in many things: in their contempt for amusements, for what was graceful in man or beautiful in woman; in their scorn of art, of elegant literature, even of music; in their general condemnation of the past, from which they would preserve little excepting what was Hebrew, which, of course, they over-honered as much as they undervalued all the rest. In their notions respecting the Sunday they went to the same extreme. The general reason is obvious. They wished to avoid old abuses, and thought they were not out of the water till they were in the fire. But there was a special reason, also: the English are the most empirical of all nations. They love a fact more than an idea, and often cling to an historical precedent rather than obey a great truth which transcends all precedents. The national tendency to external things, perhaps, helped lead them to these peculiar notions of the Sabbath. The precedent they found in "The chosen people," and established, as they thought, by God himself.

The ideas of the Puritans respecting the Sunday are still cherished in the popular theology of New England. There is one party in our churches possessed of many excellences, which has always had the merit of speaking out fully what it thinks and feels. At this day that party still represents the Puritanic opinions about the Sunday, though a little modified. They teach that God created the world in six days, and rested the seventh; that he commanded mankind, also, to rest on that day; commanded a man to be stoned to death for picking up sticks of a Saturday; that by divine authority the first day of the week was substituted for the seventh, and therefore that it is the religious duty of all men to rest from work on that day, for the Hebrew law of the Sabbath is binding on Christians for ever. It is maintained that abstinence from work on Sunday is as much a religious duty as abstinence from theft or hatred; that the day must be exclusively devoted to religion, in the technical sense of that word, to public or private worship, to religious reading, thought, or conversation. To attend church on that day is thought to be a good in itself, though it should lead to no further good, and therefore a duty as imperative as the duty of loving man and God. The preacher may not edify, still the duty of attending to his ministration of the word remains the same; for the attendance is a good in itself. It is taught that work, that amusement, common conversation, the reading of a book not technically religious, is a sin, just as clearly a sin as theft or hatred, though perhaps not so great. Writing a letter, even, is denounced as a sin, though the letter be written for the purpose of arresting the progress of a war, and securing life and freedom to millions of men.

Now, it is very plain that such ideas are not consistent with the truth. In the language of the church, they are a heresy. As we learn the facts of the case we must give up such ideas concerning the Sunday. It is like any other day. Christianity knows no classes of days, as holy or profane; all days are the Lord's days, all time holy time.

But then comes the other question, What is the best use to be made of the day; the use most conducive to the highest interests of mankind? Will it be most profitable to "give up the Sunday," to use it as the Catholics do, as the Puritans did, or to adopt some other method? To answer these questions fairly, let us look and see the effects of the present notions about the Sunday, and the stricter mode of observing it here in New England. The experience of two hundred years is worth looking at. Let us look at the good effects first.

The good and evil of any age are commonly bound so closely together, that in plucking up the tares, there is danger lest the wheat also be uprooted, at least trodden down. In America, especially in New England, every thing is intense, with of course a tendency to extravagance, to fanaticism. Look at some of the most obvious signs of that intensity. No conservatism in the world is so bigoted as American conservatism; no democracy so intense. Nowhere else can you find such thorough-going defenders of the existing state of things, social, ecclesiastical, civil; such defenders of drunkenness, ignorance, superstition, slavery, and war; nowhere such radical enemies to the existing state of things; such foes of drunkenness, ignorance, superstition, slavery, and war. No "Revivals of religion" are like the American; none of old were like these. See how the American soldiers fight; how the American men will work. Puritanism was intense enough in England; in the New World it was yet more so. Our fathers were intense Calvinists; more Calvinistic than Calvin — they became Hopkinsian. They hated the Pope; kings and bishops were their aversion. They feared God. Did they love him — love him as much? They had an intense religious activity, but they had another intensity. It is better that we should say it, rather than men who do not honor them. That intensity of action, when turned towards material things, or, as they called them, "carnal things," needed some powerful check. It was found in their bigotry and superstition. In such an age as theirs, when the Reformation broke down all the ordinary restraints of society, and rent asunder the golden ties which bound man to the past; when the Anglican church ended in fire, and the English monarchy in blood; when men full of piety thanked God for the fire and the bloodshed, and felt the wrongs of a thousand years driving them almost to madness — what was there to keep such men within bounds, and restrain them from the wildest license and unbridled anarchy? Nothing but superstition; nothing short of fear of hell. They broke down the monarchy; they trod the church under their feet. She who had once been counted as the queen and mother of society, was now to be regarded only as the Apocalyptical woman in scarlet, the mother of abominations, bride of the devil, and queen of hell. The Old Testament wrought on the minds of these men like a charm, to stimulate and to soothe. "One day," said they, "is made holy by God; in it shall no work be done by man or beast, or thing inanimate. On that day all must attend church as an act of religion." Here, then, was a bar extending across the stream of worldliness, filling one seventh part of its channel, wide and deep, and wonderfully interrupting its whelming tide. I admire the divine skill which compounds the gases in the air; which balances centripetal and centrifugal forces into harmonious proportions, — those fair ellipses in the unseen air; but still more marvellous is that same skill, diviner now, which compounds the folly and the wisdom of mankind; balances centripetal and centrifugal forces here, stilling the noise of kings and the tumult of the people, making their wrath to serve him, and the remnant thereof restraining forever.

On Sunday, master and man, the slave stolen from the wilderness, the servant — a Christian man bought from some Christian conqueror, — must cease from their work. Did the covetous, the cruel, the strong, oppress the weak for six days, the Sabbath said, "Hitherto shalt thou come, but no further." The servant was free from his master, and the weary was at rest. The plough stood still in the furrow; the sheaf lay neglected in the field; the horse and the ox enjoyed their master's Sabbath of rest, all heedless of the divine decrees, of election or reprobation, yet not the less watched over by that dear Providence which numbered the hairs of the head, and overruled the falling of a sparrow for the sparrow's good. All must attend church, master and man, rich and poor, oppressor and oppressed. Good things and great things got read out of the Bible, it was the book of the people, the New Testament, written much of it in the interest of all mankind, with special emphasis laid on the rights of the weak and the duties of the strong. Good things got said in sermon and in prayer. The speakers must think, the hearers think, as well as tremble. Begin to think in a circle narrow as a lady's ring, or the Assembly's Catechism, you will think out; for thought, like all movement, tends to the right line. Calvinism has always bred thinkers, and when barbarism was the first danger was perhaps the only thing which could do it. Calvinism, too, has always shown itself in favor of popular liberty to a certain degree, and though it stops far short of the mark, yet goes far beyond the Catholic or Episcopalian.

Sunday, thus enforced by superstition, has yet been the education-day of New England; the national school-time for the culture of man's highest powers; therein have the clergy been our educators, and done a vast service which mankind will not soon forget. It was good seed they sowed on this soil of the New World; the harvest is proof of that. They builded wiser than they knew. Their unconscious hands constructed the thought of God. Even their superstition and bigotry did much to preserve church and clergy to us; much also to educate and develop the highest powers of man. But for that superstition we might have seen the same anarchy, the same unbridled license in the seventeenth century, which we saw in the eighteenth, as a consequence of a similar revolution, a similar reaction; only it would have been carried out with the intensity of that most masculine and earnest race of men. How much further English atrocities would have gone than the French did go; how long it would have taken mankind, by their proper motion, to reascend from a fall so adverse and so low, I cannot tell. I see what saved them from the plunge.

True, the Sunday was not what it should be, more than the week; preaching was not what it should be, more than practice. But without that Sunday, and without that preaching, New England would have been a quite different land; America another nation altogether; the world by no means so far advanced as now. New England with her descendants has always been the superior portion of America. I flatter no man's prejudice, but speak a plain truth. She is superior in intelligence, in morality — that is too plain for proof. The prime cause of that superiority must be sought in the character of the fathers of New England; but a secondary and most powerful cause is to be found also in those two institutions — Sunday and preaching. Why is it that all great movements, from the American Revolution down to anti-slavery, have begun here? Why is it that education societies, missionary societies, Bible societies, and all the movements for the advance of mankind, begin here? Why, it is no more an accident than the rising of the tide. Find much of the cause in the superior character, and therefore in the superior aims of the forefathers, much also will be found due to this — Once in the week they paused from all work; they thought of their God, who had delivered them from the iron house and yoke of bondage; they listened to the words of able men, exhorting them to justice, piety, and a heavenly walk with God; they trembled at fear of hell; they rejoiced at hope of heaven. The church — no, the "meeting-house" — was the common property of all; the minister the common friend. The slave looked up to him; the chief magistrate dared not look down on him. For more than a hundred years the ablest men of New England went into the pulpit. No talent was thought too great, no learning too rich and profound, no genius too holy and divine, for the work of teaching men their highest duty, and helping to their highest bliss. He was the minister to all. There was not then a church for the rich, and a chapel for the poor; the rich and the poor met together, for one God was the maker of them all — their Father too; they had one Gospel, one Redeemer, — their Brother not less than their God; they journeyed toward the same heaven, which had but one entrance for great and little; they prayed all the same prayer. The effect of this socialism of religion is seldom noticed; so we walk on moist earth, not thinking that we tread on the thunder-cloud and the lightning. But it is not in human nature for men of intense religious activity to meet in the same church, sing the same psalm, pray the same prayer, partake the same elements of communion, and not be touched with compassion — each for all, and all for each. The same causes which built up religion in New England, built up democracy along with it. Is it not easy to see the cause which made the rich men of New England the most benevolent of rich men; gave them their character for generosity and public spirit — yes, for eminent humanity? The acorn is not more obviously the parent of the oak than those two institutions of New England the parent of such masculine virtues as distinguish her sons.

Regarded merely as a day of rest from labor, the Sunday has been of great value to us. Considering the intense character of the nation, our tendency to material things, and our restless love of work, it seems as if a Moses of the nineteenth century, legislating for us, would enact two rest-days in the week, rather than one. It is a good thing that a man once a week pauses from his work, arrays himself in clean garments, and is at rest.

Regarded in its other aspects, Sunday has aided the intellectual culture of the people to a degree not often appreciated. To many a man, yes, to most men, it is their only reading day, and they will read "secular" books, spite of the clerical admonition. Many a poor boy in New England, who has toiled all the week, and would gladly have studied all the night, did not obstinate Nature forbid, has studied stealthily all Sunday, not Jeremiah and the prophets, but Homer and the mathematics, and risen at length to eminence amongst cultivated men; — he has to thank the Sunday for the beginnings of that manly growth.

The moral and religious effect of the day is yet more important. One seventh part of the time was to be devoted to moral and religious culture. The clergy watched diligently over Sunday, as their own day. Work was then the accident; religion was the business. Every thing with us becomes earnest; Sunday as earnest as the week. It must not be spent idly. Perhaps no body of clergymen, for two hundred years, on the whole, were ever so wakeful and active as the American. They also are earnest and full of intensity, especially in the more serious sects. I think I am not very superstitious; not often inclined to lean on my father's staff rather than walk on my own feet; not over-much accustomed to take things on trust because they have been trusted to all along: but I must confess that I see a vast amount of good achieved by the aid of these two institutions, the Sunday and preaching, which could not have been done without them. I know I have my prejudices; I love the Sunday; a professional bias may warp me aside, for I am a preacher— the pulpit is my joy and my throne. Judge you how far my profession and my prejudice have led me astray in estimating the value of the Sunday, its preaching, and the good they have achieved for us in New England. I know what superstition, what bigotry, has been connected with both; I know it has kept grim and terrible guard about these institutions. I look upon that superstition and bigotry, as on the old New England guns which were fought with in the Indian wars, the French wars, and the Revolution;—things that did service when men knew not how to defend what they valued most with better tools and more Christian. I look on both with the same melancholy veneration, but honor them the more that now they are old, battered, unfit for use and covered with rust. I would respectfully hang them up, superstition and the musket, side by side; honorable, but harmless, with their muzzles down, and pray God it might never be my lot to handle such ungodly weapons, though in a cause never so humane and holy.

Let us look a little at the ill effects of these notions of the Sunday and the observance which they led to. It is thought an act of religion to attend church and give a mere bodily presence there. Hence the minister often relies on this circumstance to bring his audience together; preaches sermons on the duty of going to church, while ingenuous boys blush for his weakness, and ask, "Were it not better to rely on your goodness, your piety, your wisdom; on your superior ability to teach men, even on your eloquence, rather than tell them it is an act of religion to come and hear you, when both they and you are painfully conscious that they are thereby made no wiser, no better, nor more Christian?" This notion is a dangerous one for a clergyman. It flatters his pride and encourages his sloth. It blinds him to his own defects, and leads him to attribute his empty benches to the perverseness of human nature and the carnal heart, which a few snow-flakes can frighten from his church, while a storm will not keep them from a lecture on science or literature. No doubt it is a man's duty to seek all opportunities of becoming wiser and better. So far as church-going helps that work, so far it is a duty. But to count it in itself, irrespective of its consequences, an act of religion, is to commit a dangerous error, which has proved fatal to many a man's growth in goodness and piety. Let us look to the end, not merely at the means.

This notion has also a bad effect on the hearers. It is thought an act of religion to attend church, whether you are edified or not by sermon, by psalm, or prayer; an act of religion, though you could more profitably spend the time in your own closet at home, or with your own thoughts in the fields. Of course, then, he who attends once a day is thought a Christian to a certain degree; if twice, more so; if thrice, why that denotes an additional amount of growth in grace. In this way the day is often spent in a continual round of meetings. Sermon follows sermon; prayer treads upon the footsteps of prayer; psalm effaces psalm, till morning, afternoon, evening, all are gone. The Sunday is ended and over; the man is tired — but has he been profited and made better thereby? The sermons and the prayers have cancelled one another, been heard and forgot. They were too numerous to remember or produce their effect. So on a summer's lake, as the winds loiter and then pass by, ripple follows ripple, and wave succeeds to wave, yet the next day the wind has ceased and the unstable water bears no trace left there by all the blowings of the former day, but bares its incontinent bosom to the frailest and most fleeting clouds.

Another ill effect follows from regarding attendance at church as an act of religion in itself: — It is forgotten that a man cannot teach what he does not know. If you have more manhood than I, more religion; if you are the more humane and the more divine, it is idle for me to try and teach you divinity and humanity; idle in you to make believe you are taught. The less must learn of the greater, not the greater directly of the less. It is too often forgotten by the preacher that his hearers may be capable of teaching him; that he cannot fill them out of an emptiness, but a fulness. Hence, it comes to pass that no one, how advanced soever, is allowed to graduate, so to say, from the church. Perhaps it may do a great man, mature in Christianity, good to sit down with his fellows and hear a little man talk who knows nothing of religion; it may increase his sympathy with mankind. It can hardly be an act of religion to such a man so advanced in his goodness and piety; perhaps not the best use he could make of the hour.

The current opinion hinders social tendencies. A man must not meet with his friend and neighbor, or if he does, he must talk with bated breath, with ghostly countenance, and of a ghostly theme. From this abuse of the Sunday comes much of the cold and unsocial character which strangers charge us with. As things now go, there are many who have no opportunity for social intercourse except the hours of the Sunday. Then it is forbidden them. So they suffer and lose much of the charm of life; become ungenial, unsocial, stiff, and hard, and cold.

This notion hinders men, also, from intellectual culture. They must read no book but one professedly religious. Such works are commonly poor and dull; written mainly by men of little ability, of little breadth of view; not written in the interest of mankind, but only of a sect — the Calvinists or Unitarians. A good man groans when he looks over the immense piles of sectarian books written with good motives, and read with the most devout of intentions, but which produce their best effect when they lead only to sleep. Yet it is commonly taught that it is religion to spend a part of Sunday in reading such works, in listening, or in trying to listen, or in affecting to try and listen, to the most watery sermons, while it is wicked to read some "secular" book, philosophy, history, poem, or tale, which expands the mind and warms the heart. Our poor but wisdom-seeking boy must read his Homer only by stealth. There are many men who have no time for intellectual pursuits, none for reading, except on Sunday. It is cruel to tell them they shall read none but sectarian books or listen only to sectarian words.

But there are other evils yet. These notions and the corresponding practice tend to make religion external, consisting in obedience to form, in compliance with custom; while religion is and can be only piety and goodness, love to God and love to man. To keep the Sunday idle, to attend church, is not being religious. It is easy to do that; easy to stop there, and then to look at real, manly saints, who live in the odor of sanctity, whose sentiment is a prayer, their deeds religion, and their whole life a perpetual communion with God, and say, "Infidel! Unbeliever."

Then, as one day is devoted to religion, it is thought that is enough; that religion has no more business in the world than the world in religion. So division is made of the territory of mortal life, in which partition worldliness has six days, while poor religion has only the Sunday, and content with her own limits, feels no salient wish to absorb or annex the week! It is painful to see this abuse of an institution so noble. No commonness of its occurrence renders it less painful. It is painful to be told that men of the most scrupulous sects on Sunday, are in the week the least scrupulous of men.

But even in religious matters it is thought all things which pertain directly to the religious welfare of men are not proper to be discussed on Sunday. One must not preach against intemperance, against slavery, against war, on Sunday. It is not "evangelical;" not "preaching the gospel." Yet it is thought proper to preach on total depravity, on eternal damnation; to show that God will damn forever the majority of mankind; that the apostle Peter was a Unitarian. The Sunday is not the time, the pulpit not the place, preaching not the instrument, wherewith to oppose the monstrous sins of our day, and secure education, temperance, peace, freedom, for mankind. It is not evangelical, not Christian, to do that of a Sunday! Yet wonderful to say, it is not thought very wicked to hold a political caucus on Sunday for the merest party purposes; not wicked at all to work all day at the navy-yards in fitting out vessels, if they are only vessels of war; not at all wicked to toil all Sunday, if it is only in aiming to kill men in regular battle. Theological newspapers can expend their cheap censure on a member of Congress for writing a letter on Sunday, yet have no word of fault to find with the order which sets hundreds to work on Sunday in preparing armaments of war; not a word against the war which sets men to butcher their Christian brothers on the day which Christians celebrate as the anniversary of Christ's triumph over death! These things show that we have not yet arrived at the most profitable and Christian mode of using the Sunday; and when I consider these abuses I wonder not that the cry of "Infidel" is met by the unchristian taunt, yet more deserved and biting, "Thou hypocrite!" I wonder not that some men say, "Let us away with the Sunday altogether; and if we have no place for rest, we will have none for hypocrisy."

The efforts honestly made by good and honest men, to Judaize the day still more; to revive the sterner features of ancient worship; to put a yoke on us which neither we nor our fathers could bear; to transform the Christian Sunday into the Jewish Sabbath, must lead to a reaction. Abuse on one side will be met by abuse on the other; despotic asceticism by license; Judaism by heathenism. Superstition is the mother of denial. Men will scorn the Sunday; abuse its timely rest. Its hours that may be devoted to man's highest interests will be prostituted to low aims, and worldliness make an unbroken sweep from one end of the month to the other; and then it will take years of toil before mankind can get back and secure the blessings now placed within an easy reach. I put it to you, men whose heads time has crowned with white, or sprinkled with a sober gray, if you would deem it salutary to enforce on your grandchildren the Sabbath austerities which your parents imposed on you? In your youth was the Sunday a welcome day; a genial day; or only wearisome and sour? Was religion, dressed in her Sabbath dress, a welcome guest; was she lovely and to be desired? Your faces answer. Let us profit by your experience.

How can we make the Sunday yet more valuable? If we abandon the superstitious notions respecting its origin and original design, the evils that have hitherto hindered its use will soon perish of themselves. They all grow out of that root. If men are not driven into a reaction by pretensions for the Sunday which facts will not warrant; if unreasonable austerities are not forced upon them in the name of the law, and the name of God; there is no danger in our day that men will abandon an institution which already has done so much service to mankind. Let Sunday and preaching stand on their own merits, and they will encounter no more opposition than the common school and the work-days of the week. Then men will be ready enough to appropriate the Sunday to the highest objects they know and can appreciate. Tell men the Sunday is made for man, and they will use it for its highest use. Tell them man is made for it, and they will war on it as a tyrant. I should be sorry to see the Sunday devoted to common work; sorry to hear the clatter of a mill, or the rattle of the wheels of business on that day. I look with pain on men engaged needlessly in work on that day; not with the pain of wounded superstition, but a deeper regret. I would not water my garden with perfumes when common water was at hand. We shall always have work enough in America; hand-work, and head-work, for common purposes. There is danger that we shall not have enough of rest, of intellectual cultivation, of refinement, of social intercourse; that our time shall be too much devoted to the lower interests of life, to the means of living and not the end.

I would not consider it an act of religion to attend

church: only a good thing to go there when the way of improvement leads through it; when you are made wiser and better by being there. I am pained to see a man spend the whole of a Sunday in going to church, — and forgetting himself in getting acquainted with the words of the preachers. I think most intelligent hearers, and most intelligent and Christian preachers, will confess that two sermons are better than three, and one is better than two. One need only look at the afternoon face of a congregation in the city, to be satisfied of this. If one half the day were devoted to public worship, the other half might be free for private studies of men at home, for private devotion, for social relaxation, for intercourse with one's own family and friends. Then Sunday afternoon and evening would afford an excellent opportunity for meetings for the promotion of the great humane movements of the day, which some would think not evangelical enough to be treated of in the morning. Would it be inconsistent with the great purposes of the day, inconsistent with Christianity, to have lectures on science, literature, and similar subjects delivered then? I do not believe the Catholic custom of spending the Sunday afternoon in England, before the Reformation, was a good one. It diverted men from the higher end to the lower. I cannot think that here and now we need amusement so much as society, instruction, refinement, and devotion. Yet it seems to me unwise to restrain the innocent sports of children of a Sunday, to the same degree that our fathers did; to make Sunday to them a day of gloom and sadness. Thoughtful parents are now much troubled in this matter; they cannot enforce the old discipline, so disastrous to themselves; they fear to trust their own sense of what is right; — so, perhaps, get the ill of both schemes, and the good of neither. There are in Boston about thirty thousand Catholics, twenty-five thousand of them, probably, too ignorant to read with pleasure or profit any book. At home, amusement formed a part of their Sunday service; it was a part of their religion to make a festive use of Sunday afternoon. What shall they do? Is it Christian in us by statute to interdict them from their recreation? With the exception of children and these most ignorant persons, it does not appear that there is any class amongst us who need any part of the Sunday for sport.

I am not one of those who wish "to give up the Sunday;" indeed there are few such men amongst us; I would make it yet more useful and profitable. I would remove from it the superstition and the bigotry which have so long been connected with it; I would use it freely, as a Christian not enslaved by the letter of Judaism, but made free by an obedience to the law of the spirit of life. I would use the Sunday for religion in the wide sense of that word; use it to promote piety and goodness, for humanity, for science, for letters, for society. I would not abuse it by impudent license on the one hand, nor by slavish superstition on the other. We can easily escape the evils which come of the old abuse; can make the Sunday ten times more valuable than it is even now; can employ it for all the highest interests of mankind, and fear no reaction into libertinism.

The Sunday is made for man, as are all other days; not man for the Sunday. Let us use it, then, not consuming its hours in a Jewish observance; not devote it to the lower necessities of life, but the higher; not squander it in idleness, sloth, frivolity, or sleep; let us use it for the body's rest, for the mind's culture, for head and heart and soul.

Men and women, you have received the Sunday from your fathers, as a day to be devoted to the highest interests of man. It has done great service for them and for you. But it has come down accompanied with superstition which robs it of half its value. It is easy for you to make the day far more profitable to yourselves than it ever was to your fathers; easy to divest it of all bigotry, to free it from all oldness of the letter; easy to leave it for your children an institution which shall bless them for ages yet to come: or it is easy to bind on their necks unnatural restraints; to impose on their conscience and understanding absurdities which at last they must repel with scorn and contempt. It is in your hands to make the Sunday Jewish or Christian.

III.

A SERMON OF IMMORTAL LIFE.—PREACHED AT THE MELODEON, ON SUNDAY, SEPTEMBER 20, 1846.

WISDOM OF SOLOMON III. 1, 4.

The souls of the righteous are in the hands of God: their hope is full of immortality.

IT is the belief of mankind that we shall all live forever. This is not a doctrine of Christianity alone. It belongs to the human race. You may find nations so rude that they live houseless, in caverns of the earth; nations that have no letters, not knowing the use of bows and arrows, fire or even clothes, but no nation without a belief in immortal life. The form of that belief is often grotesque and absurd; the mode of proof ridiculous; the expectations of what the future life is to be are often childish and silly. But notwithstanding all that, the fact still remains, the belief that the soul of a man never dies.

How did mankind come by this opinion? "By a miraculous revelation," says one. But according to the common theory of miraculous revelations, the race could not have obtained it in this way, for according to that theory the heathen had no such revelations; yet we find this doctrine the settled belief of the whole heathen world. The Greeks and Romans believed it long before Christ; the Chaldees, with no pretence to miraculous inspiration, taught the idea of immortality; while the Jews, spite of their alleged revelations, rested only in the dim sentiment thereof.

It was not arrived at by reasoning. It requires a good deal of hard thinking to reason out and prove this matter. Yet you find this belief among nations not capable as yet of that art of thinking and to that degree, nations who never tried to prove it, and yet believe it as confidently as we. The human race did not sit down and think it out; never waited till they could prove it by logic and metaphysics; did not delay their belief till a miraculous revelation came to confirm it. It came to mankind by intuition; by instinctive belief, the belief which comes unavoidably from the nature of man. In this same way came the belief in God; the love of man; the sentiment of justice. Men could see, and knew they could see, before they proved it; before they had theories of vision; without waiting for a miraculous revelation to come and tell them they had eyes, and might see if they would look. Some faculties of the body act spontaneously at first — so others of the spirit.

Immortality is a fact of man's nature, so it is a

part of the universe, just as the sun is a fact in the heavens and a part of the universe. Both are writings from God's hand; each therefore a revelation from Him, and of Him; only not miraculous, but natural, regular, normal. Yet each is just as much a revelation from Him as if the great Soul of all had spoken in English speech to one of us and said, "There is a sun there in the heavens, and thou shalt live for ever." Yes, the fact is more certain than such speech would make it, for this fact speaks always — a perpetual revelation, and no words can make it more certain.

As a man attains consciousness of himself, he attains consciousness of his immortality. At first he asks proof no more of his eternal existence than of his present life; instinctively he believes both. Nay, he does not separate the two; this life is one link in that golden and electric chain of immortality; the next life another and more bright, but in the same chain. Immortality is what philosophers call an ontological fact; it belongs essentially to the being of man, just as the eye is a physiological fact and belongs to the body of man. To my mind this is the great proof of immortality: the fact that it is written in human nature; written there so plain that the rudest nations have not failed to find it, to know it; written just as much as form is written on the circle, and extension on matter in general. It comes to our consciousness as naturally as the notions of time and space. We feel it as a desire; we feel it as a fact. What is thus in man is writ there of God who writes no lies. To suppose that this universal desire has no corresponding gratification, is to represent Him, not as the father of all but as only a deceiver. I feel the longing after immortality, a desire essential to my nature, deep as the foundation of my being; I find the same desire in all men. I feel conscious of immortality; that I am not to die; no, never to die, though often to change. I cannot believe this desire and consciousness are felt only to mislead, to beguile, to deceive me. I know God is my father, and the father of the nations. Can the Almighty deceive his children? For my own part, I can conceive of nothing which shall make me more certain of my immortality. I ask no argument from learned lips. No miracle could make me more sure; no, not if the sheeted dead burst cerement and shroud, and rising forth from their honored tombs stood here before me, the disenchanted dust once more enchanted with that fiery life; no, not if the souls of all my sires since time began came thronging round, and with miraculous speech told me they lived and I should also live. I could only say, "I knew all this before, why waste your heavenly speech!" I have now indubitable certainty of eternal life. Death removing me to the next state, can give me infallible certainty.

But there are men who doubt of immortality.

They say they are conscious of the want, not of the fact. They need a proof. The exception here proves the rule. You do not doubt your personal and conscious existence now; you ask no proof of that; you would laugh at me should I try to convince you that you are alive and self-conscious. Yet one of the leaders of modern philosophy wanted a proof of his as a basis for his science, and said, — "I am because I think." But his thought required proof as much as his being; yes, logically more, for being is the ground of thinking, not thinking of being. At this day there are sound men who deny the existence of this outward world, declaring it only a dream-world. This ground, they say, and yonder sun have being but in fancy, like the sun and ground you perchance dreamed of last night whose being was only a being-dreamed. These are exceptional men, and help prove the common rule, that man trusts his senses and believes an outward world. Yet such are more common amongst philosophers than men who doubt of their immortal life. You cannot easily reason those men out of their philosophy and into their senses, nor by your own philosophy perhaps convince them that there is an outward world.

I think few of you came to your belief in everlasting life through reasoning. Your belief grew out of your general state of mind and heart. You could not help it. Perhaps few of you ever sat down and weighed the arguments for and against it, and so made up your mind. Perhaps those who have the firmest consciousness of the fact are least familiar with the arguments which confirm that consciousness. If a man disbelieves it, if he denies it, his opinion is not often to be changed immediately or directly by argument. His special conviction has grown out of his general state of mind and heart, and is only to be removed by a change in his whole philosophy. I am not honoring men for their belief, nor blaming men who doubt or deny. I do not believe any one ever willingly doubted this; ever purposely reasoned himself into the denial thereof. Men doubt because they cannot help it; not because they will, but must.

There are a great many things true which no man as yet can prove true; some things so true that nothing can make them plainer, or more plainly true. I think it is so with this doctrine, and therefore, for myself, ask no argument. With my views of man, of God, of the relation between the two, I want no proof, satisfied with my own consciousness of immortality. Yet there are arguments which are fair, logical, just, which satisfy the mind, and may, perhaps, help persuade some men who doubt, if such men there are amongst you. I think that immortality is a fact of consciousness; a fact given in the constitution of man: therefore a matter of sentiment. But it requires thought to pick it out from amongst the other facts of consciousness. Though at first merely a feeling, a matter of sentiment, on examination it becomes an idea — a matter of thought. It will bear being looked at in the sharpest and dryest light of logic. Truth never flinches before reason. It is so with our consciousness of God; that is an ontological fact, a fact given in the nature of man. At first it is a feeling, a matter of sentiment. By thought we abstract this fact from other facts; we find an idea of God. That is a matter of philosophy, and the analyzing mind legitimates the idea and at length demonstrates the existence of God, which we first learned without analysis, and by intuition. A great deal has been written to prove the existence of God, and that by the ablest men; yet I cannot believe that any one was ever reasoned directly into a belief in God, by all those able men, nor directly out of it by all the skeptics and scoffers. Indirectly such works affect men, change their philosophy and modes of thought, and so help them to one or the other conclusion.

The idea of immortality, like the idea of God, in a certain sense, is born in us, and fast as we come to consciousness of ourselves we come to consciousness of God, and of ourselves as immortal. The higher we advance in wisdom, goodness, piety, the larger place do God and immortality hold in our experience and inward life. I think that is the regular and natural process of a man's development. Doubt of either seems to me an exception, an irregularity. Causes that remove the doubt must be general more than special.

However, in order to have a basis of thought and reasoning, as well as of intuition and reason, let me mention some of the arguments for everlasting life.

I. The first is drawn from the general belief of mankind. The greatest philosophers and the most profound and persuasive religious teachers of the whole world have taught this. That is an important fact, for these men represent the consciousness of mankind in the highest development it has yet reached, and in such points are the truest representatives of man. What is more, the human race believes it, not merely as a thing given by miraculous revelation, not as a matter proven by science, not as a thing of tradition resting on some man's authority, but believes it instinctively, not knowing and not asking why, or how; believes it as a fact of consciousness. Now in a matter of this sort the opinion of the human race is worth considering. I do not value very much the opinion of a priesthood in Rome or Judea, or elsewhere on this point, or any other, for they may have designs adverse to the truth. But the general sentiment of the human race in a matter like this is of the greatest importance. This general sentiment of mankind is a quite different thing from public opinion, which favors freedom in one country and slavery in another; this sentiment of mankind relates to what is a matter of feeling with most men. It is only a few thinkers that have made it a matter of thought. The opinion of mankind, so far as we know, has not changed on this point for four thousand years. Since the dawn of history, man's belief in immortality has continually been developing and getting deeper fixed.

Still more, this belief is very dear to mankind. Let me prove that. If it were true that one human soul was immortal and yet was to be eternally damned, getting only more clotted with crime and deeper bit by agony as the ages went slowly by, then immortality were a curse, not to that man only, but to all mankind — for no amount of happiness, merited or undeserved, could ever atone or make up for the horrid wrong done to that one most miserable man. Who of you is there that could relish Heaven, or even bear it for a moment, knowing that a brother was doomed to smart with ever greatening agony, while year on year, and age on age, the endless chain of eternity continued to coil round the flying wheels of hell? I say the thought of one such man would fill even Heaven with misery, and the best man of men would scorn the joys of everlasting bliss, would spurn at Heaven and say, "Give me my brother's place; for me there is no Heaven while he is there!" Now it has been popularly taught, that not one man alone, but the vast majority of all mankind, are thus to be condemned; immortal only to be everlastingly wretched. That is the popular doctrine now in this land. It has been so taught in the Christian churches these sixteen centuries and more — taught in the name of Christ! Such an immortality would be a curse to men, to every man; as much so to the "saved" as to the "lost;" for who would willingly stay in Heaven, and on such terms? Surely not he who wept with weeping men! Yet in spite of this vile doctrine drawn over the world to come, mankind religiously believes that each shall live for ever. This shows how strong is the instinct which can lift up such a foul and hateful doctrine and still live on. Tell me not that scoffers and critics shall take away man's faith in endless life: it has stood a harder test than can ever come again.

II. The next argument is drawn from the nature of man.

1. All men desire to be immortal. This desire is instinctive, natural, universal. In God's world such a desire implies the satisfaction thereof equally natural and universal. It cannot be that God has given man this universal desire of immortality, this belief in it, and yet made it all a mockery. Man loves truth; tells it; rests only in it; how much more God who is the trueness of truth. Bodily senses imply their objects — the eye light, the ear sound; the touch, the taste, the smell, things relative thereto.

Spiritual senses likewise foretell their object, — are silent prophecies of endless life. The love of justice, beauty, truth, of man and God, points to realities unseen as yet. We are ever hungering after noblest things, and what we feed on makes us hunger more. The senses are satisfied, but the soul never.

2. Then, too, while this composite body unavoidably decays, this simple soul which is my life decays not. Reason, the affections, all the powers that make the man, decay not. True, the organs by which they act become impaired. But there is no cause for thinking that love, conscience, reason, will, ever become weaker in man; but cause for thinking that all these continually become more strong. Was the mind of Newton gone when his frame, long overtasked, refused its wonted work?

3. Here on earth, every thing in its place and time matures. The acorn and the chestnut, things natural to this climate, ripen every year. A longer season would make them no better nor bigger. It is so with our body — that, under proper conditions, becomes mature. It is so with all the things of earth. But man is not fully grown as the acorn and the chestnut; never gets mature. Take the best man and the greatest — all his faculties are not developed, fully grown and matured. He is not complete in the qualities of a man; nay, often half his qualities lie all unused. Shall we conclude these are never to obtain development and do their work? The anal-

ogy of nature tells us that man, the new-born plant, is but removed by death to another soil, where he shall grow complete and become mature.

4. Then, too, each other thing under its proper conditions not only ripens but is perfect also after its kind. Each clover-seed is perfect as a star. Every lion, as a general rule, is a common representation of all lionhood; the ideal of his race made real in him, a thousand years of life would not make him more. But where is the Adamitic man; the type and representative of his race, who makes actual its idea? Even Jesus bids you not call him good; no man has all the manhood of mankind. Yes, there are rudiments of greatness in us all, but abortive, incomplete, and stopped in embryo. Now all these elements of manhood point as directly to another state as the unfinished walls of yonder rising church intimate that the work is not complete, that the artist here intends a roof, a window there, here a tower, and over all a heaven-piercing spire. All men are abortions, our failure pointing to the real success. Nay, we are all waiting to be born, our whole nature looking to another world, and dimly presaging what that world shall be. Death, however we misname him, seasonable or out of time, is the birth-angel, that alone.

5. Besides, the presence of injustice, of wrong, points the same way. The fact that one man goes out of this life in childhood, in manhood, at any time

before the natural measure of his days is full; the fact that any one is by circumstances made wretched; that he is hindered from his proper growth and has not here his natural due — all intimates to me his future life. I know that God is just. I know His justice too shall make all things right, for He must have the power, the wish, the will therefor, to speak in human speech. I see the injustice in this city, its pauperism, suffering, and crime, men smarting all their life, and by no fault of theirs. I know there must be another hemisphere to balance this; another life, wherein justice shall come to all and for all. Else God were unjust; and an unjust God to me is no God at all, but a wretched chimera which my soul rejects with scorn. I see the autumn prefigured in the spring. The flowers of May-day foretold the harvest, its rosy apples and its yellow ears of corn. As the bud now lying cold and close upon the bark of every tree throughout our northern clime is a silent prophecy of yet another spring and other summers, and harvests too; so this instinctive love of justice scantly budding here and nipped by adverse fate, silently but clearly tells of a kingdom of heaven. I take some miserable child here in this city, squalid in dress and look, ignorant and wicked too as most men judge of vagrant vice, made so by circumstances over which that child had no control; I turn off with a shudder at the public wrong we have done and still are doing; but in that child I see proof of another world, yes, Heaven glittering from behind those saddened eyes. I know that child has a man's nature in him, perhaps a Channing's trusting piety; perhaps a Newton's mind; has surely rudiments of more than these; for what were Channing, Newton, both of them, but embryo men? I turn off with a shudder at the public wrong, but a faith in God's justice, in that child's eternal life, which nothing can ever shake.

III. A third argument is drawn from the nature of God. He, as the infinite, the unconditioned, the absolute, is all-powerful, all-wise, all-good. Therefore he must wish the best of all possible things; must know the best of all possible things; must will the best of all possible things, and so bring it to pass. Life is a possible thing; eternal life is possible. Neither implies a contradiction; yes, to me they seem necessary, more than possible. Now, then, as life, serene and happy life, is better than non-existence, so immortality is better than perpetual death. God must know that, wish that, will that, and so bring that about. Man, therefore, must be immortal. This argument is brief indeed, but I see not how it can be withstood.

I do not know that one of you doubts of eternal life. If any does, I know not if these thoughts will ever affect his doubt. Still, I think each argument is powerful; to one that thinks, reasons, balances, and then decides, exceeding powerful. All put together form a mass of argument which, as it seems to me, no logic can resist. Yet I beg you to understand that I do not rest immortality on any reasoning of mine, but on reason itself; not on these logical arguments, but on man's consciousness, and the instinctive belief which is common to the human race. I believed my immortality before I proved it; believed it just as strongly then as now. Nay, could some doubter rise, and, to my thinking, vanquish all these arguments, I should still hold fast my native faith, nor fear the doubter's arms. The simple consciousness of men is stronger than all forms of proof. Still, if men want arguments — why, there they are.

The belief in immortality is one thing; the special form thereof, the definite notion of the future life, another and quite different. The popular doctrine in our churches I think is this: That this body which we lay in the dust shall one day be raised again, the living soul joined on anew, and both together live the eternal life. But where is the soul all this time, between our death-day and our day of rising? Some say it sleeps unconscious, dead all this time; others, that it is in Heaven now, or else in hell; others, in a strange and transient home, imperfect in its joy or woe, waiting the final day and more complete account. It seems to me this notion is absurd and impossible: absurd in its doctrine relative to the present condition of departed souls; impossible in what it teaches of the resurrection of this body. If my soul is to claim the body again, which shall it be, the body I was born into, or that I died out of? If I live to the common age of men, changing my body as I must, and dying daily, then I have worn some eight or ten bodies. So at the last, which body shall claim my soul, for the ten had her? The soul herself may claim them all. But to make the matter still more intricate, there is in the earth but a certain portion of matter out of which human bodies can be made. Considering all the millions of men now living, the myriads of millions that have been before, it is plain, I think, that all the matter suitable for human bodies has been lived over many times. So if the world were to end to-day, instead of each old man having ten bodies from which to choose the one that fits him best, there would be ten men, all clamoring for each body! Shall I then have a handful of my former dust, and that alone? That is not the resurrection of my former body. This whole doctrine of the resurrection of the flesh seems to me impossible and absurd.

I know men refer this, as many other things no better, to Jesus. I find no satisfactory evidence that he taught the resurrection of the body; there is some evidence that he did not. I know it was the doctrine of the Pharisees of his time, of Paul, the early Christians, and more or less of the Christian churches to this day. In Christ's time in Judea, there were the Sadducees, who taught the eternal death of men; the Pharisees who taught the resurrection of the flesh and its reunion with the soul; the Essenes, who taught the immortality of the soul, but rejected the resurrection of the body. Paul was a Pharisee, and in his letters taught the resurrection of the dead, the belief of the Pharisees. From him it has come down to us, and in the creed of many churches it is still written, "I believe in the resurrection of the flesh." Many doubted this in early times, but the council of Nice declared all men accursed who dared to doubt the resurrection of the flesh. I mention this as absurd and impossible, because it is still, I fear, the popular belief, and lest some should confound the doctrine of immortality with this tenet of the Pharisees. Let it be remembered the immortality of the soul is one thing, the resurrection of the body another and quite different.

What is this future life? what can we know of it besides its existence? Some men speak as if they knew the way around Heaven as around the wards of their native city. What we can know in detail is cautiously to be inferred from the nature of man and the nature of God. I will modestly set down what seems to me.

It must be a conscious state. Man is by his nature conscious; yes, self-conscious. He is progressive in his self-consciousness. I cannot think a removal out of the body destroys this consciousness; rather that it enhances and intensifies this. Yet consciousness in the next life must differ as much from consciousness here as the ripe peach differs from the blossom, or the bud, or the bark, or the earthly materials out of which it grew. The child is no limit to the man, nor my consciousness now to what I may be, must be hereafter.

It must be a social state. Our nature is social; our joys social. For our progress here, our happiness, we depend on one another. Must it not be so there? It must be an advance upon our nature and condition here. All the analogy of nature teaches that. Things advance from small to great; from base to beautiful. The girl grows into a woman; the bud swells into the blossom, that into the fruit. The process over, the work begins anew. How much more must it be so in the other life. What old powers we shall discover now buried in the flesh; what new powers shall come upon us in that new state, no man can know; it were but poetic idleness to talk of them. We see in some great man, what power of intellect, imagination, justice, goodness, piety, he reveals, lying latent in us all. How men bungle in their works of art! No Raphael can paint a dew-drop or a flake of frost. Yet some rude man, tired with his work, lies down beneath a tree, his head upon his swarthy arm, and sleep shuts, one by one, these five scant portals of the soul, and what an artist is he made at once! How brave a sky he paints above him, with what golden garniture of clouds set off; what flowers and trees, what men and women does he not create, and moving in celestial scenes! What years of history does he condense in one short minute, and when he wakes, shakes off the purple drapery of his dream as if it were but worthless dust and girds him for his work anew! What other powers there are shut up in men less known than this artistic phantasy; powers of seeing the distant, recalling the past, predicting the future, feeling at once the character of men — of this we know little, only by rare glimpses at the unwonted side of things. But yet we know enough to guess there are strange wonders there waiting to be revealed.

What form our conscious, social, and increased activity shall take, we know not. We know of that no more than before our birth we knew of this world, of sight, smell, hearing, taste, and touch, or the things which they reveal. We are not born into that world, have not its senses yet. This we know, that the same God, all-powerful, all-wise, all-good, rules there and then, as here and now. Who cannot trust him to do right and best for all? For my own part, I feel no wish to know how or where, or what I shall be hereafter. I know it will be right for my truest welfare; for the good of all. I am satisfied with this trust.

Yet the next life must be a state of retribution. Thither we carry nothing but ourselves, our naked selves. Our fortune we leave behind us; our honors and rank return to such as gave; even our reputation, the good or ill men thought we were, clings to us no more. We go thither without our staff or scrip; nothing but the man we are. Yet that man is the result of all life's daily work; it is the one thing which we have brought to pass. I cannot believe men who have voluntarily lived mean, little, vulgar and selfish lives, will go out of this and into that, great, noble, generous, good, and holy. Can the practical saint and the practical hypocrite enter on the same course of being together? I know the sufferings of bad men here, the wrong they do their nature, and what comes of that wrong. I think that suffering is the best part of sin, the medicine to heal it with. What men suffer here from their wrongdoing is its natural consequence; but all that suffering is a mercy, designed to make them better. Every thing in this world is adapted to promote the welfare of God's creatures. Must it not be so in the next? How many men seem wicked from our point of view, who are not so from their own; how many become infamous through no fault of theirs; the victims of circumstances, born into crime, of low and corrupt parents, whom former circumstances made corrupt! Such men cannot be sinners before God. Here they suffer from the tyranny of appetites they never were taught to subdue; they have not the joy of a cultivated mind. The children of the wild Indian are capable of the same cultivation as children here; yet they are savages. Is it always to be so? Is God to be partial in granting the favors of another life? I cannot believe it. I doubt not that many a soul rises up from the dungeon and the gallows, yes, from dens of infamy amongst men, clean and beautiful before God. Christ, says the Gospel, assured the penitent thief of sharing heaven with him — and that day. Many seem inferior to me, who in God's sight must be far before me; men who now seem too low to learn of me here, may be too high to teach me there.

I cannot think the future world is to be feared, even by the worst of men. I had rather die a sinner than live one. Doubtless justice is there to be done; that may seem stern and severe. But remember God's justice is not like a man's; it is not vengeance, but mercy; not poison, but medicine. To me it seems tuition more than chastisement. God is not the Jailer of the Universe, but the Shepherd of the people; not the Hangman of mankind, but their Physician; yes, our Father. I cannot fear Him as I fear men. I cannot fail to love. I abhor sin, I loathe and nauseate thereat; most of all at my own.

I can plead for others and extenuate their guilt, perhaps they for mine; not I for my own. I know God's justice will overtake me, giving me what I have paid for. But I do not, cannot fear it. I know His justice is love; that if I suffer, it is for my everlasting joy. I think this is a natural state of mind. I do not find that men ever dread the future life, or turn pale on their death-bed at thought of God's vengeance, except when a priesthood has frightened them to that. The world's literature, which is the world's confession, proves what I say. In Greece, in classic days, when there was no caste of priests, the belief in immortality was current and strong. But in all her varied literature I do not remember a man dying, yet afraid of God's vengeance. The rude Indian of our native land did not fear to meet the Great Spirit, face to face. I have sat by the bedside of wicked men, and while death was dealing with my brother, I have watched the tide slow ebbing from the shore, but I have known no one afraid to go. Say what we will, there is nothing stronger and deeper in men than confidence in God, a solemn trust that He will do us good. Even the worst man thinks God his Father; and is he not? Tell me not of God's vengeance, punishing men for his own glory! There is no such thing. Talk not to me of endless hell, where men must suffer for suffering's sake, be damned for an eternity of woe. I tell you there is no such thing, nor can there ever be. Does not even the hireling shepherd, when a single lamb has gone astray, leave the ninety and nine safe in their fold, go forth some stormy night and seek the wanderer, rejoicing to bring home the lost one on his shoulders? And shall God forget His child, his frailest or most stubborn child; leave him in endless misery, a prey to insatiate Sin, that grim, bloodthirsty wolf, prowling about the human fold? I tell you No; not God. Why, this eccentric earth forsakes the sun awhile, careering fast and far away, but that attractive power prevails at length, and the returning globe comes rounding home again. Does a mortal mother desert her son, wicked, corrupt and loathsome though he be? If so, the wiser world cries, Shame! But she does not. When her child becomes loathsome and hateful to the world, drunk with wickedness, and when the wicked world puts him away out of its sight, strangling him to death, that mother forgets not her child. She had his earliest kiss from lips all innocent of coming ill, and she will have his last. Yes, she will press his cold and stiffened form to her own bosom; the bosom that bore and fed the innocent babe yearns yet with mortal longing for the murdered murderer. Infamous to the world, his very dust is sacred dust to her. She braves the world's reproach, buries her son, piously hoping, that as their lives once mingled, so their ashes shall. The world, cruel and forgetful oft, honors the mother in its deepest heart. Do you tell me that culprit's mother loves her son more than God can love him? Then go and worship her. I know that when father and mother both forsake me, in the extremity of my sin, I know my God loves on. Oh yes, ye sons of men, Indian and Greek, ye are right to trust your God. Do priests and their churches say No!—bid them go and be silent forever. No grain of dust gets lost from off this dusty globe; and shall God lose a man from off this sphere of souls? Believe it not.

I know that suffering follows sin, lasting long as the sin. I thank God it is so; that God's own angel stands there to warn back the erring Balaams, wandering towards woe. But God, who sends the rain, the dew, the sun, on me as on a better man, will, at last, I doubt it not, make us all pure, all just, all good, and so, at last, all happy. This follows from the nature of God himself, for the All-good must wish the welfare of His child; the All-wise know how to achieve that welfare; the All-powerful bring it to pass. Tell me He wishes not the eternal welfare of all men, then I say, That is not the God of the universe. I own not that as God. Nay, I tell you it is not God you speak of, but some heathen fancy, smoking up from your unhuman heart. I would ask the worst of mothers, Did you forsake your child because he went astray, and mocked your word? "Oh no," she says; "he was but a child, he knew no better, and I led him right, corrected him for his good, not mine!" Are we not all children before

God; the wisest, oldest, wickedest, God's child! I am sure He will never forsake me, how wicked soever I become. I know that he is love; love, too, that never fails. I expect to suffer for each conscious, wilful wrong; I wish, I hope, I long to suffer for it. I am wronged if I do not; what I do not outgrow, live over and forget here, I hope to expiate there. I fear a sin; not to outgrow a sin.

A man who has lived here a manly life, must enter the next under the most favorable circumstances. I do not mean a man of mere negative goodness, starting in the road of old custom, with his wheels deep in the ruts, not having life enough to go aside, but a positively good man, one bravely good. He has lived heaven here, and must enter higher up than a really wicked man, or a slothful one, or one but negatively good. He can go from earth to heaven, as from one room to another, pass gradually, as from winter to spring. To such an one, no revolution appears needed. The next life, it seems, must be a continual progress, the improvement of old powers, the disclosure or accession of new ones. What nobler reach of thought, what profounder insight, what more heavenly imagination, what greater power of conscience, faith and love, will bless us there and then, it were vain to calculate, it is far beyond our span. You see men now, whose souls are one with God, and so His will works through them as the magnetic fire runs on along the unimpeding line. What happiness they have, it is they alone can say. How much greater must it be there; not even they can tell. Here the body helps us to some things. Through these five small loop-holes the world looks in. How much more does the body hinder us from seeing? Through the sickly body yet other worlds look in. He who has seen only the daylight, knows nothing of that heaven of stars, which all night long hang overhead their lamps of gold. When death has dusted off this body from me, who will dream for me the new powers I shall possess? It were vain to try. Time shall reveal it all.

I cannot believe that any state in Heaven is a final state, only a condition of progress. The bud opens into the blossom, the flower matures into the fruit. The salvation of to-day is not blessedness enough for to-morrow. Here we are first babes of earth, with a few senses, and those imperfect, helpless and ignorant; then children of earth; then youths; then men, armed with reason, conscience, affection, piety, and go on enlarging these without end. So methinks it must be there, that we shall be first babes of Heaven, then children, next youths, and so go on growing, advancing and advancing — our being only a becoming more and more, with no possibility of ever reaching the end. If this be true, then there must be a continual increase of being.

So, in some future age, the time will come, when each one of us shall have more mind, and heart, and soul, than Christ on earth; more than all men now on earth have ever had; yes, more than they and all the souls of men now passed to Heaven;— shall have, each one of us, more being than they all have had, and so more truth, more soul, more faith, more rest and bliss of life.

Do men of the next world look in upon this? Are they present with us, conscious of our deeds or thoughts? Who knows? Who can say aye or no? The unborn know nothing of the life on earth; yet the born of earth know somewhat of them, and make ready for their coming. Who knows but men born to heaven are waiting for your birth to come— have gone to prepare a place for us? All that is fancy, and not fact; it is not philosophy, but poetry; no more. Of this we may be sure, that what is best will be; what best for saint or sinner; what most conducive to their real good. That is no poetry, but unavoidable truth, which all mankind may well believe.

There are many who never attained their true stature here, yet without blameworthiness of theirs; men cheated of their growth. Many a Milton walks on his silent way, and goes down at last, not singing and unsung. How many a possible Newton or Descartes has dug the sewers of a city, and dies, giving no sign of the wealthy soul he bore!

> "Chill penury repressed his noble rage,
> And froze the genial current of the soul."

What if the best of you had been born slaves in North Carolina, or among savages at New Zealand; nay, in some of the filthy cellars of Boston, and turned friendless into the streets; what might you have become? Surely not what you are; yet, before God, you might, perhaps, be more deserving, and, at death, go to a far higher place. What is so terribly wrong here, must be righted there. It cannot be that God will thrust a man out of Heaven, because his mother was a savage, a slave, a pauper, or a criminal. It is men's impiety which does so here, not Heaven's justice there! How the wrong shall be righted I know not, care not now to know; of the fact I ask no further certainty. Many that are last shall be first. It may be that the pirate, in heaven, having outgrown his earthly sins, shall teach justice to the judge who hanged him here. They who were oppressed and trampled on, kept down, dwarfed, stinted and emaciate in soul, must have justice done them there, and will doubtless stand higher in Heaven than we, who, having many talents, used them poorly, or hid them idle in the dirt, knowing our Father's will, yet heeding not. It was Jesus that said, Many shall come from the east and the west, and sit down in the kingdom of God, and men, calling themselves saints, be thrust out.

Shall we remember the deeds of the former life; this man that he picked rags out of the mud in the streets, and another that he ruled nations? Who can tell; nay, who need care to ask? Such a remembrance seems not needed for retribution's sake. The oak remembers not each leaf it ever bore, though each helped to form the oak, its branch and bole. How much has gone from our bodies! we know not how it came or went! How much of our past life is gone from our memory, yet its result lives in our character! The saddler remembers not every stitch he took while an apprentice, yet each stitch helped form the saddle.

Shall we know our friends again? For my own part I cannot doubt it; least of all when I drop a tear over their recent dust. Death does not separate them from us here. Can life in heaven do it? They live in our remembrance; memory rakes in the ashes of the dead, and the virtues of the departed flame up anew, enlightening the dim cold walls of our consciousness. Much of our joy is social here; we only half enjoy an undivided good. God made mankind, but sundered that into men, that they might help one another. Must it not be so there, and we be with our real friends? Man loves to think it; yet to trust is wiser than to prophesy. But the girl who went from us a little one may be as parent to her father when he comes, and the man who left us have far outgrown our dream of an angel when we meet again. I cannot doubt that many a man who not long ago left his body here, now far surpasses the radiant manliness which Jesus won and wore; yes, is far better, greater, too, than many poorly conceive of God.

There are times when we think little of a future life. In a period of success, serene and healthy life; the day's good is good enough for that day. But there comes a time when this day's good is not enough; its ill too great to bear. When death comes down and wrenches off a friend from our side; wife, child, brother, father, a dear one taken; this life is not enough. Oh, no, not to the coldest, coarsest, and most sensual man. I put it to you, to the most heartless of you all, or the most cold and doubting — When you lay down in the earth your mother, sister, wife, or child, remembering that you shall see their face no more, is life enough? Do you not reach out your arms for heaven, for immortality, and feel you cannot die? When I see men at a feast, or busy in the street, I do not think of their eternal life; perhaps feel not my own. But when the stiffened body goes down to the tomb, sad, silent, remorseless, I feel there is no death for the man. That clod which yonder dust shall cover is not my brother. The dust goes to its place, the man to his own. It is then I feel my immortality. I look through the grave into heaven. I ask no miracle, no proof, no reasoning for me. I ask no risen dust to teach me immortality. I am conscious of eternal life.

But there are worse hours than these: seasons bitterer than death, sorrows that lie a latent poison in the heart, slowly sapping the foundations of our peace. There are hours when the best life seems a sheer failure to the man who lived it, his wisdom folly, his genius impotence, his best deed poor and small; when he wonders why he was suffered to be born; when all the sorrows of the world seem poured upon him; when he stands in a populous loneliness, and though weak, can only lean in upon himself. In such hour he feels the insufficiency of this life. It is only his cradle-time, he counts himself just born; all honors, wealth and fame are but baubles in his baby hand; his deep philosophy but nursery rhymes. Yet he feels the immortal fire burning in his heart. He stretches his hands out from the swaddling-clothes of flesh, reaching after the topmost star, which he sees, or dreams he sees, and longs to go alone. Still worse, the consciousness of sin comes over him; he feels that he has insulted himself. All about him seems little; himself little, yet clamoring to be great. Then we feel our immortality; through the gairish light of day we see a star or two beyond. The soul within us feels her wings, contending to be born, impatient for the sky, and wrestles with the earthly worm that folds us in.

"Mysterious Night! when our first Parent knew
  Thee from report divine, and heard thy name,
Did he not tremble for this lovely frame,
  This glorious canopy of light and blue?
Yet 'neath a curtain of translucent dew,
  Bathed in the rays of the great setting flame,
Hesperus with the host of heaven came;
  And lo, Creation widened in man's view.
Who could have thought such darkness lay concealed
  Within thy beams, O Sun? or who could find,
Whilst fly and leaf and insect stood revealed,
  That to such countless orbs thou mad'st us blind?
Why do we then shun Death with anxious strife?
  If Light can thus deceive, wherefore not Life?"

I would not slight this wondrous world. I love its day and night. Its flowers and its fruits are dear to me. I would not wilfully lose sight of a departing cloud. Every year opens new beauty in a star; or in a purple gentian fringed with loveliness. The laws too of matter seem more wonderful the more I study them, in the whirling eddies of the dust, in the curious shells of former life buried by thousands in a grain of chalk, or in the shining diagrams of light above my head. Even the ugly becomes beautiful when truly seen. I see the jewel in the bunchy toad. The more I live, the more I love this lovely world; feel more its Author in each little thing; in all that is great. But yet I feel my immortality the more. In childhood the consciousness of immortal life buds forth feeble, though full of promise. In the man it unfolds its fragrant petals, his most celestial flower, to mature its seed throughout eternity. The prospect of that everlasting life, the perfect justice yet to come, the infinite progress before us, cheer and comfort the heart. Sad and disappointed, full of self-reproach, we shall not be so forever. The light of heaven breaks upon the night of trial, sorrow, sin; the sombre clouds which overhung the east, grown purple now, tell us the dawn of heaven is coming in. Our faces, gleamed on by that, smile in the new-born glow; we are beguiled of our sadness before we are aware. The certainty of this provokes us to patience, it forbids us to be slothfully sorrowful. It calls us to be up and doing. The thought that all will at last be right with the slave, the poor, the weak, and the wicked, inspires us with zeal to work for them here, and make it all right for them even now.

There is small merit in being willing to die; it seems almost sinful in a good man to wish it when the world needs him here so much. It is weak and unmanly to be always looking and sighing voluptuously for that. But it is of great comfort to have in your soul a sure trust in immortality; of great value here and now to anticipate time and live to-day the eternal life. That we may all do. The joys of heaven will begin as soon as we attain the character of heaven and do its duties. That may begin to-day. It is everlasting life to know God, to have His Spirit dwelling in you, yourself at one with Him. Try that and prove its worth. Justice, usefulness, wisdom, religion, love, are the best things we hope for in Heaven. Try them on — they will fit you here not less becomingly. They are the best things of earth. Think no outlay of goodness and piety too great. You will find your reward begin here. As much goodness and piety, so much Heaven. Men will not pay you — God will; pay you now; pay you hereafter and for ever.

IV.

THE PUBLIC EDUCATION OF THE PEOPLE.—AN ADDRESS DELIVERED BEFORE THE ONONDAGA TEACHERS' INSTITUTE, AT SYRACUSE, NEW YORK, OCTOBER 4, 1849.

EDUCATION is the developing and furnishing of the faculties of man. To educate the people is one of the functions of the State. It is generally allowed in the free States of America, that the community owes each child born into it a chance for education, intellectual, moral, and religious. Hence the child has a just and recognized claim on the community for the means of this education, which is to be afforded him, not as a charity, but as a right.

The fact indicates the progress mankind has made in not many years. Once the state only took charge of the military education of the people; not at all of their intellectual, moral, or religious culture. They received their military discipline, not for the special and personal advantage of the individuals, Thomas and Oliver, but for the benefit of the state. They received it, not because they were men claim ing it in virtue of their manhood, but as subjects of the state, because their military training was needful for the state, or for its rulers who took the name thereof. Then the only culture which the community took public pains to bestow on its members, was training them to destroy. The few, destined to command, learned the science of destruction, and the kindred science of defence; the many, doomed to obey, learned only the art to destroy, and the kindred art of defence.

The ablest men of the nation were sought out for military teachers, giving practical lessons of the science and the art; they were covered with honor and loaded with gold. The wealth of the people and their highest science went to this work. Institutions were founded to promote this education, and carefully watched over by the state, for it was thought the Commonwealth depended on disciplined valor. The soldier was thought to be the type of the state, the archetype of man; accordingly the highest spiritual function of the state was the production of soldiers.

Most of the civilized nations have passed through that stage of their development: though the few or the many are still taught the science or the art of war in all countries called Christian, there is yet a class of men for whom the state furnishes the means of education that is not military; means of education which the individuals of that class could not provide for themselves. This provision is made at the cost of the state; that is, at the cost of every man in the state, for what the public pays, you pay and I pay, rich or poor, willingly and consciously, or otherwise. This class of men is different in different countries, and their education is modified to suit the form of government and the idea of the state. In Rome the state provides for the public education of priests. Rome is an ecclesiastical state; her government is a Theocracy — a government of all the people, but by the priests, for the sake of the priests, and in the name of God. Place in the church is power, bringing honor and wealth; no place out of the church is of much value. The offices are filled by priests, the chief magistrate is a priest, supposed to derive his power and right to rule, not democratically, from the people, or royally, by inheritance, — for in theory the priest is as if he had no father, as theoretically he has no child, — but theocratically from God.

In Rome the priesthood is thought to be the flower of the state. The most important spiritual function of the state, therefore, is the production of priests; accordingly the greatest pains are taken with their education. Institutions are founded at the public cost, to make priests out of men; these institutions are the favorites of government, well ordered, well watched over, well attended, and richly honored. Institutions for the education of the people are of small account, ill endowed, watched over but poorly, thinly attended, and not honored at all. The people are designed to be subjects of the church, and as little culture is needed for that, though much to make them citizens thereof, so little is given.

As there are institutions for the education of the priests, so there is a class of men devoted to that work; able men, well disciplined, sometimes men born with genius, and always men furnished with the accomplishments of sacerdotal and scientific art; very able men, very well disciplined, the most learned and accomplished men in the land. These men are well paid and abundantly honored, for on their faithfulness the power of the priesthood, and so the welfare of the state, is thought to depend. Without the allurement of wealth and honors, these able men would not come to this work; and without the help of their ability, the priests could not be well educated. Hence their power would decline; the class, tonsured and consecrated but not instructed, would fall into contempt; the theocracy would end. So the educators of the priests are held in honor, surrounded by baits for vulgar eyes; but the public educators of the people, chiefly women or ignorant men, are held in small esteem. The very buildings destined to the education of the priests are conspicuous and stately; the colleges of the Jesuits, the Propaganda, the seminaries for the education of priests, the monasteries for training the more wealthy and *regular* clergy, are great establishments, provided with libraries, and furnished with all the apparatus needful for their important work. But the school-houses for the people are small and mean buildings, ill made, ill furnished, and designed for a work thought to be of little moment. All this is in strict harmony with the idea of the theocracy, where the priesthood is mighty and the people are subjects of the Church; where the effort of the state is toward producing a priest.

In England the state takes charge of the education of another class, the nobility and gentry; that is, of young men of ancient and historical families, the nobility, and young men of fortune, the gentry. England is an oligarchical state; her government an aristocracy, the government of all by a few, the nobility and gentry, for the sake of a few, and in the name of a king. There the foundation of power is wealth and birth from a noble family. The union of both takes place in a wealthy noble. There, nobility is the blossom of the state; aristocratic birth brings wealth, office, and their consequent social distinction. Political offices are chiefly monopolized by men of famous birth or great riches. The king, the chief officer of the land, must surpass all others in wealth, and the pomp and circumstance which comes thereof, and in aristocracy of birth. He is not merely noble but royal; his right to rule is not at all derived from the people, but from his birth. Thus he has the two essentials of aristocratic influence, birth and wealth, not merely in the heroic degree, but in the supreme degree.

As the state is an aristocracy, its most important spiritual function is the production of aristocrats; each noble family transmits the full power of its blood only to a single person — the oldest son; of the highest form, the royal, only one is supposed to be born in a generation, only one who receives and transmits in full the blood royal.

As the nobility are the blossom of the state, great pains must be taken with the education of those persons born of patrician or wealthy families. As England is not merely a military or ecclesiastical state, though partaking largely of both, but commercial, agricultural and productive in many ways; as she holds a very prominent place in the politics of the world, so there must be a good general education provided for these persons; otherwise their power would decline, the nobility and gentry sink into contempt, and the government pass into other hands, — for though a man may be born to rank and wealth, he is not born to knowledge, nor to practical skill. Hence institutions are founded for the education of the aristocratic class: Oxford and Cambridge, "those twins of learning," with their preparatories and help-meets.

The design of these institutions is to educate the young men of family and fortune. The aim in their academic culture is not as in Pagan Rome, a military state, to make soldiers, nor as in Christian Rome, to turn out priests; it is not, as in the German universities, to furnish the world with scholars and philosophers, men of letters and science, but to mature and furnish the gentleman, in the technical sense of that word, a person conventionally fitted to do the work of a complicated aristocratic state, to fill with honor its various offices, military, political, ecclesiastical or social, and enjoy the dignity which comes thereof. These universities furnish the individual who resorts thither with opportunities not otherwise to be had; they are purchased at the cost of the state, at the cost of each man in the state. The alumnus at Oxford pays his term-bills, indeed, but the amount thereof is a trifle compared to the actual cost of his residence there; mankind pays the residue.

These institutions are continually watched over by the state, which is the official guardian of aristocratic education; they are occasionally assisted by grants from the public treasury, though they are chiefly endowed by the voluntary gifts of individual men. But these private gifts, like the public grants, come from the earnings of the whole nation. They are well endowed, superintended well, and richly honored; their chancellors and vice-chancellors are men of distinguished social rank; they have their representatives in Parliament; able men are sought out for teachers, professors, heads of houses; men of good ability, of masterly education, and the accomplishments of a finished gentleman; they are well paid, and copiously rewarded with honors and social distinction. Gentility favors these institutions; nobility watches over them, and royalty smiles upon them. In this threefold sunlight, no wonder that they thrive. The buildings at their service are among the most costly and elegant in the land; large museums are attached to them, and immense libraries; every printer in England, at his own cost, must give a copy of each book he publishes to Cambridge and Oxford. What wealth can buy, or artistic genius can create, is there devoted to the culture of this powerful class.

But while the nobility and gentry are reckoned the flower of the state, the common people are only the leaves, and therefore thought of small importance in the political botany of the nation. Their education is amazingly neglected; is mainly left to the accidental piety of private Christians, to the transient charity of philanthropic men, or the "enlightened self-interest" of mechanics and small-traders, who now and then found institutions for the education of some small fraction of the multitude. But such institutions are little favored by the government, or the spirit of the dominant class; gentility does not frequent them, nor nobility help them, nor royalty watch over to foster and to bless. The Parliament, which voted one hundred thousand pounds of the nation's money for the queen's horses and hounds, had but thirty thousand to spare for the education of her people. No honor attends the educators of the people; no wealth is heaped up for them; no beautiful buildings are erected for their use; no great libraries got ready at the public charge; no costly buildings are provided. You wonder at the colleges and collegiate churches of Oxford and of Cambridge; at the magnificence of public edifices in London, new or ancient — the House of Parliament, the Bank, the palaces of royal and noble men, the splendor of the churches — but you ask, where are the school-houses for the people? You go to Bridewell and Newgate for the answer. All this is consistent with the idea of an aristocracy. The gentleman is the type of the state; and the effort of the state is towards producing him. The people require only education enough to become the servants of the gentleman, and seem not to be valued for their own sake, but only as they furnish pabulum for the flower of the oligarchy.

In Rome and England, great sums have been given by wealthy men, and by the state itself, to furnish the means of a theocratic or aristocratic education to a certain class; and to produce the national priests, and the national gentlemen. There public education is the privilege of a few, but bought at the cost of the many; for the plough-boy in Yorkshire, who has not culture enough to read the petition for daily bread in the Lord's Prayer, helps pay the salary of the Master of Trinity, and the swine-herd in the Roman Campagna, who knows nothing of religion, except what he learns at Christmas and Easter, by seeing the Pope carried on men's shoulders into St. Peter's, helps support the Propaganda and the Roman College. The privileged classes are to receive an education under the eye of the state, which considers itself bound to furnish them the means of a public education, partly at the individual's cost, chiefly at the cost of the public. The amount of education depends on three things: — on the educational attainments of the human race; on the wealth and tranquillity of the special nation, enabling it to avail itself of that general attainment; and on the natural powers and industry of the particular individual in the nation. Such is the solidarity of mankind that the development of the individual thus depends on that of the race, and the education of a priest in Rome or a gentleman in England is the resultant of these three forces, — the attainment of mankind, the power of the nation, and the private character and conduct of the man himself. Each of these three is a variable and not a constant quantity. So the amount of education which a man can receive at Oxford or at Rome fluctuates and depends on the state of the nation and of the world; but as the attainments of mankind have much increased within a few years, as the wealth of England has increased, and her tranquillity become more secure, you see how easy it becomes for the state to offer each gentleman an amount of education which it would have been quite impossible to furnish in the time of the Yorks and the Lancasters.

In America things are quite other and different. I speak of the Free States of the North; the Slave States have the worst features of an oligarchy combined with a theocratic pride of caste, which generates continual unkindness; there the idea of the state is found inconsistent with the general and public education of the people; it is as much so in South Carolina as in England or Rome; even more so, for the public and general culture of all is only dangerous to a theocracy or aristocracy while it is directly fatal to slavery. In England, and still more in Catholic Rome, the churches — themselves a wonderful museum of curiosities, and open all the day to all persons — form an important element for the education of the most neglected class. But slavery and education of the people are incommensurable quantities. No amount of violence can be their common measure. The republic, where master and slave were equally educated, would soon be a red-republic. The slave-master knows this, and accordingly puts education to the ban, and glories in keeping three million barbarians in the land, and, of course, suffers the necessary degradation which comes thereof. But in the free states of the North the government is not a theocracy, or an aristocracy; the state, in theory is not for the few, nor even for the majority, but for all; classes are not recognized, and therefore not protected in any privilege. The government is a democracy, the government of all, by all, for all, and in the name of all. A man is born to all the rights of mankind; all are born to them, so all are equal. Therefore, what the state pays for, not only comes at the cost of all, but must be for the use and benefit of all. Accordingly, as a theocracy demands the education of priests, and an aristocracy that of the nobility and the gentry, so a democracy demands the education of all. The aim must be, not to make priests and gentlemen of a few, a privileged class, but to make men of all; that is, to give a normal and healthy development of their intellectual, moral, affectional and religious faculties, to furnish and instruct them with the most important elementary knowledge, to extend this development and furnishing of the faculties as far as possible.

Institutions must be founded for this purpose — to educate all, rich and poor, men well-born with good abilities, men ill-born with slender natural powers. In New England, these institutions have long since been founded at the public cost, and watched over with paternal care, as the ark of our covenant, the palladium of our nation. It has been recognized as a theory, and practised on as a fact, that all the property in the land is held by the state for the public education of the people, as it is for their defence; that property is amenable to education as to military defence.

In a democracy there are two reasons why this theory and practice prevail. One is a political reason. It is for the advantage of the state; for each man that keeps out of the jail and the poor-house, becomes a voter at one-and-twenty; he may have some office of trust and honor; the highest office is open before him. As so much depends on his voting wisely, he must have a chance to qualify himself for his right of electing and of being elected. It is as necessary now in a democracy, and as much demanded by the idea thereof, that all should be thus qualified by education, as it once was in a military state, that all should be bred up soldiers.

The other is a philosophical reason. It is for the advantage of the individual himself, irrespective of the state. The man is a man, an integer, and the state is for him; as well as a fraction of the state, and he for it. He has a man's rights; and, however inferior in might to any other man, born of parentage how humble soever, to no wealth at all, with a body never so feeble, he is yet a man, and so equal in rights to any other man born of a famous line, rich and able; of course he has a right to a chance for the best culture which the educational attainment of mankind, and the circumstances of the nation render possible to any man; to so much thereof as he has the inborn power and the voluntary industry to acquire. This conclusion is getting acted on in New England, and there are schools for the dumb and the blind, even for the idiot and the convict.

So, then, as the idea of our government demands the education of all, the amount of education must depend on the same three variables mentioned before; it must be as good as it is possible for them to afford. The democratic state has never done its political and educational duty, until it affords every man a chance to obtain the greatest amount of education which the attainment of mankind renders it possible for the nation, in its actual circumstances, to command, and the man's nature and disposition render it possible for him to take.

Looking at the matter politically, from the point of view of the State, each man must have education enough to exercise his rights of electing and being elected. It is not easy to fix the limits of the amount; it is also a variable continually increasing. Looking at the matter philosophically, from the point of view of the individual, there is no limit but the attainment of the race and the individual's capacity for development and growth. Only a few men will master all which the circumstances of the nation and the world render attainable; some will come short for lack of power, others for lack of inclination. Make education as accessible as it can now be made, as attractive as the teachers of this age can render it, the majority will still get along with the smallest amount that is possible or reputable. Only a few will strive for the most they can get. There will be many a thousand farmers, traders, and mechanics in their various callings, manual and intellectual, to a single philosopher. This also is as it should be, and corresponds with the nature of man and his function on the earth. Still all have the natural right to the means of education to this extent, by fulfilling its condition.

To accomplish this work, the democratic education of the whole people, with the aim of making them men, we want public institutions founded by the people, paid for by the public money; institutions well endowed, well attended, watched over well, and proportionably honored; we want teachers, able men, well disciplined, well paid, and honored in proportion to their work. It is a good thing to educate the privileged classes, priests in a theocracy, and gentlemen in an aristocracy. Though they are few in number, it is a great work; the servants thereof are not too well paid, nor too much held in esteem in England, nor in Rome, nor too well furnished with apparatus. But the public education of a whole people is a greater work, far more difficult, and should be attended with corresponding honor, and watched over even more carefully by the state.

After the grown men of any country have provided for their own physical wants, and insured the needful physical comforts, their most important business is to educate themselves still further, and train up the rising generation to their own level. It is important to leave behind us cultivated lands, houses and shops, railroads and mills, but more important to leave behind us men grown, men that are men; such are the seed of material wealth,—not it of them. The highest use of material wealth is its educational function.

Now the attainments of the human race increase with each generation; the four leading nations of Christendom, England, France, Germany, and the United States, within a hundred years, have apparently, at the least, doubled their spiritual attainments; in the free states of America, there is a constant and rapid increase of wealth, far beyond the simultaneous increase of numbers; so not only does the educational achievement of mankind become greater each age, but the power of the state to afford each man a better chance for a better education, greatens continually, the educational ability of the state enlarging as those two factors get augmented. The generation now grown up, is, therefore, able and bound to get a better culture than their fathers, and leave to their own children a chance still greater.

Each child of genius, in the nineteenth century, is born at the foot of the ladder of learning, as completely as the first child, with the same bodily and spiritual nakedness; though of the most civilized race, with six, or sixty thousands of years behind him, he must begin with nothing but himself. Yet such is the union of all mankind, that, with the aid of the present generation, in a few years he will learn all that mankind has learned in its long history; next go beyond that, discovering and creating anew; and then draw up to the same height the new generation, which will presently surpass him.

A man's education never ends, but there are two periods thereof, quite dissimilar, the period of the Boy, and that of the Man. Education in general is the developing and instructing the faculties, and is, therefore, the same in kind to both man and boy, though it may be brought about by different forces. The education of the boy, so far as it depends on institutions, and conscious modes of action, must be so modified as to enable him to meet the influences which will surround him when he is a man; otherwise, his training will not enable him to cope with the new forces he meets, and so will fail of the end of making him a man. I pass over the influence of the family, and of nature, which do not belong to my present theme. In America, the public education of men is chiefly influenced by four great powers, which I will call educational forces, and which correspond to four modes of national activity:

I. The political action of the people, represented by the State;

II. The industrial action of the people, represented by Business;

III. The ecclesiastical action of the people, represented by the Church;

IV. The literary action of the people, represented by the Press.

I now purposely name them in this order, though I shall presently refer to them several times, and in a different succession. These forces act on the people, making us such men as we are; they act indirectly on the child before he comes to consciousness; directly, afterwards, but most powerfully on the man. What is commonly and technically called education — the development and instruction of the faculties of children, is only preparatory; the scholastic education of the boy is but introductory to the practical education of the man. It is only this preparatory education of the children of the people that is the work of the school-masters. Their business is to give the child such a development of his faculties, and such furniture of preliminary knowledge, that he can secure the influence of all these educational forces, appreciating and enhancing the good, withstanding, counteracting, and at last ending the evil thereof, and so continue his education; and at the same time that he can work in one or more of those modes of activity, serving himself and mankind, politically by the state, ecclesiastically by the church, literarily by the press, or at any rate, industrially by his business. To give children the preparatory education necessary for this fourfold receptivity, or activity, we need three classes of public institutions:

I. Free common schools;

II. Free high schools;

III. Free colleges.

Of these I will presently speak in detail, but now, for the sake of shortness, let me call them all collectively by their generic name — the School. It is plain the teachers who work by this instrument ought to understand the good and evil of the four educational forces which work on men grown, in order to prepare their pupils to receive the good thereof, and withstand the evil. So then let us look a moment at the character of these educational forces, and see what they offer us, and what men they are likely to make of their unconscious pupils. Let us look at the good qualities first, and next at the evil.

It is plain that business, the press, and politics all tend to promote a great activity of body and mind. In business, the love of gain, the enterprising spirit of our practical men in all departments, their industry, thrift and forecast, stimulate men to great exertions, and produce a consequent development of the faculties called out. Social distinction depends almost wholly on wealth; that never is accumulated by mere manual industry, such is the present constitution of society, but it is acquired by the higher forms of industry, in which the powers of nature serve the man, or he avails himself of the creations of mere manual toil. Hence there is a constant pressure towards the higher modes of industry for the sake of money; of course, a constant effort to be qualified for them. So in the industrial departments the mind is more active than the hand. Accordingly it has come to pass that most of the brute labor of the free states is done by cattle, or by the forces of nature — wind, water, fire — which we have harnessed by our machinery, and set to work. In New England most of the remaining work which requires little intelligence is done by Irishmen, who are getting a better culture by that very work. Men see the industrial handiwork of the North, and wonder; they do not always see the industrial head-work, which precedes, directs and causes it all; they seldom see the complex forces of which this enterprise and progress are the resultant.

There is no danger that we shall be sluggards. Business now takes the same place in the education of the people that was once held by war: it stimulates activity, promotes the intercourse of man with man, nation with nation; assembling men in masses, it elevates their temperature, so to say; it leads to new and better forms of organization; it excites men to invention, so that thereby we are continually acquiring new power over the elements, peacefully annexing to our domain new provinces of nature — water, wind, fire, lightning — setting them to do our work, multiplying the comforts of life, and setting free a great amount of human time. It is not at all destructive; not merely conservative, but continually creates anew. Its creative agent is not brute force, but educated mind. A man's trade is always his teacher, and industry keeps a college for mankind, much of our instruction coming through our hands; with us, where the plough is commonly in the hands of him who owns the land it furrows, business affords a better education than in most other countries, and develops higher qualities of mind. There is a marked difference in this respect between the North and South. There was never before such industry, such intense activity of head and hand in any nation in a time of peace.

The press encourages the same activity, enterprise, perseverance. Both of these encourage generosity; neither honors the miser, who gets for the sake of getting, or "starves, cheats, and pilfers to enrich an heir;" he does not die respectably in Boston, who dies rich and bequeaths nothing to any noble public charity. It encourages industry which accumulates with the usual honesty, and for a rather generous use.

The press furnishes us with books exceedingly cheap. We manufacture literature cheaper than any nation except the Chinese. Even the best books, the works of the great masters of thought, are within the reach of an industrious farmer or mechanic, if half a dozen families combine for that purpose. The educational power of a few good books scattered through a community, is well known.

Then the press circulates, cheap and wide, its newspapers, emphatically the literature of men who read nothing else: they convey intelligence from all parts of the world, and broaden the minds of home-keeping youths, who need not now have homely wits.

The state, also, promotes activity, enterprise, hardihood, perseverance and thrift. The American Government is eminently distinguished by these five qualities. The form of government stimulates patriotism, each man has a share in the public lot. The theocracies, monarchies, and aristocracies of old time have produced good and great examples of patriotism, in the few or the many; but the nobler forms of love of country, of self-denial and disinterested zeal for its sake, are left for a democracy to bring to light.

Here all men are voters, and all great questions are, apparently and in theory, left to the decision of the whole people. This popular form of government is a great instrument in developing and instructing the mind of the nation. It helps extend and intensify the intelligent activity which is excited by business and the press. Such is the nature of our political institutions that, in the free states, we have produced the greatest degree of national unity of action, with the smallest restriction of personal freedom, have reconciled national unity with individual variety, not seeking uniformity; thus room is left for as much individualism as a man chooses to take; a vast power of talent, enterprise and invention is left free for its own work. Elsewhere, save in England, this is latent, kept down by government. Since this power is educated and has nothing to hold it back; since so much brute work is done by cattle and the forces of nature, now domesticated and put in harness, and much time is left free for thought, more intelligence is demanded, more activity, and the citizens of the free states have become the most active, enterprising and industrious people in the world; the most inventive in material work.

In all these three forms of action there is much to stir men to love of distinction. The career is open to talent, to industry; open to every man; the career of letters, business, and politics. Our rich men were poor men; our famous men came of sires else not heard of. The laurel, the dollar, the office, and the consequent social distinction of men successful in letters, business and politics, these excite the obscure or needy youth to great exertions, and he cannot sleep; emulation wakes him early, and keeps him late astir. Behind him, scattering "the rear of darkness," stalk poverty and famine, gaunt and ugly forms, with scorpion whip to urge the tardier, idler man. The intense ambition for money, for political power, and the social results they bring, keeps men on the alert. So ambition rises early, and works with diligence that never tires.

The Church, embracing all the churches under that name, cultivates the memory of men, and teaches reverence for the past; it helps keep activity from wandering into unpopular forms of wickedness or of unbelief. Men who have the average intelligence, goodness and piety, it keeps from slipping back, thus blocking to rearward the wheels of society, so that the ascent gained shall not be lost; men who have less than this average it urges forward, addressing them in the name of God, encouraging by hope of heaven, and driving with fear of hell. It turns the thought of the people towards God; it sets before us some facts in the life, and some parts of the doctrine, of the noblest One who ever wore the form of man, bidding us worship him. The ecclesiastical worship of Jesus of Nazareth is, perhaps, the best thing in the American church. It has the Sunday and the institution of preaching under its control. A body of disciplined men are its servants; they praise the ordinary virtues; oppose and condemn the unpopular forms of error and of sin. Petty vice, the vice of low men, in low places, is sure of their lash. They promote patriotism in its common form. Indirectly, they excite social and industrial rivalry, and favor the love of money by the honor they bestow upon the rich and successful. But at the same time they temper it a little, sometimes telling men, as business or the state does not, that there is in man a conscience, affection for his brother-man, and a soul which cannot live by bread alone; no, not by wealth, office, fame and social rank. They tell us, also, of eternity, where worldly distinctions, except of orthodox and heterodox, are forgotten, where wealth is of no avail; they bid us remember God.

Such are the good things of these great national forces; the good things which in this fourfold way we are teaching ourselves. The nation is a monitorial school, wonderfully contrived for the education of the people. I do not mean to say that it is by the forethought of men that the American democracy is at the same time a great practical school for the education of the human race. This result formed no part of our plan, and is not provided for by the Constitution of the United States; it comes of the forethought of God, and is provided for in the Constitution of the Universe.

Now each of these educational forces has certain defects, negative evils, and certain vices, positive evils, which tend to misdirect the nation, and so hinder the general education of the people: of these, also, let me speak in detail.

The state appeals to force, not to justice; this is its last appeal; the force of muscles aided by force of mind, instructed by modern science in the art to kill. The nation appeals to force in the settlement of affairs out of its borders. We have lately seen an example of this, when we commenced war against a feeble nation, who, in that special emergency, had right on her side, about as emphatically as the force was on our side. The immediate success of the enterprise, the popular distinction acquired by some of the leaders, the high honor bestowed on one of its heroes, all this makes the lesson of injustice attractive. It may be that a similar experiment will again be tried, and doubtless with like success. Certainly there is no nation this side of the water which can withstand the enterprise, the activity, the invention, industry and perseverance of a people so united, and yet so free and intelligent. Another successful injustice of this character, on a large scale, will make right still less regarded, and might honored yet more.

The force we employ out of our borders, might opposed to right, we employ also at home against our brethren, and keep three millions of them in bondage; we watch for opportunities to extend the institution of slavery over soil unpolluted by that triple curse, and convert the Constitution, the fundamental law of the land, into an instrument for the defence of slavery.

The men we honor politically, by choosing them to offices in the state, are commonly men of extraordinary force, sometimes, it is true, only of extraordinary luck, but of only ordinary justice; men who, perhaps, have mind in the heroic degree, but conscience of the most vulgar pattern. They are to keep the law of the United States when it is wholly hostile to the law of the universe, to the everlasting justice of God.

I am not speaking to politicians, professional representatives of the state; not speaking for political effect; not of the state as a political machine for the government of the people. I am speaking to teachers, for an educational purpose; of the state as an educational machine, as one of the great forces for the spiritual development of the people. Now by this preference of force and postponement of justice at home and abroad, in the selection of men for office, with its wealth, and rank, and honor, by keeping the law of the land to the violation of the law of God, it is plain we are teaching ourselves to love wrong; at least to be insensible to the right. What we practise on a national scale as a people, it is not easy to think wrong when practised on a personal scale, by this man and that.

The patriotism, also, which the state nurses, is little more than that Old Testament patriotism which loves your countryman, and hates the stranger; the affection which the Old Testament attributes to Jehovah, and which makes him say, "I loved Jacob, and I hated Esau;" a patriotism which supports our country in the wrong as readily as in the right, and is glad to keep one sixth part of the nation in bondage without hope. It is not a patriotism which, beginning here, loves all the children of God, but one that robs the Mexican, enslaves the African, and exterminates the Indian.

These are among the greater evils taught us by the political action of the people as a whole. If you look at the action of the chief political parties, you see no more respect for justice in the politics of either party, than in the politics of the nation, the resultant of both; no more respect for right abroad, or at home. One party aims distinctively at preserving the property already acquired; its chief concern is for that, its sympathy there; where its treasure is, is also its heart. It legislates, consciously or otherwise, more for accumulated wealth, than for the laboring man who now accumulates. This party goes for the dollar; the other for the majority, and aims at the greatest good of the greatest number, leaving the good of the smaller number to most uncertain mercies. Neither party seems to aim at justice, which protects both the wealth that labor has piled up, and the laborer who now creates it; justice, which is the point of morals common to man and God, where the interests of all men, abroad and at home, electing and elected, greatest number and smallest number, exactly balance. Falsehood, fraud, a willingness to deceive, a desire for the power and distinction of office, a readiness to use base means in obtaining office — these vices are sown with a pretty even hand upon both parties, and spring up with such blossoms and such a fruitage as we all see. The third political party has not been long enough in existence to develop any distinctive vices of its own.

I shall not speak of the public or private character of the politicians who direct the state; no doubt that is a powerful element in our national education; but as a class, they seem no better and no worse than merchants, mechanics, ministers and farmers, as a class; so in their influence there is nothing peculiar, only their personal character ceases to be private, and becomes a public force in the education of the people.

The Churches have the same faults as the State. There is the same postponement of justice and preference of force, the same neglect of the law of God in their zeal for the statutes of men; the same crouching to dollars or to numbers. However, in the churches these faults appear negatively, rather than as an affirmation. The worldliness of the church is not open, self-conscious and avowed; it is not, as a general thing, that human injustice is openly defended, but rather justice goes by default. But if the churches do not positively support and teach injustice, as the state certainly does, they do not teach the opposite, and, so far as that goes, are allies of the state in its evil influence. The fact that the churches, as such, did not oppose the war, and do not oppose slavery, its continuance, or its extension; nay, that they are often found its apologists and defenders, seldom its opponents; that they not only pervert the sacred books of the Christians to its defence, but wrest the doctrines of Christianity to justify it; the fact that they cannot, certainly do not, correct the particularism of the political parties, the love of wealth in one, of mere majorities in the other; that they know no patriotism not bounded by their country, none coextensive with mankind; that they cannot resist the vice of party spirit — these are real proofs that the church is but the ally of the state in this evil influence.

But the church has also certain specific faults of its own. It teaches injustice by continually referring to the might of God, not His justice; to His ability and will to damn mankind, not asking if He has the right? It teaches that in virtue of His infinite power, He is not amenable to infinite justice, and to infinite love. Thus, while the state teaches, in the name of expediency and by practice, that the strong may properly be the tyrants of the weak, the mighty nation over the feeble, the strong race over the inferior, that the government may dispense with right at home and abroad — the church, as theory in Christ's name, teaches that God may repudiate His own justice and His own love.

The churches have little love of truth, as such, only of its uses. It must be such a truth as they can use for their purposes; canonized truth; truth long known; that alone is acceptable and called "religious truth;" all else is "profane and carnal," as the reason which discovers it. They represent the average intelligence of society; hence, while keeping the old, they welcome not the new. They promote only popular forms of truth, popular in all Christendom, or in their special sect. They lead in no intellectual reforms; they hinder the leaders. Negatively and positively, they teach, that to believe what is clerically told you in the name of religion, is better than free, impartial search after the truth. They dishonor free thinking, and venerate constrained believing. When the clergy doubt, they seldom give men audience of their doubt. Few scientific men not clerical believe the Bible account of creation, — the universe made in six days, and but a few thousand years ago, — or that of the formation of woman, and of the deluge. Some clerical men still believe these venerable traditions, spite of the science of the times; but the clerical men who have no faith in these stories not only leave the people to think them true and miraculously taught, but encourage men in the belief, and calumniate the men of science who look the universe fairly in the face and report the facts as they find them.

The church represents only the popular morality, not any high and aboriginal virtue. It represents not the conscience of human nature, reflecting the universal and unchangeable moral laws of God, touched and beautified by his love, but only the conscience of human history, reflecting the circumstances man has passed by, and the institutions he has built along the stream of time. So, while it denounces unpopular sins, vices below the average vice of society, it denounces also unpopular excellence, which is above the average virtue of society. It blocks the wheels rearward, and the car of humanity does not roll down hill; but it blocks them forward also. No great moral movement of the age is at all dependent directly on the church for its birth; very little for its development. It is in spite of the church that reforms go forward; it holds the curb to check more than the rein to guide. In morals, as in science, the church is on the anti-liberal side, afraid of progress, against movement, loving "yet a little sleep, a little slumber;" conservative and chilling, like ice, not creative, nor even quickening, as water. It doffs to use and wont; has small confidence in human nature, much in a few facts of human history. It aims to separate Piety from Goodness, her natural and heaven-appointed spouse, and marry her to Bigotry, in joyless and unprofitable wedlock. The church does not lead men to the deep springs of human nature, fed ever from the far heights of the Divine nature, whence flows that river of God, full of living water, where weary souls may drink perennial supply. While it keeps us from falling back, it does little directly to advance mankind. In common with the state, this priest and Levite pass by on the other side of the least developed classes of society, leaving the slave, the pauper, and the criminal, to their fate, hastening to strike hands with the thriving or the rich.

These faults are shared in the main by all sects; some have them in the common, and some in a more eminent degree, but none is so distinguished from the rest as to need emphatic rebuke, or to deserve a special exemption from the charge. Such are the faults of the church of every land, and must be from the nature of the institution; like the state, it can only represent the average of mankind.

I am not speaking to clergymen, professional representatives of the church, not of the church as an ecclesiastical machine for keeping and extending certain opinions and symbols; not for an ecclesiastical purpose; I speak to teachers, for an educational purpose, of the church as an educational machine, one of the great forces for the spiritual development of the people.

The Business of the land has also certain vices of

its own; while it promotes the virtues I have named before, it does not tend to promote the highest form of character. It does not promote justice and humanity, as one could wish; it does not lead the employer to help the operative as a man, only to use him as a tool, merely for industrial purposes. The average merchant cares little whether his ship brings cloth and cotton, or opium and rum. The average capitalist does not wish the stock of his manufacturing company divided into small shares, so that the operatives can invest their savings therein and have a portion of the large dividends of the rich; nor does he care whether he takes a mortgage on a ship or a negro slave, nor whether his houses are rented for sober dwellings, or for drunkeries; whether the state hires his money to build harbors at home, or destroy them abroad. The ordinary manufacturer is as ready to make cannons and cannon-balls to serve in a war which he knows is unjust, as to cast his iron into mill-wheels, or forge it into anchors. The common farmer does not care whether his barley feeds poultry for the table, or, made into beer, breeds drunkards for the almshouse and the jail; asks not whether his rye and potatoes become the bread of life, or, distilled into whiskey, are deadly poison to men and women. He cares little if the man he hires become more manly or not; he only asks him to be a good tool. Whips for the backs of negro slaves are made, it is said, in Connecticut with as little compunction as Bibles are printed there; "made to order," for the same purpose — for the dollar. The majority of blacksmiths would as soon forge fetter-chains to enslave the innocent limbs of a brother-man, as draught-chains for oxen. Christian mechanics and pious young women, who would not hurt the hair of an innocent head, have I seen at Springfield, making swords to slaughter the innocent citizens of Vera Cruz and Jalapa. The ships of respectable men carry rum to intoxicate the savages of Africa, powder and balls to shoot them with; they carry opium to the Chinese; nay, Christian slaves from Richmond and Baltimore to New Orleans and Galveston. In all commercial countries, the average vice of the age is mixed up with the industry of the age, and unconsciously men learn the wickedness long intrenched in practical life. It is thought industrial operations are not amenable to the moral law, only to the law of trade. "Let the supply follow the demand" is the maxim. A man who makes as practical a use of the golden rule as of his yard-stick, is still an exception in all departments of business.

Even in the commercial and manufacturing parts of America, money accumulates in large masses; now in the hands of an individual, now of a corporation. This money becomes an irresponsible power, acting by the laws, but yet above them. It is wielded by a few men, to whom it gives a high social position and consequent political power. They use this triple form of influence, pecuniary, social and political, in the spirit of commerce, not of humanity, not for the interest of mankind; thus the spirit of trade comes into the state. Hence it is not thought wrong in politics to buy a man, more than in commerce to buy a ship; hence the rights of a man, or a nation, are looked on as articles of trade, to be sold, bartered, and pledged; and in the Senate of the United States, we have heard a mass of men, more numerous than all our citizens seventy years ago, estimated as worth twelve hundred millions of dollars.

In most countries business comes more closely into contact with men than the state, or the church, or the press, and is a more potent educator. Here it not only does this, but controls the other three forces, which are mainly instruments of this; hence this form of evil is more dangerous than elsewhere, for there is no power organized to resist it as in England or Rome; so it subtly penetrates everywhere, bidding you place the accidents before the substance of manhood, and value money more than man.

Notwithstanding the good qualities of the Press, the books it multiplies, and the great service it renders, it also has certain vices of its own. From the nature of the thing the greater part of literature represents only the public opinion of the time. It must therefore teach deference to that, not deference to truth and justice. It is only the eminent literature which can do more than this; books, which at first fall into few hands though fit, and like the acorns sown with the mulleins and the clover, destined to germinate but slowly, long to be overtopped by an ephemeral crop, at last, after half an hundred years, shall mature their own fruit for other generations of men. The current literature of this age only popularizes the thought of the eminent literature of the past. Great good certainly comes from this, but also great evil.

Of all literature, the newspapers come most into contact with men—they are the literature of the people, read by such as read nothing else; read also by such as read all things beside. Taken in the mass, they contain little to elevate men above the present standard. The political journals have the general vice of our politics, and the special faults of the particular party; the theological journals have the common failings of the church, intensified by the bigotry of the sects they belong to; the commercial journals represent the bad qualities of business. Put all three together, and it is not their aim to tell the truth, the whole truth, and nothing but the truth, nor to promote justice, the whole of justice, and nothing but justice. The popular literature helps bring to consciousness the sentiments and ideas which prevail in the state, the church, and business. It brings those sentiments and ideas intimately into connection with men, magnetizing them with the good and ill of those three powers, but it does little directly to promote a higher form of human character.

So, notwithstanding the good influence of these four modes of national activity in educating the grown men of America, they yet do not afford the highest teaching which the people require, to realize individually the idea of a man, and jointly that of a democracy. The state does not teach perfect justice; the church does not teach that, or love of truth. Business does not teach perfect morality, and the average literature, which falls into the hands of the million, teaches men to respect public opinion more than the word of God, which transcends that. Thus these four teach only the excellence already organized or incorporated in the laws, the theology, the customs, and the books of the land. I cannot but think these four teachers are less deficient here than in other lands, and have excellences of their own, but the faults mentioned are inseparable from such institutions. An institution is an organized thought; of course, no institution can represent a truth which is too new or too high for the existing organizations, yet that is the truth which it is desirable to teach. So there will always be exceptional men, with more justice, truth and love than is represented by the institutions of the time, who seem therefore hostile to these institutions, which they seek to improve and not destroy. Contemporary with the priests of Judah and Israel were the prophets thereof, antithetic to one another as the centripetal and centrifugal forces, but, like them, both necessary to the rhythmic movement of the orbs in heaven, and the even poise of the world.

In Rome and in England the idea of a theocracy and an aristocracy has become a fact in the institutions of the land, which accordingly favor the formation of priests and gentlemen. The teachers of the educated class, therefore, may trust to the machinery already established to do their work, only keeping off the spirit of the age which would make innovations; and such is the respectability and popular esteem of the institutions, that this is done easier than men think, by putting an exceptional book in the index at Rome or in the academical fire at Oxford. But here, the idea of a democracy is by no means so well established and organized in institutions. It is new, and while a theocrat and an aristocrat are respected everywhere, a democrat is held in suspicion; accordingly, to make men, the teacher cannot trust his educational machinery, he must make it, and invent anew as well as turn his mill.

These things being so, it is plain the teachers in the schools should be of such a character that they can give the children what they will most want when they become men; such an intellectual and moral development that they can appreciate and receive the good influence of these four educational forces, and withstand, resist, and exterminate the evil thereof. In the schools of a democracy which are to educate the people and make them men, you need more aboriginal virtue than in the schools of an aristocracy or a theocracy, where a few are to be educated as gentlemen or priests. Since the institutions of the land do not represent the idea of a democracy, and the average spirit of the people, which makes the institutions, represents it no more, if the children of the people are to become better than their fathers, it is plain their teachers must be prophets, and not priests merely; must animate them with a spirit higher, purer and more holy than that which inspires the state, the church, business, or the common literature of the times. As the teacher cannot impart and teach what he does not possess and know, it is also plain that the teacher must have this superior spirit.

To accomplish the public education of the children of the people, we need the three classes of institutions just mentioned: free Common Schools, free High Schools and free Colleges. Let me say a word of each.

The design of the Common School is to take children at the proper age from their mothers, and give them the most indispensable development, intellectual, moral, affectional and religious; to furnish them with as much positive, useful knowledge as they can master, and, at the same time, teach them the three great scholastic helps or tools of education — the art to read, to write and calculate.

The children of most parents are easily brought to school, by a little diligence on the part of the teachers and school committee; but there are also children of low and abandoned, or, at least, neglected parents, who live in a state of continual truancy; they are found on the banks of your canals; they swarm in your large cities. When those children become men, through lack of previous development, instruction and familiarity with these three instruments of education, they cannot receive the full educational influence of the state and church, of business and the press: they lost their youthful education, and therefore they lose, in consequence, their manly culture. They remain dwarfs, and are barbarians in the midst of society; there will be exceptional men whom nothing can make vulgar; but this will be the lot of the mass. They cannot perform the intelligent labor which business demands, only the brute work, so they lose the development which comes through the hand that is active in the higher modes of industry, which, after all, is the greatest educational force; accordingly, they cannot compete with ordinary men, and remain poor; lacking also that self-respect which comes of being respected, they fall into beggary, into intemperance, into crime; so, from being idlers at first, a stumbling-block in the way of society, they become paupers, a positive burden which society must take on its shoulders; or they turn into criminals, active foes to the industry, the order, and the virtue of society.

Now if a man abandons the body of his child, the state adopts that body for a time; takes the guardianship thereof, for the child's own sake; sees that it is housed, fed, clad, and cared for. If a man abandons his child's spirit, and the child commits a crime, the state, for its own sake, assumes the temporary guardianship thereof, and puts him in a jail. When a man deserts his child, taking no concern about his education, I venture to make the suggestion, whether it would not be well, as a last resort, for the State to assume the guardianship of the child for its own sake, and for the child's sake. We allow no one, with ever so thick a skin, to grow up in nakedness; why should we suffer a child, with however so perverse a parent, to grow up in ignorance and degenerate into crime? Certainly, a naked man is not so dangerous to society as an ignorant man, nor is the spectacle so revolting. I should have less hope of a state where the majority were so perverse as to continue ignorant of reading, writing and calculating, than of one where they were so thick-skinned as to wear no clothes. In Massachusetts, there is an Asylum for juvenile offenders, established by the city of Boston, a Farm School for bad boys, established by the characteristic benevolence of the rich men of that place, and a State Reform School under the charge of the Commonwealth: all these are for lads who break the laws of the land. Would it not be better to take one step more, adopt them before they offended, and allow no child to grow up in the barbarism of ignorance? Has any man an unalienable right to live a savage in the midst of civilization?

We need also public High Schools, to take children where the common schools leave them, and carry them further on. Some States have done something towards establishing such institutions; they are common in New England. Some have established Normal Schools, special High Schools for the particular and professional education of public teachers. Without these, it is plain there would not be a supply of competent educators for the public service.

Then we need free Colleges, conducted by public officers, and paid for by the public purse. Without these the scheme is not perfect. The idea which lies at the basis of the public education of a people in a democracy, is this: Every man, on condition of doing his duty, has a right to the means of education, as much as a right, on the same condition, to the means of defence from a public enemy in time of war, or from starvation in time of plenty and of peace. I say every man, I mean every woman also. The amount of education must depend on the three factors named before, — on the general achievement of mankind, the special ability of the state, and the particular power of the individual.

If all is free, common schools, high schools, and colleges, boys and girls of common ability and common love of learning, will get a common education; those of greater ability, a more extended education, and those of the highest powers, the best culture which the race can now furnish, and the state afford. Hitherto no nation has established a public college, wholly at the public cost, where the children of the poor and the rich could enjoy together the great national charity of superior education. To do this is certainly not consistent with the idea of a theocracy or an aristocracy, but it is indispensable to the complete realization of a democracy. Otherwise the children of the rich will have a monopoly of superior education, which is the case with the girls everywhere — for only the daughters of rich men can get a superior education, even in the United States — and with boys in England and France, and of course the offices, emoluments and honors which depend on a superior education; or else the means thereof will be provided for poor lads by private benefactions, charity-funds and the like, which some pious and noble man has devoted to this work. In this case the institutions will have a sectarian character, be managed by narrow, bigoted men, and the gift of the means of education be coupled with conditions which must diminish its value, and fetter the free spirit of the young man. This takes place in many of the collegiate establishments of the North, which, notwithstanding those defects, have done a great good to mankind.

The Common Schools giving their pupil the power of reading, writing and calculating, developing his faculties and furnishing him with much elementary knowledge, put him in communication with all that is written in a common form, in the English tongue; its treasures lie level to his eye and hand. The High School and the College, teaching him also other languages, afford him access to the treasures contained there; teaching him the mathematics and furnishing him with the discipline of science, they enable him to understand all that has hitherto been recorded in the compendious forms of philosophy, and thus place the child of large ability in connection with all the spiritual treasures of the world. In the mean time, for all these pupils, there is the material and the human world about them, the world of consciousness within. They can study both and add what they may to the treasures of human discovery or invention.

It seems to me that it is the duty of the state to place the means of this education within the reach of all children of superior ability, — a duty that follows from the very idea of a democracy, not to speak of the idea of Christianity. It is not less the interest of the state to do so, for then, youths, well born, with good abilities, will not be hindered from getting a breeding proportionate to their birth, and from occupying the stations which are adequately filled only by men of superior native abilities, enriched by culture, and developed to their highest power. Then the work of such stations will fall to the lot of such men, and of course be done. Eminent ability, talent, or genius, should have eminent education, and so serve the nation in its eminent kind; for when God makes a million-minded man, as once or twice in the ages, or a myriad-minded man, as He does now and then, it is plain that this gift also is to be accounted precious, and used for the advantage of all.

I say no state has ever attempted to establish such institutions; yet the Government of the United States has a seminary for the public education of a few men at the public cost. But it is a school to qualify men to fight; they learn the science of destruction, the art thereof, the kindred art and science of defence. If the same money we now pay for military education at West Point were directed to the education of teachers of the highest class, say professors and presidents of colleges; if the same pains were taken to procure able men, to furnish them with the proper instruction for their special work, and give them the best possible general development of their powers, not forgetting the moral, the affectional and the religious, and animating them with the philanthropic spirit needed for such a work, how much better results would appear! But in the present intellectual condition of the people it would be thought unworthy of a nation to train up schoolmasters! But is it only soldiers that we need?

All these institutions are but introductory, a preparatory school, in three departments, to fit youths for the great educational establishment of practical life. This will find each youth and maiden as the schools leave him, moulding him to their image, or moulded by him to a better. So it is plain what the teachers are to do:—besides teaching the special branches which fall to their lot, they are to supply for the pupils, the defects of the State, of the Church, of Business, and the Press, especially the moral defects. For this great work of mediating between the mother and the world, for so furnishing and fitting the rising generation, introducing them into practical life, that they shall receive all the good of these public educational forces with none of the ill, but enhance the one while they withstand the other, and so each in himself realize the idea of man, and all in their social capacity, the idea of a democracy —it is also plain what sort of men we need for teachers: we need able men, well endowed by nature, well disciplined by art; we need superior men

— men juster than the state, truer and better than the churches, more humane than business, and higher than the common literature of the press. There are always men of that stamp born into the world; enough of them in any age to do its work. How shall we bring them to the task? Give young men and women the opportunity to fit themselves for the work, at free common schools, high schools, normal schools, and colleges; give them a pay corresponding to their services, as in England and Rome; give them social rank and honor in that proportion, and they will come; able men will come; men well disciplined will come; men of talent and even genius for education will come.

In the state you pay a man of great political talents large money and large honors; hence there is no lack of ability in politics, none of competition for office. In the church you pay a good deal for a "smart minister," one who can preach an audience into the pews and not himself out of the pulpit. Talent enough goes to business; educated talent too, at least with a special education for this, honor, and social distinction. Private colleges and theological schools, often, have powerful men for their professors and presidents; sometimes, men of much talent for education; commonly, men of ripe learning and gentlemanly accomplishments. Even men of genius seek a place as teachers in some private college, where they are under the control of the leaders of a sect — and must not doubt its creed, nor set science a-going freely lest it run over some impotent theological dogma — or else of a little coterie, or close corporation of men selected because radical or because conservative, men chosen not on account of any special fitness for superintending the superior education of the people, but because they were one-sided, and leaned this way in Massachusetts and that in Virginia. Able men seek such places because they get a competent pay, competent honors, competent social rank. Senators and ambassadors are not ashamed to be presidents of a college, and submit to the control of a coterie, or a sect, and produce their results. If such men can be had for private establishments to educate a few to work in such trammels and such company, certainly, it is not difficult to get them for the public and for the education of all. As the state has the most children to educate, the most money to pay with, it is clear, not only that they need the best ability for this work, but that they can have it soon as they make the teacher's calling gainful and respectable.

In England and Rome, the most important spiritual function of the state is the production of the gentleman and the priest; in democratic America it is the production of the man. Some nations have taken pains with the military training of all the people, for the sake of the state, and made every man a soldier. No nation has hitherto taken equivalent pains with the general education of all, for the sake of the state and the sake of the citizens; — "the heathens of China" have done more than any Christian people, for the education of all. This was not needed in a theocracy, nor an aristocracy; it is essential to a democracy. This is needed politically; for where all men are voters, the ignorant man, who cannot read the ballot which he casts; the thief, the pirate, and the murderer, may, at any time, turn the scale of an election, and do us a damage which it will take centuries to repair. Ignorant men are the tools of the demagogue; how often he uses them, and for what purposes, we need not go back many years to learn. Let the people be ignorant and suffrage universal, a very few men will control the state, and laugh at the folly of the applauding multitude whose bread they waste, and on whose necks they ride to insolence and miserable fame.

America has nothing to fear from any foreign foe; for nearly forty years she has had no quarrel but of her own making. Such is our enterprise and our strength, that few nations would, carelessly, engage in war with us; none, without great provocation. In the midst of us, is our danger; not in foreign arms, but in the ignorance and the wickedness of our own children, the ignorance of the many, the wickedness of the few who will lead the many to their ruin. The bulwark of America is not the army and navy of the United States, with all the men at public cost instructed in the art of war; it is not the swords and muskets idly bristling in our armories; it is not the cannon and the powder carefully laid by; no, nor is it yet the forts, which frown in all their grim barbarity of stone along the coast, defacing the landscape, else so fair: these might all be destroyed to-night, and the nation be as safe as now. The more effectual bulwark of America is her schools. The cheap spelling-book, or the vane on her school-house is a better symbol of the nation than "The star-spangled banner;" the printing press does more than the cannon; the press is mightier than the sword. The army that is to keep our liberties — you are part of that, the noble army of teachers. It is you, who are to make a great nation greater, even wise and good, — the next generation better than their sires.

Europe shows us, by experiment, that a republic cannot be made by a few well-minded men, however well-meaning. They tried for it at Rome, full of enlightened priests; in Germany, the paradise of the scholar, but there was not a people well educated, and a democracy could not stand upright long enough to be set a-going. In France, where men are better fitted for the experiment than elsewhere in continental Europe, you see what comes of it — the first step is a stumble, and for their president, the raw republicans chose an autocrat, not a democrat; not a mere soldier, but only the name of a soldier;

one that thinks it an insult if liberty, equality, and fraternity be but named!

Think you a democracy can stand without the education of all; not barely the smallest pittance thereof which will keep a live soul in a live body, but a large, generous cultivation of mind and conscience, heart and soul? A man, with half an eye, can see how we suffer continually in politics for lack of education among the people. Some nations are priest-ridden, some king-ridden, some ridden of nobles; America is ridden by politicians, a heavy burden for a foolish neck.

Our industrial interests demand the same education. The industrial prosperity of the North, our lands yearly enriching, while they bear their annual crop; our railroads, mills and machines, the harness with which we tackle the elements, — for we domesticate fire and water, yes, the very lightning of heaven — all these are but material results of the intelligence of the people. Our political success and our industrial prosperity, both come from the pains taken with the education of the people. Halve this education, and you take away three fourths of our political welfare, three fourths of our industrial prosperity; double this education, you greaten the political welfare of the people, you increase their industrial success fourfold. Yes, more than that, for the results of education increase by a ratio of much higher powers.

It seems strange that so few of the great men in politics have cared much for the education of the people; only one of those, now prominent before the North, is intimately connected with it. He, at great personal sacrifice of money, of comfort, of health, even of respectability, became superintendent of the common schools of Massachusetts, a place whence we could ill spare him, to take the place of the famous man he succeeds. Few of the prominent scholars of the land interest themselves in the public education of the people. The men of superior culture think the common school beneath their notice; but it is the mother of them all.

None of the States of the North has ever given this matter the attention it demands. When we legislate about public education, this is the question before us:—Shall we give our posterity the greatest blessing that one generation can bestow upon another? Shall we give them a personal power which will create wealth in every form, multiply ships, and roads of earth, or of iron; subdue the forest, till the field, chain the rivers, hold the winds as its vassals, bind with an iron yoke the fire and water, and catch and tame the lightning of God? Shall we give them a personal power which will make them sober, temperate, healthy, and wise; that shall keep them at peace, abroad and at home, organize them so wisely that all shall be united, and yet, each left free, with no tyranny of the few over the many, or the little over the great? Shall we enable them to keep, to improve, to double manifold the political, social, and personal blessings they now possess; shall we give them this power to create riches, to promote order, peace, happiness — all forms of human welfare, or shall we not? That is the question. Give us intelligent men, moral men, men well developed in mind and conscience, heart and soul, men that love man and God, industrial prosperity, social prosperity, and political prosperity, are sure to follow. But without such men, all the machinery of this threefold prosperity is but a bauble in a child's hand, which he will soon break or lose, which he cannot replace when gone, nor use while kept.

Rich men, who have intelligence and goodness, will educate their children, at whatever cost. There are some men, even poor men's sons, born with such native power that they will achieve an education, often a most masterly culture; men whom no poverty can degrade, or make vulgar, whom no lack of means of culture can keep from being wise and great. Such are exceptional men; the majority, nine tenths of the people, will depend, for their culture, on the public institutions of the land. If there had never been a free public school in New England, not half of her mechanics and farmers would now be able to read, not a fourth part of her women. I need not stop to tell what would be the condition of her agriculture, her manufactures, her commerce;

they would have been, perhaps, even behind the agriculture, commerce and manufactures of South Carolina. I need not ask what would be the condition of her free churches, or the republican institutions which now beautify her rugged shores and sterile soil; there would be no such churches, no such institutions. If there had been no such schools in New England, the Revolution would yet remain to be fought. Take away the free schools, you take away the cause of our manifold prosperity; double their efficiency and value, you not only double and quadruple the prosperity of the people, but you will enlarge their welfare — political, social, personal — far more than I now dare to calculate. I know men object to public schools; they say, education must be bottomed on religion, and that cannot be taught unless we have a State religion, taught "by authority" in all our schools; we cannot teach religion, without teaching it in a sectarian form. This objection is getting made in New York; we have got beyond it in New England. It is true, all manly education must be bottomed on religion; it is essential to the normal development of man, and all attempts at education, without this, must fail of the highest end. But there are two parts of religion which can be taught in all the schools, without disturbing the denominations, or trenching upon their ground, namely, piety, the love of God, and goodness, the love of man. The rest of religion, after piety and goodness are removed, may safely be left to the institutions of any of the sects, and so the state will not occupy their ground.

It is often said that superior education is not much needed; the common schools are enough, and good enough, for it is thought that superior education is needed for men as lawyers, ministers, doctors, and the like, not for men as men. It is not so. We want men cultivated with the best discipline, everywhere, not for the profession's sake, but for man's sake. Every man with a superior culture, intellectual, moral, and religious, every woman thus developed, is a safeguard and a blessing. He may sit on the bench of a judge or a shoemaker, be a clergyman or an oysterman, that matters little, he is still a safeguard and a blessing. The idea that none should have a superior education but professional men — they only for the profession's sake — belongs to dark ages, and is unworthy of a democracy.

It is the duty of all men to watch over the public education of the people, for it is the most important work of the state. It is particularly the duty of men who, hitherto, have least attended to it, men of the highest culture, men, too, of the highest genius. If a man with but common abilities has attained great learning, he is is one of the "public administrators," to distribute the goods of men of genius, from other times and lands, to mankind, their legal heirs. Why does God sometimes endow a man with great intellectual power, making, now and then, a million-minded man? Is that superiority of gift solely for the man's own sake? Shame on such a thought. It is of little value to him unless he use it for me; it is for your sake and my sake, more than for his own. He is a precious almoner of wisdom; one of the public guardians of mankind, to think for us, to help us think for ourselves; born to educate the world of feebler men. I call on such men, men of culture, men of genius, to help build up institutions for the education of the people. If they neglect this, they are false to their trust. The culture which hinders a man from sympathy with the ignorant, is a curse to both, and the genius which separates a man from his fellow-creatures, lowlier born than he, is the genius of a demon.

Men and women, practical teachers now before me, a great trust is in your hands; nine tenths of the children of the people depend on you for their early culture, for all the scholastic discipline they will ever get; their manly culture will depend on that, their prosperity thereon, all these on you. When they are men, you know what evils they will easily learn from state and church, from business and the press. It is for you to give them such a developing and such a furnishing of their powers, that they will withstand, counteract and exterminate that evil. Teach them to love justice better than their native land, truth better than their church, humanity more than money, and fidelity to their own nature better than the public opinion of the press. As the chief thing of all, teach them to love man and God. Your characters will be the inspiration of these children; your prayers their practice, your faith their works.

The rising generation is in your hands, you can fashion them in your image, you will, you must do this. Great duties will devolve on these children when grown up to be men; you are to fit them for these duties. Since the Revolution, there has not been a question before the country, not a question of constitution or confederacy, free trade or protective tariff, sub-treasury or bank, of peace or war, freedom or slavery, the extension of liberty, or the extension of bondage — not a question of this sort has come up before Congress, or the people, which could not have been better decided by seven men, honest, intelligent, and just, who loved man and God, and looked, with a single eye, to what was right in the case. It is your business to train up such men. A representative, a senator, a governor may be made, any day, by a vote. Ballots can make a president out of almost any thing; the most ordinary material is not too cheap and vulgar for that. But all the votes of all the conventions, all the parties, are unable to make a people capable of self-government. They cannot put intelligence and justice into the head of a single man. You are to do that. You are the "Sacred Legion," the "Theban Brothers" to repel the greatest foes that can invade the land, the only foes to be feared; you are to repel ignorance, injustice, unmanliness, and irreligion. With none else to help you, in ten years' time you can double the value of your schools; double the amount of development and instruction you annually furnish. So doing, you shall double, triple, quadruple, multiply manifold the blessings of the land. You can, if you will. I ask If you will? If your works say "Yes," then you will be the great benefactors of the land, not giving money, but a charity far nobler yet, education, the greatest charity. You will help fulfil the prophecy which noble men long since predicted of mankind, and help found the kingdom of heaven on earth; you will follow the steps of that noblest man of men, the Great Educator of the human race, whom the Christians still worship as their God. Yes, you will work with God himself; He will work with you, work for you, and bless you with everlasting life.

V.

THE POLITICAL DESTINATION OF AMERICA AND THE SIGNS OF THE TIMES.—DELIVERED BEFORE SEVERAL LITERARY SOCIETIES, 1848.

EVERY nation has a peculiar character, in which it differs from all others that have been, that are, and possibly from all that are to come; for it does not yet appear that the Divine Father of the nations ever repeats himself and creates either two nations or two men exactly alike. However, as nations, like men, agree in more things than they differ, and in obvious things too, the special peculiarity of any one tribe does not always appear at first sight. But if we look through the history of some nation which has passed off from the stage of action, we find certain prevailing traits which continually reappear in the language and laws thereof; in its arts, literature, manners, modes of religion — in short, in the whole life of the people. The most prominent thing in the history of the Hebrews is their continual trust in God, and this marks them from their first appearance to the present day. They have accordingly done little for art, science, philosophy, little for commerce and the useful arts of life, but much for religion; and the psalms they sung two or three thousand years ago are at this day the hymns and prayers of the whole Christian world. Three great historical forms of religion, Judaism, Christianity, and Mahometanism, all have proceeded from them.

He that looks at the Ionian Greeks finds in their story always the same prominent characteristic, a devotion to what is beautiful. This appears often to the neglect of what is true, right, and therefore holy. Hence, while they have done little for religion, their literature, architecture, sculpture, furnish us with models never surpassed, and perhaps not equalled. Yet they lack the ideal aspiration after religion that appears in the literature and art, and even language of some other people, quite inferior to the Greeks in elegance and refinement. Science, also, is most largely indebted to these beauty-loving Greeks for truth is one form of loveliness.

If we take the Romans, from Romulus their first king, to Augustulus the last of the Cæsars, the same traits of national character appear, only the complexion and dress thereof changed by circumstances. There is always the same hardness and materialism, the same skill in organizing men, the same turn for affairs and genius for legislation. Rome borrowed her theology and liturgical forms; her art, science, literature, philosophy, and eloquence; even her art of war was an imitation. But law sprung up indigenous in her soil; her laws are the best gift she offers to the human race, — the "monument more lasting than brass," which she has left behind her.

We may take another nation, which has by no means completed its history, the Saxon race, from Hengist and Horsa to Sir Robert Peel: there also is a permanent peculiarity in the tribe. They are yet the same bold, handy, practical people as when their bark first touched the savage shores of Britain; not over religious; less pious than moral; not so much upright before God, as downright before men; servants of the understanding more than children of reason; not following the guidance of an intuition, and the light of an idea, but rather trusting to experiment, facts, precedents, and usages; not philosophical, but commercial; warlike through strength and courage, not from love of war or its glory; material, obstinate, and grasping, with the same admiration of horses, dogs, oxen, and strong drink; the same willingness to tread down any obstacle, material, human or divine, which stands in their way; the same impatient lust of wealth and power; the same disposition to colonize and reannex other lands; the same love of liberty and love of law; the same readiness in forming political confederations.

In each of these four instances, the Hebrews, the Ionians, the Romans, and the Anglo-Saxon race, have had a nationality so strong, that while they have mingled with other nations in commerce and in war, as victors and vanquished, they have stoutly held their character through all; they have thus modified feebler nations joined with them. To take the last, neither the Britons nor the Danes affected very much the character of the Anglo-Saxons; they never turned it out of its course. The Normans gave the Saxon manners, refinement, letters, elegance. The Anglo-Saxon bishop of the eleventh century, dressed in untanned sheep-skins, "the woolly side out and the fleshy side in;" he ate cheese and flesh, drank milk and mead. The Norman taught him to wear cloth, to eat also bread and roots, to drink wine. But in other respects the Norman left him as he found him. England has received her kings and her nobles from Normandy, Anjou, the Provence, Scotland, Holland, Hanover, often seeing a foreigner ascend her throne; yet the sturdy Anglo-Saxon character held its own, spite of the new element infused into its blood: change the ministries, change the dynasties often as they will, John Bull is obstinate as ever, and himself changes not; no philosophy or religion makes him less material. No nation but the English could have produced a Hobbes, a Hume, a Paley, or a Bentham; they are all instantial and not exceptional men in that race.

Now this idiosyncrasy of a nation is a sacred gift; like the genius of a Burns, a Thorwaldsen, a Franklin, or a Bowditch, it is given for some divine purpose, to be sacredly cherished and patiently unfolded. The cause of the peculiarities of a nation or an individual man we cannot fully determine as yet, and so we refer it to the chain of causes which we call Providence. But the national persistency in a common type is easily explained. The qualities of father and mother are commonly transmitted to their children, but not always, for peculiarities may lie latent in a family for generations, and reappear in the genius or the folly of a child — often in the complexion and features: and besides, father and mother are often no match. But such exceptions are rare, and the qualities of a race are always thus reproduced, the deficiency of one man getting counterbalanced by the redundancy of the next: the marriages of a whole tribe are not far from normal.

Some nations, it seems, perish through defect of this national character, as individuals fail of success through excess or deficiency in their character. Thus the Celts, that great flood of a nation which once swept over Germany, France, England, and, casting its spray far over the Alps, at one time threatened destruction to Rome itself, seem to have been so filled with love of individual independence that they could never accept a minute organization of human rights and duties, and so their children would not group themselves into a city, as other races, and submit to a strong central power, which should curb individual will enough to insure national unity of action. Perhaps this was once the excellence of the Celts, and thereby they broke the trammels and escaped from the theocratic or despotic traditions of earlier and more savage times, developing the power of the individual for a time, and the energy of a nation loosely bound; but when they came in contact with the Romans, Franks and Saxons, they melted away as snow in April — only, like that, remnants thereof yet lingering in the mountains and islands of Europe. No external pressure of famine or political oppression now holds the Celts in Ireland together, or gives them national unity of action enough to resist the Saxon foe. Doubtless in other days this very peculiarity of the Irish has done the world some service. Nations succeed each other as races of animals in the geological epochs, and like them, also, perish when their work is done.

The peculiar character of a nation does not appear nakedly, without relief and shadow. As the waters of the Rhone, in coming from the mountains, have caught a stain from the soils they have traversed which mars the cerulean tinge of the mountain snow that gave them birth, so the peculiarities of each nation become modified by the circumstances to which it is exposed, though the fundamental character of a nation, it seems, has never been changed. Only when the blood of the nation is changed by additions from another stock is the idiosyncrasy altered.

Now, while each nation has its peculiar genius or character which does not change, it has also and accordingly a particular work to perform in the economy of the world, a certain fundamental idea to unfold and develop. This is its national task, for in God's world, as in a shop, there is a regular division of labor. Sometimes it is a limited work, and when it is done the nation may be dismissed, and go to its repose. *Non omnia possumus omnes* is as true of nations as of men; one has a genius for one thing, another for something different, and the idea of each nation and its special work will depend on the genius of the nation. Men do not gather grapes of thorns.

In addition to this specific genius of the nation and its corresponding work, there are also various accidental or subordinate qualities, which change with circumstances, and so vary the nation's aspect that its peculiar genius and peculiar duty are often hid from its own consciousness, and even obscured to that of the philosophic looker-on. These subordinate peculiarities will depend first on the peculiar genius, idea and work of the nation, and next on the transient circumstances, geographical, climactic, historical and secular, to which the nation has been exposed. The past helped form the circumstances of the present age, and they the character of the men now living. Thus new modifications of the national type continually take place; new variations are played, but on the same old strings and of the same old tune. Once circumstances made the Hebrews entirely pastoral, now as completely commercial; but the same trust in God, the same national exclusiveness appear, as of old. As one looks at the history of the Ionians, Romans, Saxons, he sees unity of national character, a continuity of idea and of work; but it appears in the midst of variety, for while these remained ever the same to complete the economy of the world, subordinate qualities — sentiments, ideas, actions — changed to suit the passing hour. The nation's *course* was laid towards a certain point, but they stood to the right hand or the left, they sailed with much canvas or little, and swift or slow, as the winds and waves compelled: nay, sometimes the national ship "heaves to," and lies with her "head to the wind," regardless of her destination; but when the storm is overblown resumes her course. Men will carelessly think the ship has no certain aim, but only drifts.

The most marked characteristic of the American nation is Love of Freedom; of man's natural rights. This is so plain to a student of American history, or of American politics, that the point requires no arguing. We have a genius for liberty: the American idea is freedom, natural rights. Accordingly, the work providentially laid out for us to do seems this, — to organize the rights of man. This is a problem hitherto unattempted on a national scale, in human history. Often enough attempts have been made to organize the powers of priests, kings, nobles, in a theocracy, monarchy, oligarchy, powers which had no foundation in human duties or human rights, but solely in the selfishness of strong men. Often enough have the mights of men been organized, but not the rights of man. Surely there has never been an attempt made on a national scale to organize the rights of man as man; rights resting on the nature of things; rights derived from no conventional compact of men with men; not inherited from past generations, nor received from parliaments and kings, nor secured by their parchments; but rights that are derived straightway from God, the Author of Duty and the Source of Right, and which are secured in the great charter of our being.

At first view it will be said, the peculiar genius of America is not such, nor such her fundamental idea, nor that her destined work. It is true that much of the national conduct seems exceptional when measured by that standard, and the nation's course as crooked as the Rio Grande; it is true that America sometimes seems to spurn liberty, and sells the freedom of three million men for less than three million annual bales of cotton; true, she often tramples, knowingly, consciously, tramples on the most unquestionable and sacred rights. Yet, when one looks through the whole character and history of America, spite of the exceptions, nothing comes out with such relief as this love of freedom, this idea of liberty, this attempt to organize right. There are numerous subordinate qualities which conflict with the nation's idea and work, coming from our circumstances, not our soul, as well as many others which help the nation perform her providential work. They are signs of the times, and it is important to look carefully among the most prominent of them, where, indeed, one finds striking contradictions.

The first is an impatience of authority. Every thing must render its reason, and show cause for its being. We will not be commanded, at least only by such as we choose to obey. Does some one say, "Thou shalt," or "Thou shalt not," we ask, "Who are you?" Hence comes a seeming irreverence. The shovel hat, the symbol of authority, which awed our fathers, is not respected unless it covers a man, and then it is the man we honor, and no longer the shovel hat. "I will complain of you to the government!" said a Prussian nobleman to a Yankee stage-driver, who uncivilly threw the nobleman's trunk to the top of the coach. "Tell the government to go to the devil!" was the symbolical reply.

Old precedents will not suffice us, for we want something anterior to all precedents; we go beyond what is written, asking the cause of the precedent and the reason of the writing. "Our fathers did so," says some one. "What of that?" say we. "Our fathers—they were giants, were they? Not at all, only great boys, and we are not only taller than they, but mounted on their shoulders to boot, and see twice as far. My dear wise man, or wiseacre, it is we that are the ancients, and have forgotten more than all our fathers knew. We will take their wisdom joyfully, and thank God for it, but not their authority, we know better; and of their nonsense not a word. It was very well that they lived, and it is very well that they are dead. Let them keep decently buried, for respectable dead men never walk."

Tradition does not satisfy us. The American scholar has no folios in his library. The antiquary unrolls his codex, hid for eighteen hundred years in the ashes of Herculaneum, deciphers its fossil wisdom, telling us what great men thought in the bay of Naples, and two thousand years ago. "What do you tell of that for?" is the answer to his learning. "What has Pythagoras to do with the price of cotton? You may be a very learned man; you can read the hieroglyphics of Egypt, I dare say, and know so much about the Pharaohs, it is a pity you had not lived in their time, when you might have been good for something; but you are too old-fashioned for our business, and may return to your dust." An eminent American, a student of Egyptian history, with a scholarly indignation declared, "There is not a man who cares to know whether Shoophoo lived one thousand years before Christ, or three."

The example of other and ancient States does not terrify or instruct us. If slavery were a curse to Athens, the corruption of Corinth, the undoing of Rome, and all history shows it was so, we will learn no lesson from that experience, for we say, "We are not Athenians, men of Corinth, nor pagan Romans, thank God, but free republicans, Christians of America. We live in the nineteenth century, and though slavery worked all that mischief then and there, we know how to make money out of it, twelve hundred millions of dollars, as Mr. Clay counts the cash."

The example of contemporary nations furnishes us little warning or guidance. We will set our own precedents, and do not like to be told that the Prussians or the Dutch have learned some things in the education of the people before us, which we shall do well to learn after them. So when a good man tells us of their schools and their colleges, "patriotic" school-masters exclaim, "It is not true; our schools are the best in the world! But if it were true, it is unpatriotic to say so; it aids and comforts the enemy." Jonathan knows little of war; he has heard his grandfather talk of Lexington and Saratoga; he thinks he should like to have a little touch of battle on his own account: so when there is difficulty in setting up the fence betwixt his estate and his neighbors, he blusters for awhile, talks big, and threatens to strike his father; but, not having quite the stomach for that experiment, falls to beating his other neighbor, who happens to be poor, weak, and of a sickly constitution; and when he beats her at every step, —

> "For 'tis no war, as each one knows,
> When only one side deals the blows,
> And t' other bears 'em," —

Jonathan thinks he has covered himself "with imperishable honors," and sets up his general for a great king. Poor Jonathan — he does not know the misery, the tears, the blood, the shame, the wickedness, and the sin he has set a-going, and which one day he is to account for with God who forgets nothing!

Yet while we are so unwilling to accept the good principles, to be warned by the fate, or guided by the success, of other nations, we gladly and servilely copy their faults, their follies, their vice and sin. Like all upstarts, we pique ourselves on our imitation of aristocratic ways. How many a blusterer in Congress, — for there are two denominations of blusterers, differing only in degree, your great blusterer in Congress and your little blusterer in a bar-room, — has roared away hours long against aristocratic influence, in favor of the "pure democracy," while he played the oligarch in his native village, the tyrant over his hired help, and though no man knows who his grandfather was, spite of the herald's office, conjures up some trumpery coat of arms! Like a clown, who, by pinching his appetite, has bought a gaudy cloak for Sabbath wearing, we chuckle inwardly at our brave apery of foreign absurdities, hoping that strangers will be astonished at us — which, sure enough, comes to pass. Jonathan is as vain as he is conceited, and expects that the Fiddlers, and the Trollopes, and others, who visit us periodically as the swallows, and likewise for what they can catch, shall only extol, or at least stand aghast at the brave spectacle we offer, of "the freest and most enlightened nation in the world;" and if they tell us that we are an ill-mannered set, raw and clownish, that we pick our teeth with a fork, loll back in our chairs, and make our countenance hateful with tobacco, and that with all our excellences we are a nation of "rowdies," — why, we are offended, and our feelings are hurt. There was an African chief, long ago, who ruled over a few miserable cabins, and one day received a French traveller from Paris, under a tree. With the exception of a pair of shoes, our chief was as naked as a pestle, but with great complacency he asked the traveller, "What do they say of me at Paris?"

Such is our dread of authority, that we like not old things; hence we are always a-changing. Our house must be new, and our book, and even our church. So we choose a material that soon wears out, though it often outlasts our patience. The wooden house is an apt emblem of this sign of the times. But this love of change appears not less in important matters. We think "Of old things all are over old, of new things none are new enough." So the age asks of all institutions their right to be: What right has the government to existence? Who gave the majority a right to control the minority, to restrict trade, levy taxes, make laws, and all that? If the nation goes into a committee of the whole and makes laws, some little man goes into a committee of one and passes his counter resolves. The State of South Carolina is a nice example of this self-reliance, and this questioning of all authority. That little brazen State, which contains only about half so many free white inhabitants as the single city of New York, but which none the less claims to have monopolized most of the chivalry of the nation, and its patriotism, as well as political wisdom — that chivalrous little State says, "If the nation does not make laws to suit us; if it does not allow us to imprison all black seamen from the North; if it prevents the extension of Slavery wherever we wish to carry it — then the State of South Carolina will nullify, and leave the other nine-and-twenty States to go to ruin!"

Men ask what right have the churches to the shadow of authority which clings to them — to make creeds, and to bind and to loose! So it is a thing which has happened, that when a church excommunicates a young stripling for heresy, he turns round, fulminates his edict, and excommunicates the church. Said a sly Jesuit to an American Protestant at Rome, "But the rites and customs and doctrines of the Catholic church go back to the second century, the age after the apostles!" "No doubt of it," said the American, who had also read the Fathers, "they go back to the times of the apostles themselves; but that proves nothing, for there were as great fools in the first century as the last. A fool or a folly is no better because it is an old folly or an old fool. There are fools enough now, in all conscience. Pray don't go back to prove their apostolical succession."

There are always some men who are born out of due season, men of past ages, stragglers of former generations, who ought to have been born before Dr. Faustus invented printing, but who are unfortunately born now, or, if born long ago, have been fraudulently and illegally concealed by their mothers, and are now, for the first time, brought to light. The age lifts such aged juveniles from the ground, and bids them live, but they are sadly to seek in this day; they are old-fashioned boys; their authority is called in question; their traditions and old wives' fables are laughed at, at any rate disbelieved; they get profanely elbowed in the crowd—men not knowing their great age and consequent venerableness; the shovel hat, though apparently born on their head, is treated with disrespect. The very boys laugh pertly in their face when they speak, and even old men can scarce forbear a smile, though it may be a smile of pity. The age affords such men a place, for it is a catholic age, large-minded, and tolerant, — such a place as it gives to ancient armor, Indian Bibles, and fossil bones of the mastodon; it puts them by in some room seldom used, with other old furniture, and allows them to mumble their anilities by themselves; now and then takes off its hat; looks in, charitably, to keep the mediæval relics in good heart, and pretends to listen, as they discourse of what comes of nothing and goes to it; but in matters which the age cares about, commerce, manufactures, politics, which it cares much for, even in education, which it cares far too little about, it trusts no such counsellors, nor tolerates, nor ever affects to listen.

Then there is a philosophical tendency, distinctly visible; a groping after ultimate facts, first principles, and universal ideas. We wish to know first the fact, next the law of that fact, and then the reason of the law. A sign of this tendency is noticeable in the titles of books; we have no longer "treatises" on the eye, the ear, sleep, and so forth, but in their place we find works professing to treat of the "philosophy" of vision, of sound, of sleep. Even in the pulpits, men speak about the "philosophy" of religion; we have philosophical lectures, delivered to men of little culture, which would have amazed our grandfathers, who thought a shoemaker should never go beyond his last, even to seek for the philosophy of shoes. "What a pity," said a grave Scotchman, in the beginning of this century, "to teach the beautiful science of geometry to weavers and cobblers." Here nothing is too good or high for any one tall and good enough to get hold of it. What audiences attend the Lowell lectures in Boston — two or three thousand men, listening to twelve lectures on the philosophy of fish! It would not bring a dollar or a vote, only thought to their minds! Young ladies are well versed in the philosophy of the affections, and understand the theory of attraction, while their grandmothers, good easy souls, were satisfied with the possession of the fact. The circumstance, that philosophical lectures get delivered by men like Walker, Agassiz, Emerson, and their coadjutors, men who do not spare abstruseness, get listened to, and even understood, in town and village, by large crowds of men, of only the most common culture; this indicates a philosophical tendency, unknown in any other land or age. Our circle of professed scholars, men of culture and learning, is a very small one, while our circle of thinking men is disproportionately large. The best thought of France and Germany finds a readier welcome here than in our parent land: nay, the newest and the best thought of England, finds its earliest and warmest welcome in America. It was a little remarkable, that Bacon and Newton should be reprinted here, and La Place should have found his translator and expositor coming out of an insurance office in Salem! Men of no great pretensions object to an accomplished and eloquent politician: "That is all very well; he made us cry and laugh, but the discourse was not philosophical; he never tells us the reason of the thing; he seems not only not to know it, but not to know that there *is* a reason for the thing, and if not, what is the use of this bobbing on the surface?" Young maidens complain of the minister, that he has no philosophy in his sermons, nothing but precepts, which they could read in the Bible as well as he; perhaps in heathen Seneca. He does not feed their souls.

One finds this tendency where it is least expected: there is a philosophical party in politics, a very small party it may be, but an actual one. They aim to get at everlasting ideas and universal laws, not made by man, but by God, and for man, who only finds them; and from them they aim to deduce all particular enactments, so that each statute in the code shall represent a fact in the universe; a point of thought in God; so, indeed, that legislation shall be divine in the same sense that a true system of astronomy is divine — or the Christian religion — the law corresponding to a fact. Men of this party, in New England, have more ideas than precedents, are spontaneous more than logical; have intuitions, rather than intellectual convictions, arrived at by the process of reasoning. They think it is not philosophical to take a young scoundrel and shut him up with a party of old ones, for his amendment; not philosophical to leave children with no culture, intellectual, moral, or religious, exposed to the temptations of a high and corrupt civilization, and then, when they go astray — as such barbarians needs must, in such temptations — to hang them by the neck for the example's sake. They doubt if war is a more philosophical mode of getting justice between two nations, than blows to settle a quarrel between two men. In either case, they do not see how it follows, that he who can strike the hardest blow is always in the right. In short, they think that judicial murder, which is hanging, and national murder, which is war, are not more philosophical than homicide, which one man commits on his own private account.

Theological sects are always the last to feel any popular movement. Yet all of them, from the Episcopalians to the Quakers, have each a philosophical party, which bids fair to outgrow the party which rests on precedent and usage, to overshadow and destroy it. The Catholic church itself, though far astern of all the sects, in regard to the great movements of the age, shares this spirit, and abroad, if not here, is wellnigh rent asunder by the potent medicine which this new Daniel of philosophy has put into its mouth. Everywhere in the American churches there are signs of a tendency to drop all that rests merely on tradition and hearsay, to cling only to such facts as bide the test of critical search, and such doctrines as can be verified in human consciousness here and to-day. Doctors of divinity destroy the faith they once preached.

True, there are antagonistic tendencies, for, soon as one pole is developed, the other appears; objections are made to philosophy, the old cry is raised — "Infidelity," "Denial," "Free-thinking." It is said that philosophy will corrupt the young men, will spoil the old ones, and deceive the very elect. "Authority and tradition," say some, "are all we need consult; reason must be put down, or she will soon ask terrible questions." There is good cause for these men warring against reason and philosophy; it is purely in self-defence. But this counsel and that cry come from those quarters before mentioned, where the men of past ages have their place, where the forgotten is re-collected, the obsolete preserved, and the useless held in esteem. The counsel is not dangerous; the bird of night, who overstays his hour, is only troublesome to himself, and was never known to hurt a dovelet or a mouseling after sunrise. In the night only is the owl destructive. Some of those who thus cry out against this tendency, are excellent men in their way, and highly useful, valuable as conveyancers of opinions. So long as there are men who take opinions as real estate, "to have and to hold for themselves and their heirs forever," why should there not be such conveyancers of opinions, as well as of land? And as it is not the duty of the latter functionary to ascertain the quality or the value of the land, but only its metes and bounds, its appurtenances and the title thereto; to see if the grantor is regularly seized and possessed thereof, and has good right to convey and devise the same, and to make sure that the whole conveyance is regularly made out, — so is it with these conveyancers of opinion; so should it be, and they are valuable men. It is a good thing to know that we hold under Scotus, and Ramus, and Albertus Magnus, who were regularly seized of this or that opinion. It gives an absurdity the dignity of a relic. Sometimes these worthies, who thus oppose reason and her kin, seem to have a good deal in them, and, when one examines, he finds more than he looked for. They are like a nest of boxes from Hingham and Nuremburg, you open one, and behold another; that, and lo! a third. So you go on, opening and opening, and finding and finding, till at last you come to the heart of the matter, and then you find a box that is very little, and entirely empty.

Yet, with all this tendency — and it is now so strong that it cannot be put down, nor even howled down, much as it may be howled over — there is a lamentable want of first principles, well known and established; we have rejected the authority of tradition, but not yet accepted the authority of truth and justice. We will not be treated as striplings, and are not old enough to go alone as men. Accordingly, nothing seems fixed. There is a perpetual see-sawing of opposite principles. Somebody said ministers ought to be ordained on horseback, because they are to remain so short a time in one place. It would be as emblematic to inaugurate American politicians, by swearing them on a weathercock. The great men of the land have as many turns in their course as the Euripus or the Missouri. Even the facts given in the spiritual nature of man are called in question. An eminent Unitarian divine regards the existence of God as a matter of opinion, thinks it cannot be demonstrated, and publicly declares that it is "not a certainty." Some American Protestants no longer take the Bible as the standard of ultimate appeal, yet venture not to set up in that place reason, conscience, the soul getting help of God; others, who affect to accept the Scripture as the last authority, yet, when questioned as to their belief in the miraculous and divine birth of Jesus of Nazareth, are found unable to say yes or no, not having made up their minds.

In politics, it is not yet decided whether it is best to leave men to buy where they can buy cheapest, and sell where they can sell dearest, or to restrict that matter.

It was a clear case to our fathers, in '76, that all men were "created equal," each with "Unalienable Rights." That seemed so clear, that reasoning would not make it appear more reasonable; it was taken for granted, as a self-evident proposition. The whole nation said so. Now, it is no strange thing to find it said that negroes are not "created equal" in unalienable rights with white men. Nay, in the Senate of the United States, a famous man declares all this talk a dangerous mistake. The practical decision of the nation looks the same way. So, to make our theory accord with our practice, we ought to recommit the Declaration to the hands which drafted that great State-paper, and instruct Mr. Jefferson to amend the document, and declare that "All men are created equal, and endowed by their Creator with certain unalienable rights, if born of white mothers; but if not, not."

In this lack of first principles, it is not settled in the popular consciousness, that there is such a thing as an absolute right, a great law of God, which we are to keep, come what will come. So the nation is not upright, but goes stooping. Hence, in private affairs, law takes the place of conscience, and, in public, might of right. So the bankrupt pays his shilling in the pound, and gets his discharge, but afterwards, becoming rich, does not think of paying the other nineteen shillings. He will tell you the law is his conscience; if that be satisfied, so is he.

But you will yet find him letting money at one or two per cent. a month, contrary to law; and then he will tell you that paying a debt is a matter of law, while letting money is only a matter of conscience. So he rides either indifferently — now the public hack, and now his own private nag, according as it serves his turn.

So a rich State borrows money and "repudiates" the debt, satisfying its political conscience, as the bankrupt his commercial conscience, with the notion that there is no absolute right; that expediency is the only justice, and that King People can do no wrong. No calm voice of indignation cries out from the pulpit and the press and the heart of the people, to shame the repudiators into decent morals; because it is not settled in the popular mind that there is any absolute right. Then, because we are strong and the Mexicans weak, because we want their land for a slave-pasture and they cannot keep us out of it, we think that is reason enough for waging an infamous war of plunder. Grave men do not ask about "the natural justice" of such an undertaking, only about its cost. Have we not seen an American Congress vote a plain lie, with only sixteen dissenting voices in the whole body; has not the head of the nation continually repeated that lie; and do not both parties, even at this day, sustain the vote?

Now and then there rises up an honest man, with

a great Christian heart in his bosom, and sets free a score or two of slaves inherited from his father; watches over and tends them in their new-found freedom: or another, who, when legally released from payment of his debts, restores the uttermost farthing. We talk of this and praise it, as an extraordinary thing. Indeed it is so; justice is an unusual thing, and such men deserve the honor they thus win. But such praise shows that such honesty is a rare honesty. The northern man, born on the battle-ground of freedom, goes to the South and becomes the most tyrannical of slave-drivers. The son of the Puritan, bred up in austere ways, is sent to Congress to stand up for truth and right, but he turns out a "dough-face," and betrays the duty he went to serve. Yet he does not lose his place, for every dough-faced representative has a dough-faced constituency to back him.

It is a great mischief that comes from lacking first principles, and the worst part of it comes from lacking first principles in morals. Thereby our eyes are holden so that we see not the great social evils all about us. We attempt to justify slavery, even to do it in the name of Jesus Christ. The whig party of the North loves slavery; the democratic party does not even seek to conceal its affection therefor. A great politician declares the Mexican war wicked, and then urges men to go and fight it; he thinks a famous general not fit to be nominated for President, but then invites men to elect him. Politics are national morals, the morals of Thomas and Jeremiah, multiplied by millions. But it is not decided yet that honesty is the best policy for a politician; it is thought that the best policy is honesty, at least as near it as the times will allow. Many politicians seem undecided how to turn, and so sit on the fence between honesty and dishonesty. Mr. Facing-both-ways is a popular politician in America just now, sitting on the fence between honesty and dishonesty, and, like the blank leaf between the Old and New Testaments, belonging to neither dispensation. It is a little amusing to a trifler to hear a man's fitness for the Presidency defended on the ground that he has no definite convictions or ideas!

There was once a man who said he always told a lie when it would serve his special turn. It is a pity he went to his own place long ago. He seemed born for a party politician in America. He would have had a large party, for he made a great many converts before he died, and left a numerous kindred busy in the editing of newspapers, writing addresses for the people, and passing "resolutions."

It must strike a stranger as a little odd, that a republic should have a slave-holder for President five sixths of the time, and most of the important offices be monopolized by other slave-holders; a little surprising that all the pulpits and most of the presses should be in favor of slavery, at least not against it.

But such is the fact. Everybody knows the character of the American government for some years past, and of the American parties in politics. "Like master, like man," used to be a true proverb in old England, and "Like people, like ruler," is a true proverb in America; true now. Did a decided people ever choose dough-faces? — a people that loved God and man, choose representatives that cared for neither truth nor justice? Now and then, for dust gets into the brightest eyes; but did they ever choose such men continually? The people are always fairly represented; our representatives do actually re-present us, and in more senses than they are paid for. Congress and the Cabinet are only two thermometers hung up in the capital, to show the temperature of the national morals.

But amid this general uncertainty there are two capital maxims which prevail amongst our huxters of politics: To love your party better than your country, and yourself better than your party. There are, it is true, real statesmen amongst us, men who love justice and do the right, but they seem lost in the mob of vulgar politicians and the dust of party editors.

Since the nation loves freedom above all things, the name democracy is a favorite name. No party could live a twelvemonth that should declare itself anti-democratic. Saint and sinner, statesman and politician, alike love the name. So it comes to pass that there are two things which bear that name; each has its type and its motto. The motto of one is, "You are as good as I, and let us help one another." That represents the democracy of the Declaration of Independence, and of the New Testament; its type is a free school, where children of all ranks meet under the guidance of intelligent and Christian men, to be educated in mind, and heart, and soul. The other has for its motto, "I am as good as you, so get out of my way." Its type is the bar-room of a tavern — dirty, offensive, stained with tobacco, and full of drunken, noisy, quarrelsome "rowdies," just returned from the Mexican war, and ready for a "buffalo hunt," for privateering, or to go and plunder any one who is better off than themselves, especially if also better. That is not exactly the democracy of the Declaration, or of the New Testament; but of — no matter whom.

Then, again, there is a great intensity of life and purpose. This displays itself in our actions and speeches; in our speculations; in the "revivals" of the more serious sects; in the excitements of trade; in the general character of the people. All that we do we overdo. It appears in our hopefulness; we are the most aspiring of nations. Not content with half the continent, we wish the other half. We have this characteristic of genius: we are dissatisfied with all that we have done. Somebody once said we were too vain to be proud. It is not wholly so; the national idea is so far above us that any achievement seems little and low. The American soul passes away from its work soon as it is finished. So the soul of each great artist refuses to dwell in his finished work, for that seems little to his dream. Our fathers deemed the Revolution a great work; it was once thought a surprising thing to found that little colony on the shores of New England; but young America looks to other revolutions, and thinks she has many a Plymouth colony in her bosom. If other nations wonder at our achievements, we are a disappointment to ourselves, and wonder we have not done more. Our national idea out-travels our experience, and all experience. We began our national career by setting all history at defiance — for that said, "A republic on a large scale cannot exist." Our progress since has shown that we were right in refusing to be limited by the past. The political ideas of the nation are transcendant, not empirical. Human history could not justify the Declaration of Independence and its large statements of the new idea: the nation went behind human history and appealed to human nature.

We are more spontaneous than logical; we have ideas, rather than facts or precedents. We dream more than we remember, and so have many orators and poets, or poetasters, with but few antiquaries and general scholars. We are not so reflective as forecasting. We are the most intuitive of modern nations. The very party in politics which has the least culture, is richest in ideas which will one day become facts. Great truths — political, philosophical, religious — lie a-burning in many a young heart which cannot legitimate nor prove them true, but none the less feels, and feels them true. A man full of new truths finds a ready audience with us. Many things which come disguised as truths under such circumstances pass current for a time, but by and by their bray discovers them. The hope which comes from this intensity of life and intuition of truths is a national characteristic. It gives courage, enterprise, and strength. They can who think they can. We are confident in our star; other nations may see it or not, we know it is there above the clouds. We do not hesitate at rash experiments — sending fifty thousand soldiers to conquer a nation with eight or nine millions of people. We are up to every thing, and think ourselves a match for any thing. The young man is rash, for he only hopes, having little to remember; he is excitable, and loves excitement; change of work is his repose; he is hot and noisy, sanguine and fearless, with the courage that comes from warm blood and ignorance of dangers; he does not know what a hard, tough, sour old world he is born into. We are a nation of young men. We talked of annexing Texas and northern Mexico, and did both; now we grasp at Cuba, Central America, — all the continent, — and speak of a railroad to the Pacific as a trifle for us to accomplish. Our national deeds are certainly great, but our hope and promise far outbrags them all.

If this intensity of life and hope have its good side, it has also its evil; with much of the excellence of youth we have its faults — rashness, haste, and superficiality. Our work is seldom well done. In English manufactures there is a certain solid honesty of performance; in the French a certain air of elegance and refinement: one misses both these in American works. It is said America invents the most machines, but England builds them best. We lack the phlegmatic patience of older nations. We are always in a hurry, morning, noon and night. We are impatient of the process, but greedy of the result; so that we make short experiments but long reports, and talk much though we say little. We forget that a sober method is a short way of coming to the end, and that he who, before he sets out, ascertains where he is going and the way thither, ends his journey more prosperously than one who settles these matters by the way. Quickness is a great desideratum with us. It is said an American ship is known far off at sea by the quantity of canvas she carries. Rough and ready is a popular attribute. Quick and off would be a symbolic motto for the nation at this day, representing one phase of our character. We are sudden in deliberation; the "one-hour rule" works well in Congress. A committee of the British Parliament spends twice or thrice our time in collecting facts, understanding and making them intelligible, but less than our time in speech-making after the report; speeches there commonly being for the purpose of facilitating the business, while here one sometimes is half ready to think, notwithstanding our earnestness, that the business is to facilitate the speaking. A State revises her statutes with a rapidity that astonishes a European. Yet each revision brings some amendment, and what is found good in the constitution or laws of one State gets speedily imitated by the rest; each new State of the North becoming more democratic than its predecessor.

We are so intent on our purpose that we have no time for amusement. We have but one or two festivals in the year, and even then we are serious and reformatory. Jonathan thinks it a very solemn thing to be merry. A Frenchman said we have but two amusements in America — Theology for the women and politics for the men; preaching and voting. If this be true, it may help to explain the fact that most men take their theology from their wives, and women politics from their husbands. No nation ever tried the experiment of such abstinence from amusement. We have no time for sport, and so lose much of the poetry of life. All work and no play does not always make a dull boy, but it commonly makes a hard man.

We rush from school into business early; we hurry while in business; we aim to rich quickly, making a fortune at a stroke, making or losing it twice or thrice in a lifetime. "Soft and fair, goes safe and far," is no proverb to our taste. We are the most restless of people. How we crowd into cars and steamboats; a locomotive would well typify our fuming, fizzing spirit. In our large towns life seems to be only a scamper. Not satisfied with bustling about all day, when night comes we cannot sit still, but alone of all nations have added rockers to our chairs.

All is haste, from the tanning of leather to the education of a boy, and the old saw holds its edge good as ever—"the more haste the worse speed." The young stripling, innocent of all manner of lore, whom a judicious father has barrelled down in a college, or law-school, or theological seminary, till his beard be grown, mourns over the few years he must spend there awaiting that operation. His rule is, "to make a spoon or spoil a horn;" he longs to be out in the world "making a fortune," or "doing good," as he calls what his father better names "making noisy work for repentance, and doing mischief." So he rushes into life not fitted, and would fly towards heaven, this young Icarus, his wings not half fledged. There seems little taste for thoroughness. In our schools as our farms, we pass over much ground but pass over it poorly.

In education the aim is not to get the most we can, but the least we can get along with. A ship with over-much canvas and over-little ballast were no bad emblem of many amongst us. In no country is it so easy to get a reputation for learning — accumulated thought, because so few devote themselves to that accumulation. In this respect our standard is low. So a man of one attainment is sure to be honored, but a man of many and varied abilities is in danger of being undervalued. A Spurzheim would be warmly welcomed, while a Humboldt would be suspected of superficiality, as we have not the standard to judge him by. Yet in no country in the world is it so difficult to get a reputation for eloquence, as many speak and that well. It is surprising with what natural strength and beauty the young American addresses himself to speak. Some hatter's apprentice, or shoemaker's journeyman, at a temperance or anti-slavery meeting, will speak words like the blows of an axe, that cut clean and deep. The country swarms with orators, more abundantly where education is least esteemed — in the West or South.

We have secured national unity of action for the white citizens, without much curtailing individual variety of action, so we have at the North pretty well solved that problem which other nations have so often boggled over; we have balanced the centripetal power, the government and laws, with the centrifugal power, the mass of individuals, into harmonious proportions. If one were to leave out of sight the three million slaves, one sixth part of the population, the problem might be regarded as very happily solved. As the consequences of this, in no country is there more talent, or so much awake and active. In the South this unity is attained by sacrificing all the rights of three million slaves, and almost all the rights of the other colored population. In despotic countries this unity is brought about by the sacrifice of freedom, individual variety of action, in all except the despot and his favorites; so, much of the nation's energy is stifled in the chains of the State, while here it is friendly to institutions which are friendly to it, goes to its work, and approves itself in the vast increase of wealth and comfort throughout the North, where there is no class of men which is so oppressed that it cannot rise. One is amazed at the amount of ready skill and general ability which he finds in all the North, where each man has a little culture, takes his newspaper, manages his own business, and talks with some intelligence of many things — especially of politics and theology. In respect to this general intellectual ability and power of self-help, the mass of people seem far in advance of any other nation. But at the same time our scholars, who always represent the nation's higher modes of consciousness, will not bear comparison with the scholars of England, France, and Germany, men thoroughly furnished for their work. This is a great reproach and mischief to us, for we need most accomplished leaders, who by their thought can direct this national intensity of life. Our literature does not furnish them; we have no great men there; Irving, Channing, Cooper, are not names to conjure with in literature. One reads thick volumes devoted to the poets of America, or her prose writers, and finds many names which he wonders he never heard of before, but when he turns over their works, he finds consolation and recovers his composure.

American literature may be divided into two departments: the permanent literature, which gets printed in books, that sometimes reach more than one edition; and the evanescent literature, which appears only in the form of speeches, pamphlets, reviews, newspaper articles, and the like extempore productions. Now our permanent literature, as a general thing, is superficial, tame, and weak; it is not American; it has not our ideas, our contempt of authority, our philosophical turn, nor even our uncertainty as to first principles, still less our national intensity, our hope, and fresh intuitive perceptions of truth. It is a miserable imitation. Love of freedom is not there. The real national literature is found almost wholly in speeches, pamphlets, and newspapers. The latter are pretty thoroughly American; mirrors in which we see no very flattering likeness of our morals or our manners. Yet the picture is true: that vulgarity, that rant, that bragging violence, that recklessness of truth and justice, that disregard of right and duty, are a part of the nation's every-day life. Our newspapers are low and "wicked to a fault;" only in this weakness are they un-American. Yet they exhibit, and abundantly, the four qualities we have mentioned as belonging to the signs of our times. As a general rule, our orators are also American, with our good and ill. Now and then one rises who has studied Demosthenes in Leland or Francis, and got a second-hand acquaintance with old models: a man who uses literary commonplaces, and thinks himself original and classic because he can quote a line or so of Horace, in a Western House of Representatives, without getting so many words wrong as his reporter; but such men are rare, and after making due abatement for them, our orators all over the land are pretty thoroughly American, a little turgid, hot, sometimes brilliant, hopeful, intuitive, abounding in half truths, full of great ideas; often inconsequent; sometimes coarse; patriotic, vain, self-confident, rash, strong, and young-mannish. Of course the most of our speeches are vulgar, ranting, and worthless, but we have produced some magnificent specimens of oratory, which are fresh, original, American, and brand new.

The more studied, polished, and elegant literature is not so; that is mainly an imitation. It seems not a thing of native growth. Sometimes, as in Channing, the thought and the hope are American, but the form and the coloring old and foreign. We dare not be original; our American pine must be cut to the trim pattern of the English yew, though the pine bleed at every clip. This poet tunes his lyre at the harp of Goethe, Milton, Pope, or Tennyson. His songs might be better sung on the Rhine than the Kennebec. They are not American in form or feeling; they have not the breath of our air; the smell of our ground is not in them. Hence our poet seems cold and poor. He loves the old mythology; talks about Pluto — the Greek devil, the fates and furies — witches of old time in Greece, but would blush to use our mythology, or breathe the name in verse of our devil, or our own witches, lest he should be thought to believe what he wrote. The mother and sisters, who with many a pinch and pain sent the hopeful boy to college, must turn over the classical dictionary before they can find out what the youth would be at in his rhymes. Our poet is not deep enough to see that Aphrodite came from the ordinary waters, that Homer only hitched into rhythm and furnished the accomplishment of verse to street-talk, nursery tales, and old men's gossip in the Ionian towns; he thinks what is common is unclean. So he sings of Corinth and Athens, which he never saw, but has not a word to say of Boston, and Fall River, and Baltimore, and New York, which are just as meet for song. He raves of Thermopylæ and Marathon, with never a word for Lexington and Bunker-hill, for Cowpens, and Lundy's Lane, and Bemis's Heights. He loves to tell of the Ilyssus, of "smooth-sliding Mincius, crowned with vocal reeds," yet sings not of the Petapsco, the Susquehanna, the Aroostook, and the Willimantick. He prates of the narcissus and the daisy, never of American dandelions and blue-eyed grass; he dwells on the lark and the nightingale, but has not a thought for the brown thrasher and the bobolink, who every morning in June rain down such showers of melody on his affected head. What a lesson Burns teaches us, addressing his "rough bur-thistle," his daisy, "wee crimson tippit thing," and finding marvellous poetry in the mouse whose nest his plough turned over! Nay, how beautifully has even our sweet poet sung of our own Green river, our waterfowl, of the blue and fringed gentian, the glory of autumnal days.

Hitherto, spite of the great reading public, we have no permanent literature which corresponds to the American idea. Perhaps it is not time for that; it must be organized in deeds before it becomes classic in words; but as yet we have no such literature which reflects even the surface of American life, certainly nothing which portrays our intensity of life, our hope, or even our daily doings and drivings, as the Odyssey paints old Greek life, or Don Quixote and Gil Blas portray Spanish life. Literary men are commonly timid; ours know they are but poorly fledged as yet, so dare not fly away from the parent tree, but hop timidly from branch to branch. Our writers love to creep about in the shadow of some old renown, not venturing to soar away into the unwinged air, to sing of things here and now, making our life classic. So, without the grace of high culture, and the energy of American thought, they become weak, cold, and poor; are "curious, not knowing, not exact, but nice." Too fastidious to be wise, too unlettered to be elegant, too critical to create, they prefer a dull saying that is old to a novel form of speech, or a natural expression of a new truth. In a single American work, — and a famous one too, — there are over sixty similes, not one original, and all poor. A few men, conscious of this defect, this sin against the Holy Spirit of Literature, go to the opposite extreme, and are American-mad; they wilfully talk rude, write in-numerous verse, and play their harps all jangling, out of tune. A yet fewer few are American without madness. One such must not here be passed by, alike philosopher and bard, in whose writings "ancient wisdom shines with new-born beauty," and who has enriched a genius thoroughly American in the best sense, with a cosmopolitan culture and literary skill, which were wonderful in any land. But of American literature in general, and of him in special, more shall be said at another time.

Another remarkable feature is our excessive love of material things. This is more than a Utilitarianism, a preference of the useful over the beautiful. The Puritan at Plymouth had a corn-field, a cabbage-garden, and a patch for potatoes, a school-house, and a church, before he sat down to play the fiddle. He would have been a fool to reverse this process. It were poor economy and worse taste to have painters, sculptors, and musicians, while the rude wants of the body are uncared for. But our fault in this respect is, that we place too much the charm of life in mere material things, — houses, lands, well-spread tables, and elegant furniture, — not enough in man, in virtue, wisdom, genius, religion, greatness of soul, and nobleness of life. We mistake a perfection of the means of manliness for the end — manhood itself. Yet the housekeeping of a Shakspeare, Milton, Franklin, had only one thing worth boasting of. Strange to say, that was the master of the house. A rich and vulgar man once sported a coach and four, and at its first turn-out rode into the great commercial street of a large town in New England. "How fine you must feel with your new coach and four," said one of his old friends, though not quite so rich. "Yes," was the reply, "as fine as a beetle in a gold snuff-box." All of his kindred are not so nice and discriminating in their self-consciousness.

This practical materialism is a great affliction to us. We think a man cannot be poor and great also. So we see a great man sell himself for a little money, and it is thought "a good operation." A conspicuous man, in praise of a certain painter, summed up his judgment with this: "Why, Sir, he has made twenty thousand dollars by his pictures." "A good deal more than Michael Angelo, Leonardo, and Raphael together," might have been the reply. But it is easier to weigh purses than artistic skill. It was a characteristic praise bestowed in Boston on a distinguished American writer, that his book brought him more money than any man had ever realized for an original work in this country. "Commerce," said Mr. Pitt, "having got into both houses of Parliament, privilege must be done away," — the privilege of wit and genius, not less than rank. Clergymen estimate their own and their brothers' importance, not by their apostolical gifts, or even apostolic succession, but by the value of the living.

All other nations have this same fault, it may be said. But there is this difference: in other nations the things of a man are put before the man himself; so a materialism which exalts the accidents of the man — rank, wealth, birth, and the like — above the man, is not inconsistent with the general idea of England or Austria. In America it is a contradiction. Besides, in most civilized countries, there is a class of men living on inherited wealth, who devote their lives to politics, art, science, letters, and so are above the mere material elegance which surrounds them. That class has often inflicted a deep wound on society, which festers long and leads to serious trouble in the system, but at the same time it redeems a nation from the reproach of mere material vulgarity; it has been the source of refinement, and has warmed into life much of the wisdom and beauty which have thence spread over all the world. In America there is no such class. Young men inheriting wealth very rarely turn to any thing noble; they either convert their talents into gold, or their gold into furniture, wines, and confectionary. A young man of wealth does not know what to do with himself or it; a rich young woman seems to have no resource but marriage! Yet it must be confessed, that at least in one part of the United States wealth flows freely for the support of public institutions of education.

Here it is difficult for a man of science to live by his thought. Was Bowditch one of the first mathematicians of his age? He must be at the head of an annuity office. If Socrates should set up as a dealer in money, and outwit the brokers as formerly the Sophists, and shave notes as skilfully as of old, we should think him a great man. But if he adopted his old plan, what should we say of him?

Manliness is postponed and wealth preferred. "What a fine house is this," one often says; "what furniture; what feasting. But the master of the house! — why every stone out of the wall laughs at him. He spent all of himself in getting this pretty show together, and now it is empty, and mocks its owner. He is the emblematic coffin at the Egyptian feast." "Oh, man!" says the looker-on, "why not furnish thyself with a mind, and conscience, a heart and a soul, before getting all this brass and mahogany together; this beef and these wines?" The poor wight would answer, — "Why, Sir, there were none such in the market!" — The young man does not say, "I will first of all things be a man, and so being will have this thing and the other," putting the agreeable after the essential. But he says, "First of all, by hook or by crook, I will have money, the manhood may take care of itself." He has it, — for tough and hard as the old world is, it is somewhat fluid before a strong man who resolutely grapples with difficulty and will swim through; it can be made to serve his turn. He has money, but the man has evaporated in the process; when you look he is not there. True, other nations have done the same thing, and we only repeat their experiment. The old devil of conformity says to our American Adam and Eve, "Do this and you shall be as gods," a promise as likely to hold good as the devil's did in the beginning. A man was meant for something more than a tassel to a large estate, and a woman to be more than a rich housekeeper.

With this offensive materialism we copy the vices of feudal aristocracy abroad, making our vulgarity still more ridiculous. We are ambitious or proud of wealth, which is but labor stored up, and at the same time are ashamed of labor which is wealth in process. With all our talk about democracy, labor is thought less honorable in Boston than in Berlin and Leipsic. Thriving men are afraid their children will be shoemakers, or ply some such honorable and useful craft. Yet little pains are taken to elevate the condition or improve the manners and morals of those who do all the manual work of society. The strong man takes care that his children and himself escape that condition. We do not believe that all stations are alike honorable if honorably filled; we have little desire to equalize the burdens of life, so that there shall be no degraded class; none cursed with work, none with idleness. It is popular to endow a college; vulgar to take an interest in common schools. Liberty is a fact, equality a word, and fraternity, we do not think of yet.

In this struggle for material wealth and the social rank which is based thereon, it is amusing to see the shifting of the scenes; the social aspirations of one and the contempt with which another rebuts the aspirant. An old man can remember when the most exclusive of men, and the most golden, had scarce a penny in their purse, and grumbled at not finding a place where they would. Now the successful man is ashamed of the steps he rose by. The gentleman who came to Boston half a century ago, with all his worldly goods tied up in a cotton handkerchief, and that not of so large a pattern as are made now-a-days, is ashamed to recollect that his father was a currier, or a blacksmith, or a skipper at Barnstable or Beverly; ashamed, also, of his forty or fifty country cousins, remarkable for nothing but their large hands and their excellent memory. Nay, he is ashamed of his own humble beginnings, and sneers at men starting as he once started. The generation of English "Snobs" came in with the Conqueror, and migrated to America at an early day, where they continue to thrive marvellously — the chief "conservative party" in the land.

Through this contempt for labor, a certain affectation runs through a good deal of American society, and makes our aristocracy vulgar and contemptible. What if Burns had been ashamed of his plough, and Franklin had lost his recollection of the candle-moulds and the composing stick? Mr. Chubbs, who got rich to-day, imitates Mr. Swipes, who got rich yesterday, buys the same furniture, gives similar entertainments, and counts himself "as good a man as Swipes, any day." Nay, he goes a little beyond him, puts his servants in livery, with the "Chubbs arms" on the button; but the new-found family arms are not descriptive of the character of the Chubbses, or of their origin and history — only of their vanity. Then Mr. Swipes looks down on poor Chubbs, and curls his lip with scorn; calls him a "parvenu," "an upstart," "a plebeian;" speaks of him as one of "that sort of people," "one of your ordinary men;" "thrifty and well off in the world, but a little vulgar." At the same time Mr. Swipes looks up to Mr. Bung, who got rich the day before yesterday, as a gentleman of old family and quite distinguished, and receives from that quarter the same treatment he bestows on his left-hand neighbor. The real gentleman is the same all the world over. Such are by no means lacking here, while the pretended gentlemen swarm in America. Chaucer said a good word long ago:

"— This is not mine intendément
To clepen no wight in no age
Only gentle for his lineáge;
But whoso that is virtuous,
And in his port not outragéous:
When such one thou see'st thee beforn,
Though he be not gentle born,
Thou mayest well see this in soth,
That he is gentle, because he doth
As 'longeth to a gentleman;
Of them none other deem I can;
For certainly withouten drede,
A churl is deeméd by his deed,
Of high or low, as ye may see,
Or of what kindred that he be."

It is no wonder vulgar men, who travel here and eat our dinners, laugh at this form of vulgarity. Wiser men see its cause, and prophesy its speedy decay. Every nation has its aristocracy, or controlling class: in some lands it is permanent, an aristocracy of blood; men that are descended from distinguished warriors, from the pirates and freebooters of a rude age. The nobility of England are proud of their fathers' deeds, and emblazon the symbols thereof in their family arms, emblems of barbarism. Ours is an aristocracy of wealth, not got by plunder, but by toil, thrift, enterprise; of course it is a movable aristocracy: the first families of the last century are now forgot, and their successors will give place to new names. Now earning is nobler than robbing, and work is before war; but we are ashamed of both, and seek to conceal the noble source of our wealth. An aristocracy of gold is far preferable to the old and immovable nobility of blood, but it has also its peculiar vices: it has the effrontery of an upstart, despises its own ladder, is heartless and lacks noble principle, vulgar and cursing. This lust of wealth, however, does us a service, and gives the whole nation a stimulus which it needs, and, low as the motive is, drives us to continual advancement. It is a great merit for a nation to secure the largest amount of useful and comfortable and beautiful things which can be honestly earned, and used with profit to the body and soul of man. Only when wealth becomes an idol, and material abundance is made the end, not the means, does the love of it become an evil. No nation was ever too rich, or overthrifty, though many a nation has lost its soul by living wholly for the senses.

Now and then we see noble men living apart from this vulgarity and scramble; some rich, some poor, but both content to live for noble aims, to pinch and spare for virtue, religion, for truth and right. Such men never fail from any age or land, but everywhere they are the exceptional men. Still they serve to keep alive the sacred fire in the hearts of young men, rising amid the common mob as oaks surpass the brambles or the fern.

In these secondary qualities of the people which mark the special signs of the times, there are many contradictions, quality contending with quality; all by no means balanced into harmonious relations. Here are great faults not less than great virtues. Can the national faults be corrected? Most certainly; they are but accidental, coming from our circumstances, our history, our position as a people — heterogeneous, new, and placed on a new and untamed continent. They come not from the nation's soul; they do not belong to our fundamental idea, but are hostile to it. One day our impatience of authority, our philosophical tendency, will lead us to a right method, that to fixed principles, and then we shall have a continuity of national action. Considering the pains taken by the fathers of the better portion of America to promote religion here, remembering how dear is Christianity to the heart of all, conservative and radical — though men often name as Christian what is not — and seeing how truth and right are sure to win at last, — it becomes pretty plain that we shall arrive at true principles, laws of the universe, ideas of God; then we shall be in unison also with it and Him. When that great defect — lack of first principles — is corrected, our intensity of life, with the hope and confidence it inspires, will do a great work for us. We have already secured an abundance of material comforts hitherto unknown; no land was ever so full of corn and cattle, clothing, comfortable houses, and all things needed for the flesh. The desire of those things, even the excessive desire thereof, performs an important part in the divine economy of the human race; nowhere is its good effect more conspicuous than in America, where in two generations the wild Irishman becomes a decent citizen, orderly, temperate, and intelligent. This done or even a-doing, as it is now, we shall go forth to realize our great national idea, and accomplish the great work of organizing into institutions the unalienable rights of man. The great obstacle in the way of that is African slavery — the great exception in the nation's history; the national sin. When that is removed, as soon it must be, lesser but kindred evils will easily be done away; the truth which the land-reformers, which the associationists, the free-traders, and others, have seen, dimly or clearly, can readily be carried out. But while this monster vice continues, there is little hope of any great and permanent national reform. The positive things which we chiefly need for this work, are first, education, next, education, and then education, a vigorous development of the mind, conscience, affections, religious power of the whole nation. The method and the means for that I shall not now discuss.

The organization of human rights, the performance of human duties, is an unlimited work. If there shall ever be a time when it is all done, then the race will have finished its course. Shall the American nation go on in this work, or pause, turn off, fall, and perish? To me it seems almost treason to doubt that a glorious future awaits us. Young as we are, and wicked, we have yet done something which the world will not let perish. One day we shall attend more emphatically to the rights of the hand, and organize labor and skill; then to the rights of the head, looking after education, science, literature, and art; and again to the rights of the heart, building up the State with its laws, society with its families, the church with its goodness and piety. One day we shall see that it is a shame, and a loss, and a wrong, to have a criminal, or an ignorant man, or a pauper, or an idler, in the land; that the jail, and the gallows, and the almshouse are a reproach which need not be. Out of new sentiments and ideas, not seen as yet, new forms of society will come, free from the antagonism of races, classes, men — representing the American idea in its length, breadth, depth, and height, its beauty and its truth, and then the old civilization of our time shall seem barbarous and even savage. There will be an American art commensurate with our idea and akin to this great continent; not an imitation, but a fresh, new growth. An American literature also must come with democratic freedom, democratic thought, democratic power — for we are not always to be pensioners of other lands, doing nothing but import and quote; a literature with all of German philosophic depth, with English solid sense, with French vivacity and wit, Italian fire of sentiment and soul, with all of Grecian elegance of form, and more than Hebrew piety and faith in God. We must not look for the maiden's ringlets on the baby's brow; we are yet but a girl; the nameless grace of maturity, and womanhood's majestic charm, are still to come. At length we must have a system of education, which shall uplift the humblest, rudest, worst born child in all the land; which shall bring forth and bring up noble men.

An American State is a thing that must also be; a State of free men who give over brawling, resting on industry, justice, love, not on war, cunning, and violence, — a State where liberty, equality, and fraternity are deeds as well as words. In its time the American Church must also appear, with liberty, holiness, and love for its watchwords, cultivating reason, conscience, affection, faith, and leading the world's way in justice, peace, and love. The Roman Church has been all men know what and how; the American Church, with freedom for the mind, freedom for the heart, freedom for the soul, is yet to be, sundering no chord of the human harp, but tuning all to harmony. This also must come; but hitherto no one has risen with genius fit to plan its holy walls, conceive its columns, project its towers, or lay its corner-stone. Is it too much to hope all this? Look at the arena before us — look at our past history. Hark! there is the sound of many million men, the trampling of their freeborn feet, the murmuring of their voice; a nation born of this land that God reserved so long a virgin earth, in a high day married to the human race, — rising, and swelling, and rolling on, strong and certain as the Atlantic tide; they come numerous as ocean waves when east winds blow, their destination commensurate with the continent, with ideas vast as the Mississippi, strong as the Alleghanies, and awful as Niagara; they come murmuring little of the past, but, moving in the brightness of their great idea, and casting its light far on to other lands and distant days — come to the world's great work, to organize the rights of man.

VI.

A DISCOURSE OCCASIONED BY THE DEATH OF JOHN QUINCY ADAMS. DELIVERED AT THE MELODEON, IN BOSTON, MARCH 5, 1848.

WITHIN a few days one of the most distinguished statesmen of the age has passed away; a man who has long been before the public, familiarly known in the new world and the old. He was one of the prominent monuments of the age. It becomes us to look at his life, works, and public character, with an impartial eye; to try him by the Christian standard. Let me extenuate nothing, add nothing, and set down nought from any partial love or partial hate. His individuality has been so marked in a long life, his good and evil so sharply defined, that one can scarcely fail to delineate its most important features.

God has made some men great and others little. The use of great men is to serve the little men; to take care of the human race, and act as practical interpreters of justice and truth. This is not the Hebrew rule, nor the heathen, nor the common rule, only the Christian. The great man is to be the servant of mankind, not they of him. Perhaps greatness is always the same thing in kind, differing only in mode and in form, as well as degree. The great man has more of human nature than other men, organized in him. So far as that goes, therefore, he is more me than I am myself. We feel that superiority in all our intercourse with great men, whether kings, philosophers, poets, or saints. In kind we are the same; different in degree.

In nature we find individuals, not orders and genera; but for our own convenience in understanding and recollecting, we do a little violence to nature, and put the individuals into classes. In this way we understand better both the whole and each of its parts. Human nature furnishes us with individual great men; for convenience we put them into several classes, corresponding to their several modes or forms of greatness. It is well to look at these classes before we examine any one great man; this will render it easier to see where he belongs and what he is worth. Actual service is the test of actual greatness; he who renders, of himself, the greatest actual service to mankind, is actually the greatest man. There may be other tests for determining the potential greatness of men, or the essential; this is the Christian rule for determining the actual greatness.

Let us arrange these men in the natural order of their work.

First of all, there are great men who discover general truths, great ideas, universal laws, or invent methods of thought and action. In this class the vastness of a man's genius may be measured, and his relative rank ascertained by the transcendency of his ideas, by the newness of his truth, by its practical value, and the difficulty of attaining it in his time, and under his peculiar circumstances. In literature it is such men who originate thoughts, and put them into original forms; they are the great men of letters. In philosophy we meet with such; and they are the great men of science. Thus Socrates discovered the philosophical method of minute analysis that distinguished his school, and led to the rapid advance of knowledge in the various and even conflicting academies, which held this method in common, but applied it in various ways, well or ill, and to various departments of human inquiry; thus Newton discovered the law of gravitation, universal in nature, and by the discovery did immense service to mankind. In politics we find similar, or analogous men, who discover yet other laws of God, which bear the same relation to men in society that gravitation bears to the orbs in heaven, or to the dust and stones in the street; men that discover the first truths of politics, and teach the true method of human society. Such are the great men in politics.

We find corresponding men in religion; men who discover an idea so central that all sectarianism of parties or of nations seems little in its light; who discover and teach the universal law which unifies the race, binding man to man, and men to God; who discover the true method of religion conducting to natural worship without limitation, to free piety, free goodness, free thought. To my mind such are the greatest of great men, when measured by the transcendency of their doctrine and the service they render to all. By the influence of their idea, letters, philosophy, and politics become nobler and more beautiful, both in their forms and their substance.

Such is the class of discoverers; men who get truth at first hand, truth pertaining either especially to literature, philosophy, politics, religion, or at the same time to each and all of them.

The next class consists of such as organize these ideas, methods, truths, and laws; they concretize the abstract, particularize the general; they apply philosophy to practical purposes, organizing the discoveries of science into a railroad, a mill, a steam-ship, and by their work an idea becomes fact. They organize love into families, justice into a state, piety into a church. Wealth is power, knowledge is power, religion power; they organize all these powers, wealth, knowledge, religion, into common life, making divinity humanity, and that society.

This organizing genius is a very great one, and appears in various forms. One man spreads his thought out on the soil, whitening the land with bread-corn; another applies his mind to the rivers of New England, making them spin and weave for the human race; this man will organize his thought into a machine with one idea, joining together fire and water, iron and wood, animating them into a new creature, ready to do man's bidding; while that with audacious hand steals the lightning of heaven, organizes his plastic thought within that pliant fire, and sends it of his errands to fetch and carry tidings between the ends of the earth.

Another form of this mode of greatness is seen in politics, in organizing men. The man spreads his thought out on mankind, puts men into true relations with one another and with God; he organizes strength, wisdom, justice, love, piety; balances the conflicting forces of a nation, so that each man has his natural liberty as complete as if the only man, yet, living in society, gathers advantages from all the rest. The highest degree of this organizing power is the genius for legislation, which can enact justice and eternal right into treaties and statutes, codifying the divine thought into human laws, making absolute religion common life and daily custom, and balancing the centripetal power of the mass, with the centrifugal power of the individual, into a well-proportioned state, as God has balanced these two conflicting forces into the rhythmic ellipses above our heads. It need not be disguised, that politics are the highest business for men of this class, nor that a great statesman or legislator is the greatest example of constructive skill. It requires some ability to manage the brute forces of Nature, or to combine profitably nine-and-thirty clerks in a shop; how much more to arrange twenty millions of intelligent, free men, not for a special purpose, but for all the ends of universal life!

Such is the second class of great men; the organizers, men of constructive heads, who form the institutions of the world, the little and the great.

The next class consists of men who administer the institutions after they are founded. To do this effectually and even eminently, it requires no genius for original organization of truths freshly discovered, none for the discovery of truths, outright. It requires only a perception of those truths, and an acquaintance with the institutions wherein they have become incarnate; a knowledge of details, of formulas, and practical methods, united with a strong will and a practised understanding, — what is called a turn for affairs, tact, or address; a knowledge of routine and an acquaintance with men. The success of such men will depend on these qualities; they "know the ropes" and the soundings, the signs of the times; can take advantage of the winds and the tides.

In a shop, farm, ship, factory, or army, in a church or a State, such men are valuable; they cannot be dispensed with; they are wheels to the carriage; without them cannot a city be inhabited. They are always more numerous than both the other classes; more such are needed, and therefore born. The American mind, just now, runs eminently in this direction. These are not men of theories, or of new modes of thought or action, but what are called practical men, men of a few good rules, men of facts and figures, not so full of ideas as of precedents. They are called common-sense men; not having too much common-sense to be understood. They are not likely to be fallen in with far off at sea; quite as seldom out of their reckoning in ordinary weather. Such men are excellent statesmen in common times, but in times of trouble, when old precedents will not suit the new case, and men must be guided by the nature of man, not his history, they are not strong enough for the place, and get pushed off by more constructive heads.

These men are the administrators, or managers. If they have a little less of practical sense, such men fall a little below, and turn out only critics, of whom I will not now stop to discourse.

To have a railroad, there must have been first the

discoverers, who found out the properties of wood and iron, fire and water, and their latent power to carry men over the earth; next, the organizers, who put these elements together, surveyed the route, planned the structure, set men to grade the hill, to fill the valley, and pave the road with iron bars; and then the administrators, who, after all that is done, procure the engines, engineers, conductors, ticket-distributors, and the rest of the "hands;" they buy the coal and see it is not wasted, fix the rates of fare, calculate the savings, and distribute the dividends. The discoverers and organizers often fare hard in the world, lean men, ill clad and suspected, often laughed at, while the administrator is thought the greater man, because he rides over their graves and pays the dividends, where the organizer only called for the assessments, and the discoverer told what men called a dream. What happens in a railroad happens also in a Church, or a State.

Let us for a moment compare these three classes of great men. Measured by the test referred to, the discoverers are the greatest of all. They anticipate the human race, with long steps, striding before their kind. They learn not only from the history of man, but man's nature; not by empirical experience alone, but by a transcendent intuition of truth, now seen as a law, now as an idea. They are wiser than experience, and by divination through their nobler nature know at once what the human race has not learned in its thousands of years, kindling their lamp at the central fire now streaming from the sky, now rushing broad-sheeted and terrible as ground-lightning from the earth. Of such men there are but few, especially in the highest mode of this greatness. A single One makes a new world, and men date ages after him.

Next in order of greatness comes the organizer. He, also, must have great intellect, and character. It is no light work to make thoughts things. It requires mind to make a mill out of a river, bricks, iron, and stone, and set all the Connecticut to spinning cotton. But to construct a State, to harness fittingly twenty million men, animated by such divergent motives, possessing interests so unlike — this is the greatest work of constructive skill. To translate the ideas of the discoverer into institutions, to yoke men together by mere "abstractions," universal laws, and by such yoking save the liberty of all and secure the welfare of each — that is the most creative of poetry, the most constructive of sciences. In modern times, it is said, Napoleon is the greatest example of this faculty; not a discoverer, but an organizer of the highest power and on the largest scale. In human history he seems to have had no superior, perhaps no equal.

Some callings in life afford little opportunity to develop the great qualities above alluded to. How much genius lies latent no man can know; but he that walks familiarly with humble men often stumbles over masses of unsunned gold, where men proud in emptiness, looked only for common dust. How many a Milton sits mute and inglorious in his shop; how many a Cromwell rears only corn and oxen for the world's use, no man can know. Some callings help to light, some hide and hinder. But there is none which demands more ability than politics; they develop greatness, if the man have the germ thereof within him. True, in politics, a man may get along with a very little ability, without being a discoverer or an organizer; were it otherwise we should not be blessed with a very large House, or a crowded Senate. Nay, experience shows that in ordinary times one not even a great administrator may creep up to a high place and hang on there awhile. Few able administrators sit on the thrones of Europe at this day. But if power be in the man, the hand of politics will draw out the spark.

In America, politics more than elsewhere demand greatness, for ours is, in theory, the government of all, for all, and by all. It requires greater range of thought to discover the law for all than for a few; after the discovery thereof it is more difficult to construct a democracy than a monarchy, or an aristocracy, and after that is organized, it is more difficult to administer. It requires more manhood to wield at will "the fierce democratie" of America than to rule England or France; yet the American institutions are germane to human nature, and by that fact are rendered more easy, complicated as they are.

In politics, when the institutions are established, men often think there is no room for discoverers and organizers; that administrators alone are needed, and choose accordingly. But there are ideas well known, not yet organized into institutions: that of free trade, of peace, of universal freedom, universal education, universal comfort, in a word, the idea of human brotherhood. These wait to be constructed into a State without injustice, without war, without slavery, ignorance, or want. It is hardly true that Infinity is dry of truths, unseen as yet; there are truths enough waiting to be discovered; all the space betwixt us and God is full of ideas, waiting for some Columbus to disclose new worlds. Men are always saying there is no new thing under the sun, but when the discoverer comes, they see their mistake. We want the new eye.

Now, it is quite plain where we are to place the distinguished person of whom I speak. Mr. Adams was not a discoverer; not an organizer. He added no truth to mankind, not known before, and even well known; he made no known truth a fact. He was an administrator of political institutions. Taking the whole land into consideration, comparing him with his competitors, measuring him by his apparent works, at first sight he does not seem very highly eminent in this class of political administrators. Nay, some would set him down, not an administrator so much as a political critic.

Here there is danger of doing him injustice, by neglecting a fact so obvious, that it is seldom seen. Mr. Adams was a northern man, with northern habits, methods, and opinions. By the North, I mean the free States. The chief business of the North is to get empire over nature; all tends to that. Young men of talents become merchants, merchant-manufacturers, merchant-traders. The object directly aimed at, is wealth; not wealth by plunder, but by productive work. Now, to get dominion over nature, there must be education, universal education, otherwise there is not enough intelligent industry, which alone insures that dominion. With wide-spread intelligence, property will be widely distributed, and, of course, suffrage and civil power will get distributed. All is incomplete without religion. I deny not that these peculiarities of the North, come, also, from other sources, but they all are necessary to attain the chief object thereof — dominion over the material world. The North subdues nature by thought, and holds her powers in thrall. As results of this, see the increase in wealth which is signified by northern railroads, ships, mills, and shops; in the colleges, schools, churches, which arise; see the skill developed in this struggle with nature, the great enterprises which come of that, the movements of commerce, manufactures, the efforts — and successful, too — for the promotion of education, of religion. All is democratic, and becomes more so continually, each descendant founding institutions more liberal than those of the parent State. Men designedly, and, as their business, become merchants, mechanics, and the like; they are politicians by exception, by accident, from the necessity of the case. Few northern men are politicians by profession; they commonly think it better to be a collector or a postmaster, than a Senator, estimating place by money, not power. Northern politicians are bred as lawyers, clergymen, mechanics, farmers, merchants. Political life is an accident, not an end.

In the South, the aim is to get dominion over men; so, the whole working population must be in subjection, in slavery. While the North makes brute nature half intelligent, the South makes human nature half brutal, the man becoming a thing. Talent tends to politics, not trade. Young men of ability go to the army or navy, to the public offices, to diplomatic posts, in a word, to politics. They learn to manage men. To do this, they not only learn what men think, but why they think it. The young man of the North seeks a fortune; of the South, a reputation and political power. The politician of the South makes politics the study and work of his whole life; all else is accidental and subordinate. He begins low, but ends high; he mingles with men; has bland and agreeable manners; is frank, honorable, manly, and knows how to persuade.

See the different results of causes so unlike. The North manages the commercial affairs of the land, the ships, mills, farms, and shops; the spiritual affairs, literature, science, morals, education, religion; — writes, calculates, instructs, and preaches. But the South manages the political affairs, and has free-trade or tariff, war or peace, just as she will. Of the eight Presidents who were elected in fifty years, only three were northern men. Each of them has retired from office, at the end of a single term, in possession of a fortune, but with little political influence. Each of the five southern Presidents has been twice elected; only one of them was rich. There is no accident in all this. The State of Rhode Island has men that can administer the Connecticut or the Mississippi; that can organize Niagara into a cotton factory; yes, that can get dominion over the ocean and the land: but the State of South Carolina has men that can manage the Congress, can rule the North and South, and make the nation do their bidding.

So the South succeeds in politics, but grows poor, and the North fails in politics, but thrives in commerce and the arts. There great men turn to politics, here to trade. It is so in time of peace, but, in the day of trouble, of storms, of revolution like the old one, men of tall heads will come up from the ships and the shops, the farms and the colleges of the North, born discoverers and organizers, the aristocracy of God, and sit down in the nation's councils to control the State. The North made the revolution, furnished the men, the money, the ideas, and the occasion for putting them into form. At the making of the Constitution, the South out-talked the North; put in such claims as it saw fitting, making the best bargain it could, violating the ideas of the Revolution, and getting the North, not only to consent to slavery, but to allow it to be represented in Congress itself. Now, the South breaks the Constitution just when it will, puts northern sailors in its jails, and the North dares not complain, but bears it "with a patient shrug." An eastern merchant is great on a southern exchange, makes cotton rise or fall, but no northern politician has much weight at the South, none has ever been twice elected President. The North thinks it is a great thing to get an inoffensive northern man as Speaker, in the House of Representatives. The South is an aristocracy, which the democracy of the North would not tolerate a year, were it at the North itself. Now it rules the land, has the northern masses, democrats and whigs, completely under its thumb. Does the South say, "Go," they hasten; "Come," they say "Here we are;" "Do this," they obey in a moment; "Whist," there is not a mouse stirring in all the

North. Does the South say "Annex," it is done; "Fight," men of the North put on the collar, lie lies, issue their proclamations, enroll their soldiers, and declare it is moral treason for the most insignificant clergyman to preach against the war.

All this needs to be remembered in judging of Mr. Adams. True he was regularly bred to politics, and "to the manor born;" but he was a New England man, with northern notions, northern habits, and though more than fifty years in public life, yet he seems to have sought the object of New England far more than the object of the South. Measure his greatness by his service; but that is not to be measured by immediate and apparent success.

In a notice so brief as this, I can say but little of the details of Mr. Adams's life, and purposely pass over many things, dwelling mainly on such as are significant of his character. He was born at Quincy, the 11th of July, 1767; in 1777 he went to Europe with his father, then Minister to France. He remained in Europe most of the time, his powers developing with rapidity and promise of future greatness, till 1785, when he returned and entered the junior class in Harvard College. In 1787, he graduated with distinguished honors. He studied law at Newburyport, with Judge Parsons, till 1790, and was a lawyer in Boston, till 1794.

That may be called the period of his education

He enjoyed the advantages of a residence abroad, which enabled him to acquire a knowledge of foreign languages, modes of life, and habits of thought. His father's position brought the son in contact with the ablest men of the age. He was Secretary of the American minister to Russia at the age of fourteen. He early became acquainted with Franklin and Jefferson, men who had a powerful influence on his youthful mind. For three years he was a student with Judge Parsons, a very remarkable man. These years, from 1767 to 1794, form a period marked by intense mental activity in America and in Europe. The greatest subjects which claim human attention, the laws that lie at the foundation of society, the State, the church, and the family, were discussed as never before. Mr. Adams drew in liberty and religion from his mother's breast. His cradle rocked with the Revolution. When eight years old, from a hill-top hard by his house he saw the smoke of Charlestown, burning at the command of the oppressor. The lullaby of his childhood was the roar of cannon at Lexington and Bunker Hill. He was born in the gathering of the storm, of a family that felt the blast, but never bent thereto; he grew up in its tumult. Circumstances like these make their mark on the character.

His attention was early turned to the most important matters. In 1793, he wrote several papers in the "Centinel," at Boston, on neutral rights, advising the American government to remain neutral in the quarrel between France, our ally, and others; the papers attracted the attention of Washington, who appointed the author Minister to Holland. He remained abroad in various diplomatic services in that country, in Russia and England, till 1801, when he was recalled by his father, and returned home. It was an important circumstance, that he was abroad during that time when the nation divided into two great parties. He was not called on to take sides with either; he had a vantage ground whence he could overlook both, approve their good and shun their evil. The effect of this is abundantly evident in all his life. He was not dyed in the wool by either political party, — the moral sense of the man drowned in the process of becoming a federalist or a democrat.

In 1802, he was elected to the Senate of Massachusetts, yet not wholly by the votes of one party. In 1803, he was chosen to the Senate of the United States. In the Massachusetts Legislature he was not a strict party man; he was not elected to the Senate by a strictly party vote. In 1806, he was inaugurated as Professor of Rhetoric and Oratory at Harvard University, and continued in that office about three years. In 1808, he resigned his place in the Senate. In 1809, he was sent by Mr. Madison as Minister to Russia, and remained abroad in various ministries and commissions, till 1817, when he returned, and became Secretary of State under Mr. Monroe. This office he filled till he became President, in 1825. In 1829, failing of reëlection, he retired to private life. In 1831, he was elected as one of the Representatives to Congress from Massachusetts, and continued there till his death, the first President that ever sat in an American Congress.

It will be fifty-four years the thirtieth of next May, since he began his public career. What did he aim at in that long period? At first sight, it is easy to see the aim of some of the conspicuous men of America. It has obviously been the aim of Mr. Clay to build up the "American System," by the establishment of protective duties; that of Mr. Calhoun to establish free trade, leaving a man to buy where he can buy cheapest, and sell where he can sell dearest. In respect to these matters the two are exactly opposite to one another — antithetic as the poles. But each has also, and obviously, another aim, — to build up the institution of slavery in the South. In this they agree, and if I understand them aright, this is the most important political design of each; for which Mr. Calhoun would forego even free trade, and Mr. Clay would "compromise" even a tariff. Looked at in reference to their aims, there is a certain continuity of action in both these gentlemen. I speak not now of another object which both have equally and obviously aimed at; not of the personal, but the political object.

At first sight, it does not appear that Mr. Adams had any definite scheme of measures which he aimed to establish; there is no obvious unity of idea, or continuity of action, that forces itself upon the spectator. He does not seem to have studied the two great subjects of our political economy, finance and trade, very deeply, or even with any considerable width of observation or inquiry; he had no financial or commercial hobby. He has worked with every party, and against every party; all have claimed, none held him. Now he sides with the federalists, then with the democrats; now he opposes France, showing that her policy is that of pirates; now he contends against England; now he works in favor of General Jackson, who put down the nullification of South Carolina with a rough hand; then he opposes the general in his action against the Bank; now he contends for the Indians, then for the Negroes; now attacks Masonry, and then Free trade. He speaks in favor of claiming and holding "the whole of Oregon;" then against annexing Texas.

But there is one sentiment which runs through all his life: an intense love of freedom for all men; one idea, the idea that each man has unalienable rights. These are what may be called the American sentiment, and the American idea; for they lie at the basis of American institutions, except the "patriarchal," and shine out in all our history — I should say, our early history. These two form the golden thread on which Mr. Adams's jewels are strung. Love of human freedom in its widest sense is the most marked and prominent thing in his character. This explains most of his actions. Studied with this in mind, his life is pretty consistent. This explains his love of the Constitution. He early saw the peculiarity of the American government; that it rested in theory on the natural rights of man, not on a compact, not on tradition, but on somewhat anterior to both, on the unalienable rights universal in man, and equal in each. He looked on the American Constitution as an attempt to organize these rights; resting, therefore, not on force, but natural law; not on power, but right. But with him the Constitution was not an idol; it was a means, not an end. He did more than expound it; he went back of the Constitution, to the Declaration of Independence, for the ideas of the Constitution; yes, back of the Declaration to Human Nature and the Laws of God, to legitimate these ideas. The Constitution is a compromise between those ideas and institutions and prejudices existing when it was made; not an idol, but a servant. He saw that the Constitution is "not the work of eternal justice, ruling through the people," but the work "of man; frail, fallen, imperfect man, following the dictates of his nature, and aspiring to be perfect."* Though a

* See *Social Compact*, etc. Providence, 1848, p. 31, *et al.*

"constitutionalist," he did not worship the Constitution. He was much more than a "defender of the Constitution," — a defender of Human Rights.

Mr. Adams had this American sentiment and idea in an heroic degree. Perhaps no political man now living has expressed them so fully. With a man like him, not very genial or creative, having no great constructive skill, and not without a certain pugnacity in his character, this sentiment and idea would naturally develop themselves in a negative form, that of opposition to Wrong, more often than in the positive form of direct organization of the Right; would lead to criticism oftener than to creation. Especially would this be the case if other men were building up institutions in opposition to this idea. In him they actually take the form of what he called "The unalienable right of resistance to oppression." His life furnishes abundant instances of this. He thought the Indians were unjustly treated, cried out against the wrong; when President, endeavored to secure justice to the Creeks in Georgia, and got into collision with Governor Troup. He saw, or thought he saw, that England opposed the American idea, both in the new world and the old. In his zeal for freedom he sometimes forgot the great services of England in that same cause, and hated England, hated her with great intensity of hatred, hated her political policy, her monarchy, and her aristocracy, mocked at the madness of her king, for he thought

England stood in the way of freedom.* Yet he loved the English name and the English blood, was "proud of being himself descended from that stock," thinking it worth noting, "that Chatham's language was his mother tongue, and Wolfe's great name compatriot with his own." He confessed no nation had done more for the cause of human improvement. He loved the Common Law of England, putting it far above the Roman Law, perhaps not without doing a little injustice to the latter.† The common law was a rude and barbarous code. But human liberty was there; a trial by jury was there; the habeas corpus was there. It was the law of men "regardful of human rights."

This sentiment led him to defend the right of petition in the House of Representatives, as no other man had dared to do. He cared not whether it was the petition of a majority, or a minority; of men or women, free men or slaves. It might be a petition to remove him from a committee, to expel him from the House, a petition to dissolve the Union — he

---

* See *Address at Washington*, 4th of July, 1821. Second Edition, Cambridge, *passim*.

† Reference is made to his *speech in the House of Representatives*, May 8th and 9th, 1840. (Boston, 1840.) It is a little remarkable, that the false principle of the common law, on which Mr. Adams was commenting, as laid down by Blackstone, is corrected by a writer, M. Pothier, who rests on the civil law for his authority. See pp. 6–8, and 20, 21.

presented it none the less. To him there was but one nature in all, man or woman, bond or free, and that was human nature, the most sacred thing on earth. Each human child had unalienable rights, and though that child was a beggar or slave, had rights, which all the power in the world, bent into a single arm, could not destroy nor abate, though it might ravish away. This induced him to attempt to procure the right of suffrage for the colored citizens of the District of Columbia.

This sentiment led him to oppose tyranny in the House of Representatives, the tyranny of the majority. In one of his juvenile essays, published in 1791, contending against a highly popular work, he opposed the theory that a State has the right to do what it pleases, declaring it had no right to do wrong.* In his old age he had not again to encounter the empty hypothesis of Thomas Paine, but the substantial enactment of the "Representatives" of the people of the United States. The hypothesis was trying to become a fact. The South had passed the infamous Gag-Law, which a symbolical man from New Hampshire had presented, though it originated with others.† By that law the mouth of the North

---

* *Answer to Paine's Rights of Man* (London, 1793), originally published in the Columbian Centinel. The London Edition bears the name of *John Adams* on the title-page.

† Mr. Atherton.

was completely stopped in Congress, so that not one word could be said about the matter of slavery.

The North was quite willing to have it stopped, for it did not care to speak against slavery, and the gag did not stop the mouth of the Northern purse. You may take away from the North its honor, if you can find it; may take away its rights; may imprison its free citizens in the jails of Louisiana and the Carolinas; yes, may invade the "Sacred soil of the North," and kidnap a man out of Boston itself, within sight of Faneuil Hall, and the North will not complain; will bear it with that patient shrug, waiting for yet further indignities. Only when the Northern purse is touched, is there an uproar. If the postmaster demands silver for letters, there is instant alarm; the repeal of a tariff rouses the feelings, and an embargo once drove the indignant North to the perilous edge of rebellion! Mr. Adams loved his dollars as well as most New England men; he looked out for their income as well; guarded as carefully against their outgo; though conscientiously upright in all his dealings, kind and hospitable, he has never been proved generous, and generosity is the commonest virtue of the North; is said to have been "close," if not mean. He loved his dollars as well as most men, but he loved justice more; honor more; freedom more; the Unalienable Rights of man far more.

He looked on the Constitution as an instrument for the defence of the Rights of man. The government was to act as the people had told how. The Federal government was not sovereign; the State government was not sovereign;* neither was a court of ultimate appeal; — but the People was sovereign; had the right of Eminent Domain over Congress and the Constitution, and making that, had set limits to the government. He guarded therefore against all violation of the Constitution, as a wrong done to the people; he would not overstep its limits in a bad cause; not even in a good one. Did Mr. Jefferson obtain Louisiana by a confessed violation of the Constitution, Mr. Adams would oppose the purchase of Louisiana, and was one of the six senators who voted against it. Making laws for that Territory, he wished to extend the trial by jury to all criminal prosecutions, while the law limited that form of trial to capital offences. Before that Territory had a representative in Congress, the American government wished to collect a revenue there. Mr. Adams opposed that too. It was "assuming a dangerous power;" it was government without the consent of the governed, and therefore an unjust government. "All exercise of human authority must be under the limitation of right and wrong." All other power is despotic, and "in defiance of the laws of nature and of God." †

This love of freedom led him to hate and oppose

---

* See *Oration at Quincy*, 1831, p. 12, *et seq.* (Boston, 1831.)

† The *Social Compact*, etc., etc. (Providence, 1842). p. 24.

the tyranny of the strong over the weak, to hate it most in its worst form; to hate American Slavery, doubtless the most infamous form of that tyranny now known amongst the nations of Christendom, and perhaps the most disgraceful thing on earth. Mr. Adams called slavery a vessel of dishonor so base that it could not be named in the Constitution with decency. In 1805, he wished to lay a duty on the importation of slaves, and was one of five senators who voted to that effect. He saw the power of this institution—the power of money and the power of votes which it gives to a few men. He saw how dangerous it was to the Union; to American liberty, to the cause of man. He saw that it trod three millions of men down to the dust, counting souls but as cattle. He hated nothing as he hated this; fought against nothing so manfully. It was the lion in the pathway of freedom, which frightened almost all the politicians of the North and the East and the West, so that they forsook that path; a lion whose roar could wellnigh silence the forum and the bar, the pulpit and the press; a lion who rent the Constitution, trampled under foot the Declaration of Independence, and tore the Bible to pieces. Mr. Adams was ready to rouse up this lion, and then to beard him in his den. Hating slavery, of course he opposed whatever went to strengthen its power; opposed Mr. Atherton's Gag-law; opposed the annexation of Texas; opposed the Mexican war; and, wonderful to tell, actually voted against it, and never took back his vote.

When Secretary of State, this same feeling led him to oppose conceding to the British the right of searching American vessels supposed to be concerned in the slave-trade, and when Representative to oppose the repeal of the law giving "protection" to American sailors. It appeared also in private intercourse with men. No matter what was a man's condition, Mr. Adams treated him as an equal.

This devotion to freedom and the unalienable rights of man, was the most important work of his life. Compared with some other political men, he seems inconsistent, because he now opposes one evil, then its opposite evil. But his general course is in this direction, and, when viewed in respect to this idea, seems more consistent than that of Mr. Webster, or Calhoun, or Clay, when measured by any great principle. This appears in his earlier life. In 1802, he became a member of the Massachusetts Senate. The majority of the General Court were federalists. It was a time of intense political excitement, the second year of Mr. Jefferson's administration. The custom is well known — to take the whole of the Governor's Council from the party which has a majority in the General Court. On the 27th of May, 1802, Mr. Adams stood up for the rights of the minority. He wanted some anti-federalists in the Council of Governor Strong, and as Senator threw his first vote to secure that object. Such was the first legislative action of John Quincy Adams. In the House of Representatives, in 1831, the first thing he did was to present fifteen petitions for the abolition of slavery in the District of Columbia, though, from constitutional scruples, opposed to granting the petitions. The last public act of his life was this: — The question was before the House on giving medals to the men distinguished in the Mexican war; the minority opposing it wanted more time for debate; the previous question was moved, Mr. Adams voted for the last time, — voted "No," with unusual emphasis; the great loud No of a man going home to God full of "The unalienable right of resistance to oppression," its emphatic word on his dying lips. There were the beginning, the middle, and the end, all three in the same spirit, all in favor of mankind; a remarkable unity of action in his political drama.

Somebody once asked him, What are the recognized principles of politics? Mr. Adams answered that there were none: the recognized precepts are bad ones, and so not principles. But, continued the inquirer, is not this a good one — To seek "The greatest good of the greatest number?" No, said he, that is the worst of all, for it looks specious while it is ruinous. What shall become of the minority, in that case? This is the only principle, — "To seek the greatest good of all."

I do not say there were no exceptions to this devotion to freedom in a long life; there are some passages in his history which it is impossible to justify, and hard to excuse. In early life he was evidently ambitious of place, and rank, and political power. I must confess, it seems to me, at some times, he was not scrupulous enough about the means of attaining that place and power. He has been much censured for his vote in favor of the Embargo, in 1807. His vote, howsoever unwise, may easily have been an honest vote. To an impartial spectator at this day, perhaps it will be evidently so. His defence of it I cannot think an honest defence, for in that he mentions arguments as impelling him to his vote which could scarcely have been present to his mind at the time, and, if they were his arguments then, were certainly kept in silence — they did not appear in the debate,* they were not referred to in the President's message.†

* See Pickering's *Letter to Governor Sullivan, on the Embargo.* Boston, 1808. John Quincy Adams's *Letter to the Hon. H. G. Otis*, etc. Boston, 1808. Pickering's *Interesting Correspondence*, 1808. *Review of the Correspondence between the Hon. John Adams and the late William Cunningham*, etc. 1824. But see, also, Mr. Adams's "Appendix" to the above letter, published *sixteen* years after the vote on the embargo. Baltimore, 1824. Mr. Pickering's *Brief Remarks on the Appendix.* August, 1824.

† Reference is here made to British "*Orders in Council*" of Nov. 22d, 1807. They were not officially made known to the

I am not to praise Mr. Adams simply because he is dead; what is wrong before is wrong after death. It is no merit to die; shall we tell lies about him because he is dead? No, the Egyptian people scrutinized and judged their kings after death — much more should we our fellow-citizens, intrusted with power to serve the State. "A lavish and undistinguishing eulogium is not praise." I know what coals of terrible fire lie under my feet, as I speak of this matter, and how thin and light is the coat of ashes deposited there in forty years; how easily they are blown away at the slightest breath of "Hartford Convention," or the "Embargo," and the old flame of political animosity blazes forth anew, while the hostile forms of "federalists" and "democrats" come back to light. I would not disquiet those awful shades, nor bring them up again. But a word must be said. The story of the embargo is well known: the President sent his message to the Senate recommending it, and accompanied with several documents. The message was read and assigned to a committee; the ordinary rule of business was suspended; the bill was reported by the committee; drafted, debated, engrossed, and completely passed through all its

---

American Congress till Feb. 7th, 1808. They were, however, published in the National Intelligencer, the morning on which the Message was sent to the Senate, Dec. 18th, 1807, but were not mentioned in that document, nor in the debate.

stages, the whole on the same day, in secret session, and in about four hours! Yet it was a bill that involved the whole commerce of the country, and prostrated that commerce, seriously affecting the welfare of hundreds of thousands of men. Eight hundred thousand tons of shipping were doomed to lie idle and rot in port. The message came on Friday. Some of the Senators wanted yet further information and more time for debate, at least for consideration, — till Monday. It could not be! Till Saturday, then. No; the bill must pass now, no man sleeping on that question. Mr. Adams was the most zealous for passing the bill. In that "debate," if such it can be called, while opposing a postponement for further information and reflection, he said, "The President has recommended the measure on his high responsibility; I would *not consider*, I would *not deliberate;* I would *act.* Doubtless the *President possesses such further information as will justify the measure!*"* To my mind, that is the worst act

* I copy this from the first letter of Mr. Pickering. Mr. Adams wrote a letter (to H. G. Otis) in reply to this of Mr. Pickering, but said nothing respecting the words charged upon him; but in 1824, in an appendix to that letter, he denies that he expressed the "sentiment" which Mr. Pickering charged him with. But he *does not deny the words themselves.* They rest on the authority of Mr. Pickering, his colleague in the Senate, a strong party man, it is true, perhaps not much disposed to conciliation, but a man of most unquestionable veracity. The "sentiment" speaks for itself.

of his public life; I cannot justify it. I wish I could find some reasonable excuse for it. What had become of the "sovereignty of the people," the "unalienable right of resistance to oppression?" Would *not consider;* would *not deliberate;* would *act* without doing either; leave it all to the "high responsibility" of the President, with a "doubtless" he has "further information" to justify the measure! It was a shame to say so; it would have disgraced a Senator in St. Petersburg. Why not have the "further information" laid before the Senate? What would Mr. Adams have said, if President Jackson, Tyler, or Polk, had sent such a message, and some Senator or Representative had counselled submissive action, without considering, without deliberation? With what appalling metaphors would he describe such a departure from the first duty of a statesman; how would the tempestuous eloquence of that old patriot shake the Hall of Congress till it rung again, and the nation looked up with indignation in its face! It is well known what Mr. Adams said in 1834, when Mr. Polk, in the House of Representatives, seemed over-laudatory of the President: "I shall never be disposed to interfere with any member who shall rise on this floor and pronounce a panegyric upon the chief magistrate.

> 'No, let the candied tongue lick absurd pomp,
> And crook the pregnant hinges of the knee
> Where thrift may follow fawning.'"

Yet the future of Mr. Polk was not so obvious in 1834, as the reward of Mr. Adams in 1808.

This act is particularly glaring in Mr. Adams. The North often sends men to Washington who might have done it without any great inconsistency; men, too, not so remarkable for infirmity in the head, as for that less pardonable weakness in the knees and the neck; men that bend to power "right or wrong." Mr. Adams was not afflicted with that weakness, and so the more to be censured for this palpable betrayal of a trust so important. I wish I could find some excuse for it. He was forty years old; not very old, but old enough to know better. His defence made the matter worse. The Massachusetts Legislature disapproved of his conduct; chose another man to succeed him in the Senate. Then Mr. Adams resigned his seat, and soon after was sent minister to Russia, as he himself subsequently declared,* "in consequence of the support he had for years given to the measures of Mr. Jefferson's administration against Great Britain." But his father said of that mission of his son, "Aristides is banished because he is too just."† It is easy to judge of the temper of the times, when such words

---

* Adams's *Remarks in the House of Representatives*, Jan. 5, 1846.

† *Correspondence between the Hon. John Adams and the late William Cunningham, Esq.* Boston, 1823. Letter xliii. p. 150.

as those of the father could be said on such an occasion, and that by a man who had been President of the United States! When a famine occurs, disease appears in the most hideous forms; men go back to temporary barbarism. In times of political strife, such diseases appear of the intellectual and moral powers. No man who did not live in those times can fully understand the obliquity of mind and moral depravity which then displayed themselves amongst those otherwise without reproach. Says Mr. Adams himself, referring to that period, "Imagination in her wildest vagaries can scarcely conceive the transformation of temper, the obliquities of intellect, the perversions of moral principle, effected by junctures of nigh and general excitement." However, it must be confessed that this, though not the only instance of injustice, is the only case of servile compliance with the Executive to be found in the whole life of the man. It was a grievous fault, but grievously did he answer it; and if a long life of unfaltering resistance to every attempt at the assumption of power is fit atonement, then the expiation was abundantly made.

About the same time, Mr. Adams was chairman of a committee of the Senate, appointed to consider the case of a Senator from Ohio. His conduct, on that occasion, has been the theme of violent attack, and defence as violent. To the calm spectator, at this day, his conduct seems unjustifiable, inconsistent with the counsels of justice, which, though moving with her "Pace of snail," looks always towards the right, and will not move out of her track, though the heavens fall.

While Mr. Adams was President, Hayti became free; but he did not express any desire that the United States should acknowledge her independence, and receive her minister at Washington, — an African plenipotentiary. In his message,* he says, "There are circumstances that have hitherto forbidden the acknowledgment," and mentions "additional reasons for withholding that acknowledgment." In the instructions to the American functionary, sent to the celebrated Congress of Panama, it is said, the President "is not prepared now to say that Hayti ought to be recognized as an independent sovereign power;" he "does not think it would be proper at this time to recognize it as a new State." He was unwilling to consent to the independence of Cuba, for fear of an insurrection of her slaves, and the effect at home. The duty of the United States would be "To defend themselves against the contagion of such near and dangerous examples," that would "constrain them . . . . to employ all means necessary to their security." That is, the President would be constrained to put down the blacks in Cuba, who were exercising "The unalienable right of resistance to oppression," for fear the blacks in

---

* March 15th, 1826.

the United States would discover that they also were men, and had "Unalienable rights!" Had he forgotten the famous words, "Resistance to tyrants is obedience to God?" The defence of such language on such an occasion is, that Mr. Adams's eyes were not yet open to the evil of slavery. That is a good defence, if true. To me it seems a true defence. Even great men do not see every thing. In 1800, Fisher Ames, while delivering the eulogy on General Washington, censured even the British government, because, "In the wilds of Africa, it obstructed the commerce in slaves!" No man is so wise as mankind. It must be confessed that Mr. Adams, while Secretary of State, and again, while President, showed no hostility to the institution of slavery. His influence all went the other way. He would repress the freedom of the blacks, in the West Indies, lest American slavery should be disturbed, and its fetters broke; he would not acknowledge the independence of Hayti, he would urge Spain to make peace with her descendants, for the same reason — "not for those new republics," but lest the negroes in Cuba and Porto Rico should secure their freedom. He negotiated with England, and she paid the United States more than a million of dollars* for the fugitive slaves who took refuge under

* See Mr. Adams's *Message*, Dec. 2, 1828. The exact sum was $1,197,422.18.

her flag during the late war. Mr. Adams had no scruples about receiving the money during his administration. An attempt was repeatedly made by his secretary, Mr. Clay, through Mr. Gallatin, and then through Mr. Barbour, to induce England to restore the "fugitive slaves who had taken refuge in the Canadian provinces," who, escaping from the area of freedom, seek the shelter of the British crown.* Nay, he negotiated a treaty with Mexico, which bound her to deliver up fugitive slaves, escaping from the United States — a treaty which the Mexican Congress refused to ratify! Should a great man have known better? Great men are not always wise. Afterwards, public attention was called to the matter; humble men gave lofty counsel; Mr. Adams used different language, and recommended different measures. But long before that, on the 7th of December, 1804, Mr. Pickering, his colleague in the Senate of the United States, offered a resolution, for the purpose of amending the Constitution, so as to apportion representatives, and direct taxes among the States, according to their free inhabitants.

---

* See Mr. Clay's Letter to Mr. A. H. Everett, April 27th, 1825; to Mr. Middleton, respecting the intervention of the Emperor of Russia, May 10th, and Dec. 26th, 1825; to Mr. Gallatin, May 10th, and June 19th, 1826, and Feb. 24th, 1827. *Executive Documents*, Second Session of the 20th Congress, Vol. I.

But there are other things in Mr. Adams's course and conduct, which deserve the censure of a good man. One was, the attempt to justify the conduct of England, in her late war with China, when she forced her opium upon the barbarians with the bayonet. To make out his case, he contended that "In the celestial empire . . . . the patriarchal system of Sir Robert Filmer, flourished in all its glory," and the Chinese claimed superior dignity over all others; they refused to hold equal and reciprocal commercial intercourse with other nations, and "It is time this enormous outrage upon the rights of human nature, and the first principles of the laws of nations, should cease." * It is true, the Chinese were "barbarians;" true, the English carried thither the Bible and Christianity, at least their own Christianity. But, even by the law of nations, letting alone the law of nature, the barbarians had a right to repel both Bible and Christianity, when they came in a contraband shape — that of opium and cannon balls. To justify this outrage of the strong against the weak, he quite forgets his old antipathy to England, his devotion to human freedom, and the sovereignty of the people, calling the cause of England "a righteous cause."

He defended the American claim to the whole of

---

* Report of Mr. Adams's *Lecture on the Chinese War*, in the Boston Atlas, for Dec. 4th and 5th, 1841.

Oregon, up to 54° 40′. He did not so much undertake to make out a title to either, by the law of nature or of nations, but cut the matter short, and claimed the whole of Oregon, on the strength of the first chapter of Genesis. This was the argument: God gave mankind dominion over all the earth;* between Christian nations, the command of the Creator lays the foundation of all titles to land, of titles to territory, of titles to jurisdiction. Then in the Psalms,† God gives the "uttermost part of the earth for a possession" to the Messiah, as the representative of all mankind, who held the uttermost parts of the earth in chief. But the Pope, as head of the visible church, was the representative of Christ, and so, holding under him, had the right to give to any king or prelate, authority to subdue barbarous nations, possess their territory, and convert them to Christianity. In 1493, the Pope, in virtue of the above right, gave the American continent to the Spanish monarchs, who, in time, sold their title to the people of the United States. That title may be defective, as the Pope may not be the representative of Christ, and so the passage in the Psalms will not help the American claim, but then the United States will hold under the first clause in the Testament of God, that is, in Genesis. The claim of

* Genesis i. 26–28.

† Psalms ii. 6–8.

Great Britain is not valid, for she does not want the land for the purpose specified in that clause of the Testament, to "Replenish the earth and subdue it." She wants it, "That she may keep it open as a hunting-ground," while the United States want it, that it may grow into a great nation, and become a free and sovereign republic.*

This strange hypothesis, it seems, lay at the bottom of his defence of the British in their invasion of China. It would have led him, if consistent, to claim also the greater part of Mexico. But, as he did not publicly declare his opinion on that matter, no more need be said concerning it.

Such was the most prominent idea in his history; such the departures from it. Let us look at other events in his life. While President, the most important object of his administration was the promotion of internal improvements, especially the internal communication between the States. For this purpose the government lent its aid in the construction of roads and canals, and a little more than four millions of dollars were devoted to this work in his administration. On the 4th of July, 1828, he helped break ground for the Chesapeake and Ohio canal,

---

* See Mr. Adams's *Speech on Oregon*, Feb. 9th, 1846. Arguments somewhat akin to this, may be found also in the oration delivered at Newburyport, before cited.

thinking it an important event in his life. He then said there were three great steps in the progress of America. The first was the Declaration of Independence and the achievement thereof; the second, the union of the whole country under the Constitution; but the third was more arduous than both of the others: "It is," said he, "the adaptation of the powers, physical, moral, and intellectual, of the whole Union, to the improvement of its own condition; of its *moral* and *political* condition, by wise and liberal institutions; by the cultivation of the understanding and the heart; by academies, schools, and learned institutions; by the pursuit and patronage of learning and the arts; of its *physical* condition, by associated labor to improve the bounties and supply the deficiencies of nature; to stem the torrent in its course; to level the mountain with the plain; to disarm and fetter the raging surge of the ocean." * He faithfully adhered to these words in his administration.

He was careful never to exceed the powers which the Constitution prescribed for him. He thought the acquisition of Louisiana was "accomplished by a flagrant violation of the Constitution," † and himself guarded against such violations. He revered the

* *Address on breaking ground for the Chesapeake and Ohio Canal.*

† *Jubilee of the Constitution*, p. 99.

God of Limits, who, in the Roman mythology, refused to give way or remove, even for Jupiter himself. No man was ever more conscientious on that ground. To him the Constitution meant something; his oath to keep it meant something.

No great political event occurred in his administration; the questions which now vex the country had not arisen. There was no quarrel between freedom and slavery; no man in Congress ventured to denounce slavery as a crime; the African slave-trade was thought wrong, not the slavery which caused it. Party lines, obliterated under Mr. Monroe's administration, were viewed and marked with a good deal of care and exactness; but the old lines could not be wholly restored. Mr. Adams was not the President of a section of the country; not the President of a party, but of the nation. He favored no special interest of a class, to the injury of another class. He did not reward his friends, nor punish his foes; the party of the spoils, patent or latent at all times, got no spoils from him. He never debauched his country by the removal and appointment of officers. Had he done otherwise, done as all his successors have done, used his actual power to promote his own ambition, no doubt he might have been reëlected. But he could not stoop to manage men in that way. No doubt he desired a reëlection, and saw the method and means to effect that, but conscience said, "It is not right." He forbore, lost his election, and gained — we shall soon see what he gained.

On the 19th of July, 1826, at a public dinner at Edgefield Court-house, South Carolina, Mr. McDuffie said, "Mr. Adams came into power upon principles utterly subversive of the republican system; substituting the worst species of aristocracy, that of speculating politicians and office-hunters, in the place of a sound and wholesome republican democracy." When Mr. Adams retired from office, he could remember, with the virtuous Athenian, that no man had put on mourning for him because unjustly deprived of his post. Was an office-holder or an office-wanter a political friend of Mr. Adams, that did not help him; a foe, that did not hinder. He looked only to the man's ability and integrity. I wish it was no praise to say these things; but it is praise I dare not apply to any other man since Washington. Mr. Adams once said, "There is no official act of the chief magistrate, however momentous, or however minute, but it should be traceable to a dictate of duty, pointing to the welfare of the people." That was his executive creed.

As a public servant, he had many qualities seldom united in the same person. He was simple, and unostentatious; he had none of the airs of a great man; seemed humble, modest, and retiring; caring much for the substance of manhood, he let the show take care of itself. He carried the simplicity of a plain New England man into the President's house, spending little in its decorations — about one fourth, it is said, of the amount of his successor. In his housekeeping, public or private, there was only one thing much to be boasted of and remarked upon: strange to say, that was the master of the house. He was never eclipsed by his own brass and mahogany. He had what are called democratic habits, and served himself in preference to being served by others. He treated all that were about him with a marked deference and courtesy, carrying his respect for human rights into the minutest details of common life.

He was a model of diligence, though not, perhaps, very systematic. His State papers, prepared while he was Minister, Secretary, or Member of Congress, his numerous orations and speeches, though not always distinguished for that orderly arrangement of parts which is instinctive with minds of a high philosophical character, are yet astonishing for their number, and the wide learning they display. He was well acquainted with the classic and most modern languages; at home in their literature. He was surprisingly familiar with modern history; perhaps no political man was so thoroughly acquainted with the political history of America, and that of Christian Europe for the last two hundred years. He was widely read and profoundly skilled in all that relates to diplomacy, and to international law. He was fond of belleslettres, and commented on Shakspeare more like a professor than a layman in that department. Few theologians in America, it is said, were so widely read in their peculiar lore as he. He had read much, remembered much, understood much. However, he seems to have paid little attention to physical science, and perhaps less to metaphysical. His speeches and his conversation, though neither brilliant, nor rich in ideas, astonished young men with an affluence of learning, which seemed marvellous in one all his life devoted to practical affairs. But this is a trifle: to achieve that, nothing is needed but health, diligence, memory, and a long life. Mr. Adams had all these requisites.

He had higher qualities: he loved his country, perhaps no man more so; he had patriotism in an heroic degree, yet was not thereby blinded to humanity. He thought it a vital principle of human society, that each nation should contribute to the happiness of all; and, therefore, that no nation should "regulate its conduct by the exclusive or even the paramount consideration of its own interest." * Yet he loved his country, his whole country, and when she was in the wrong he told her so, because he loved her. This, said he, would be a good sentiment: "Our country! May she be always successful; but, whether successful or not, may she be

* *Lecture on China.*

always in the right." He saw the faults of America, saw the corruption of the American government. He did not make gain by this in private, but set an honest face against it.

He was a conscientious man. This peculiarity is strongly marked in most of his life. He respected the limit between right and wrong. He did not think it unworthy of a statesman to refer to moral principles, to the absolutely right. I do not mean to say, that in his whole life there was no departure from the strict rule of duty. I have mentioned already some examples, but kept one more for this place: he pursued persons with a certain vindictiveness of spirit. I will not revive again the old quarrels, nor dig up his hard words, long ago consigned to oblivion; it would be unjust to the living. He was what is called a good hater. If he loved an idea, he seemed to hate the man who opposed it. He was not content with replying; he must also retort, though it manifestly weakened the force of the reply. In his attacks on persons he was sometimes unjust, violent, sharp, and vindictive; sometimes cruel, and even barbarous. Did he ever forgive an enemy? Every opponent was a foe, and he thrashed his foes with an iron hoof and winnowed them with a storm. The most awful specimens of invective which the language affords can be found in his words — bitter, revengeful, and unrelenting. I am sorry to say these things; it hurts my feelings to say them, yours not less to hear them. But it is not our fault they are true; it would be mine, if, knowing they were true, I did not on this occasion point them out in warning words. Mr. Adams says that Roger Williams was conscientious and contentious; it is equally true of himself. Perhaps Mr. Adams had little humor, but certainly a giant's wit; he used it tyrannously and like a giant. Wit has its place in debate; in controversy it is a legitimate weapon, offensive and defensive. After one has beaten the single barley-corn of good sense out of a whole wagon-load of chaff, the easiest way to be rid of the rubbish is to burn it up with the lightning of wit; the danger is, that the burning should begin before the separation is made; that the fire consume the good and bad indifferently. When argument is edged and pointed with wit, it is doubly effective; but when that edge is jagged with ill-will, poisoned, too, with personal spleen, then it becomes a weapon unworthy of a man. Sometimes Mr. Adams used his wit as fairly as his wisdom; and bags of wind, on which Hercules might have stamped and beaten a twelvemonth, but in vain — at a single puncture from that keen wit gave up their ghost and flattened into nothing; a vanity to all men, but a vexation of spirit to him who had blown them so full of his own soul. But sometimes, yes, often, Mr. Adams's wit performs a different part: it sits as a judge, unjust and unforgiving, " often deciding wrong, and when right from wrong motives." It was the small dagger with which he smote the fallen foe. It is a poor praise for a famous man, churchman, or statesman, to beat a blackguard with his own weapons. It must be confessed, that in controversy, Mr. Adams's arrows were sharp and deftly delivered; but they were often barbed, and sometimes poisoned.

True, he encountered more political opposition than any man in the nation. For more than forty years he has never been without bitter and unrelenting enemies, public and private. No man in America, perhaps, ever had such provocations; surely, none had ever such opportunities to reply without retorting. How much better would it have been, if, at the end of that long life and fifty years' war, he could say he had never wasted a shot; had never sinned with his lips, nor once feathered his public arrow with private spleen! Wise as he was, and old, he never learned that for undeserved calumny, for personal insult and abuse, there is one answer, Christian, manly, and irrefutable — the dignity of silence. A just man can afford to wait till the storm of abuse shall spend its rage and vanish under the rainbow, which itself furnishes and leaves behind. The retorting speech of such a man may be silvern or iron; his silence, victorious and golden.

It is easy to censure Mr. Adams for such intemperance of speech and persecution of persons; unfortunately, too easy to furnish other examples of both.

We know what he spoke — God only what he repressed. Who knows out of how deep a fulness of indignation such torrents gush? Tried by the standard of other men, his fellow politicians of America and Europe, he was no worse than they, only abler.* The mouse and the fox have as great a proportionate anger as the lion, though the one is ridiculous and the other terrific. Mr. Adams must be tried by his own standard, the rule of right, the standard of conscience and of Christianity; then surely he did wrong. For such a man the vulgarity of the offence is no excuse.

With this and the other exceptions he appears a remarkably conscientious man in his public life. He may often have erred, as all men, without violating his own sense of right.

While he was President he would not consent to any "public manifestation of honors personal to himself." He would not accept a present, for his Bible taught him what experience continually enforces, that a gift blinds the eyes of wise men and perverts their judgment. While at St. Petersburg, the Russian Minister of the Interior, then an old man, felt uneasy on account of the presents accepted during his official service, and, calculating the value of all gifts received, returned it to the imperial treas-

* See his defence of this in his *Address to his Constituents at Braintree*, Sept. 17th, 1842. Boston, 1842, p. 56, *et seq.*

ury. This fact made an impression on Mr. Adams, and led to a resolution which he faithfully kept. When a bookseller sent him a costly Bible, he kept the book, but paid its full value. No bribes, no pensions in any form, ever soiled justice in his hands. He would never be indebted to any body of men, lest they might afterwards sway him from the right path.

Because he was a conscientious man he would never be the servant of a party, and never was. It was of great advantage to him that he was absent while the two chief parties were forming in the United States. He came into the Massachusetts Legislature as a federalist, but some anti-federalists also voted for him. His first vote showed he was not limited by the common principles of a party. He was chosen to the Senate of the United States, not by a party vote. At first he acted mainly with the federalists, though not always voting with his colleague; but in 1807 acted with the administration in the matter of the Embargo. This was the eventful crisis of his life; this change in his politics, while it gave him station and political power, yet brought upon him the indignation of his former friends; it has never been forgotten nor forgiven. Be the outward occasion and inward motive what they may, this led to the sundering of friendships long cherished and deservedly dear; it produced the most bitter experience of his life. Political men would naturally undertake to judge his counsel by its probable and obvious consequences, the favor of the Executive, rather than attribute it to any latent motive of patriotism in his heart.

While at the head of the nation he would not be the President of a party, but of the people; when he became a representative in Congress he was not the delegate of a party, but of justice and the eternal right, giving his constituents an assurance that he would hold himself in allegiance to no party, national or political. He has often been accused of hatred to the South; I can find no trace of it. "I entered Congress," says he, "without one sentiment of discrimination between the North and South." At first he acted with Mr. Jackson, to arrest the progress of nullification, for the democracy of South Carolina was putting in practice what the federalists of New England have so often been alleged to have held in theory, and condemned on that allegation. Here he was consistent. In 1834, he approved the spirit of the same President in demanding justice of France; but afterwards he did not hesitate to oppose, and perhaps abuse him.

He had a high reverence for religion; none of our public men more. He aimed to be a Christian man. Signs of this have often been sought in his habits of church-going, of reading the Bible; they may be found rather in the general rectitude of his life, public and private, and in the high motives which swayed him, in his opposition to slavery, in the self-denial which cost him his reëlection. In his public acts he seems animated by the thought that he stood in the presence of God. Though rather unphilosophical in his theology, resting to a great degree on the authority of tradition and the letter, and attaching much value to forms and times, he yet saw the peculiar excellence of Christianity,—that it recognized "Love as the paramount and transcendent law of human nature." I do not say that his life indicates the attainment of a complete religious repose, but that he earnestly and continually labored to achieve that. You shall find few statesmen, few men, who act with a more continual and obvious reference to religion as a motive, as a guide, as a comfort. He was, however, no sectarian. His devotion to freedom appeared, where it seldom appears, in his notions about religion. He thought for himself, and had a theology of his own, rather old-fashioned, it is true, and not very philosophical or consistent, it may be, and in that he was not very singular, but he allowed others to think also for themselves, and have a theology of their own. Mr. Adams was a Unitarian. It is no great merit to be a Unitarian, or a Calvinist, or a Catholic, perhaps no more merit to be one than the other. But he was not ashamed of his belief when Unitarianism was little, despised, mocked at, and called "Infidelity" on all sides. When the Unitarian church at Washington, a small and feeble body, met for worship in an upper room — not large, but obscure, over a public bathing-house — John Quincy Adams, the Secretary of State and expecting to be President, came regularly to worship with them. It was not fashionable; it was hardly respectable, for the Unitarians were not then, as now, numerous and rich: but he went and worshipped. It was no merit to think with any sect, it was a great merit to dare be true to his convictions. In his theology, as in politics, he feared not to stand in a minority. If there ever was an American who loved the praise of God more than the praise of men, I believe Mr. Adams was one.

His devotion to freedom, his love of his country, his conscientiousness, his religion, are four things strong and noticeable in his character. You shall look long amongst our famous men before you find his equal in these things.*

Somebody says, no man ever used all his intel-

* In a public address, Mr. Adams once quoted the well-known words of Tacitus (Annal VI. 39), *Par negotiis neque supra,* — applying them to a distinguished man lately deceased. A lady wrote to inquire whence they came. Mr. Adams informed her, and added, they could not be adequately translated in less than seven words in English. The lady replied that they might be well translated in five — *Equal to, not above, duty,* but better in three — JOHN QUINCY ADAMS.

lectual faculties as far as possible. If any man is an exception to this rule, it is Mr. Adams. He was temperate and diligent; industrious almost to a fault, though not orderly or systematic. His diplomatic letters, his orations, his reports and speeches, all indicate wide learning, the fruit of the most remarkable diligence. The attainments of a well-bred scholar are not often found in the American Congress, or the President's house. Yet he never gives proof that he had the mind of a great man. In his special department of politics he does not appear as a master. He has no great ideas with which to solve the riddles of commerce and finance; has done little to settle the commercial problems of the world,—for that work there is needed not only a retrospective acquaintance with the habits and history of men, but the foresight which comes from a knowledge of the nature of things and of man. His chief intellectual excellence seems to have been memory; his great moral merit, a conscientious and firm honesty; his practical strength lay in his diligence. His counsels seem almost always to have come from a knowledge of human history, seldom to have been prompted by a knowledge of the nature of man. Hence he was a critic of the past, or an administrator of the present, rather than a prophetic guide for the future. He had many facts and precedents, but few ideas. Few examples of great political foresight can be quoted from his life; and therein, to his honor be it spoken, his heart seems to have out-travelled his head. The public affairs of the United States seem generally to be conducted by many men of moderate abilities, rather than by a few men of great genius for politics.

Mr. Adams wrote much. Some of his works are remarkable for their beauty, for the graceful proportions of their style, and the felicity of their decoration. Such are his celebrated Lectures on Rhetoric and Oratory, which are sufficiently learned and sagacious, not very philosophical, but written in an agreeable style, and at the present day not wholly without value. His review of the works of Fisher Ames, I speak only of the rhetoric, is, perhaps, the finest of his compositions. Some of his productions are disorderly, ill-compacted, without "joints or contexture," and homely to a fault: this oration is a growth out of a central thought, marked by an internal harmony; that, a composition, a piece of carpentry distinguished by only an outward symmetry of members; others are neither growth nor composition, only a mass of materials huddled and lumped together. Most of his later productions, with the exception of his congressional speeches, are hard, cold, and unfinished performances, with little order in the thoughts, and less beauty in the expression. His extemporaneous speeches have more of both; they are better finished than his studied orations.

He could judge and speak with fury, though he wrote with phlegm. His illustrations are usually drawn from literature, not from nature or human life; his language is commonly cold, derived from the Roman stream which has been filtered through books, rather than from the deep and original well of our Saxon home. His published letters are compact, written in a cold style, without playfulness or wit, with no elegance, and though mostly business letters, they are not remarkable for strength or distinctness. His diligence appears in verse as well as prose. He wrote much that rhymed tolerably; little that was poetical. The same absence of nature, the same coldness and lack of inspiration, mark his poetry and prose. But in all that he wrote, with the exceptions mentioned above, though you miss the genial warmth, the lofty thought, the mind that attracts, embraces, warms, and inspires the reader, you find always a spirit of humanity, of justice, and love to God.

Mr. Adams was seldom eloquent. Eloquence is no great gift. It has its place among subordinate powers, not among the chief. Alas for the statesman or preacher who has only that to save the State withal! Washington had none of it, yet how he ruled the land! No man in America has ever had a political influence so wide and permanent as Mr. Jefferson; yet he was a very indifferent writer, and never made a speech of any value. The acts of

Washington, the ideas of Jefferson, made eloquence superfluous. True, it has its value: if a man have at command the electricity of truth, justice, love, the sentiments and great ideas thereof, it is a good thing to be able with Olympian hand to condense that electric fire into bolted eloquence; to thunder and lighten in the sky. But if a man have that electric truth, it matters little whether it is Moses that speaks, or only Aaron; whether or not Paul's bodily presence be weak and his speech contemptible: it is Moses' thought which thunders and lightens out of Sinai; it is Paul's idea that is powerful and builds up the church. Of true eloquence, the best thoughts put in the best words, and uttered in the best form, Mr. Adams had little, and that appeared mainly in the latter part of his life. Hundreds have more. What passes for eloquence is common in America, where the public mouth is always a-going. His early orations are poor in their substance and faulty in their form. His ability as an orator developed late; no proofs of it appear before he entered the House of Representatives, at a good old age. In his manner of speaking there was little dignity and no grace, though sometimes there was a terrible energy and fire. He was often a powerful speaker — by his facts and figures, by his knowledge, his fame, his age, and his position, but most of all by his independent character. He spoke worthily of great men, of Madison or Lafayette, kindling with his theme, and laying aside all littleness of a party. However, he was most earnest and most eloquent not when he stood up the champion of a neglected truth, not when he dwelt on great men now venerable to us all, but when he gathered his strength to attack a foe. Incensed, his sarcasm was terrific; colossal vanity aspiring to be a Ghenghis Khan, at the touch of that Ithuriel spear shrank to the dimensions of Tom Thumb. His invective is his masterpiece of oratoric skill. It is sad to say this, and to remember, that the greatest works of ancient or of modern rhetoric, from the thundering Philippics of Demosthenes down to the sarcastic and crazy rattle of Lord Brougham, are all of the same character, are efforts against a personal foe! Men find hitherto the ablest acts and speech in the same cause,—not positive and creating, but critical and combative,—in war.

If Mr. Adams had died in 1829, he would have been remembered for awhile as a learned man; as an able diplomatist, who had served his country faithfully at home and abroad; as a President spotless and incorruptible, but not as a very important personage in American history. His mark would have been faint and soon effaced from the sands of time. But the last period of his life was the noblest. He had worn all the official honors which the nation could bestow; he sought the greater honor of serving that nation, who had now no added boon to give. All that he had done as Minister abroad, as Senator, as Secretary, and President, is little compared with what he did in the House of Representatives; and while he stood there, with nothing to hope, with nothing to fear, the hand of Justice wrote his name high up on the walls of his country. It was surprising to see at his first attendance there, men who, while he was President, had been the loudest to call out "Coalition, Bargain, Intrigue, Corruption," come forward and express the involuntary confidence they felt in his wisdom and integrity, and their fear, actual though baseless, that his withdrawal from the Committee on Manufactures would "endanger the very Union itself." * Great questions soon came up: nullification was speedily disposed of; the Bank and the tariff got ended or compromised, but slavery lay in the consciousness of the nation, like the one dear but appalling sin in a man's heart. Some wished to be rid of it, northern men and southern men. It would come up; to justify that, or excuse it, the American sentiment and idea must be denied and rejected utterly; the South, who had long known the charms of Bathsheba, was ready for her sake to make way with Uriah himself. To remove that monstrous evil, gradually but totally, and restore unity to the nation, would require a greater change than the adoption of the Constitution. To keep slavery out of sight, yet in existence, unjustified, un-

* *Remarks* of Mr. Cambreleng.

excused, unrepented of, a contradiction in the national consciousness, a political and deadly sin, the sin against the Holy Spirit of American Liberty, known but not confessed, the public secret of the people — that would lead to suppressing petitions, suppressing debate in Congress and out of Congress, to silencing the pulpit, the press, and the people.

Under these circumstances, Mr. Adams went to Congress, an old man, well known on both sides the water, the presidential laurels on his brow, independent and fearless, expecting no reward from men for services however great. In respect to the subject of slavery, he had no ideas in advance of the nation; he was far behind the foremost men. He "deprecated all discussion of slavery or its abolition, in the House, and gave no countenance to petitions for the abolition of slavery in the District of Columbia or the territories." However, he acquired new ideas as he went on, and became the congressional leader in the great movement of the American mind towards universal freedom.

Here he stood as the champion of human rights; here he fought, and with all his might. In 1836, by the celebrated resolution, forbidding debate on the subject of slavery, the South drove the North to the wall, nailed it there into shameful silence. A "Northern man with Southern principles," before entering the President's chair, declared, that if Congress should pass a law to abolish slavery in the

District of Columbia, he would exercise his veto to prevent the law.* Mr. Adams stood up manfully, sometimes almost alone, and contended for freedom of speech. Did obstinate men of the North send petitions relative to slavery, asking for its abolition in the District or elsewhere? Mr. Adams was ready to present the petitions. Did women petition? It made no difference with him. Did slaves petition? He stood up there to defend their right to be heard. The South had overcome many an obstacle, but that one fearless soul would not bend, and could not be broken. Spite of rules of order, he contrived to bring the matter perpetually before Congress, and sometimes to read the most offensive parts of the petitions. When Arkansas was made a State, he endeavored to abolish slavery in its domain; he sought to establish international relations with Hayti, and to secure the right of suffrage for the colored citizens of the District of Columbia. The laws which forbid blacks to vote in the Northern States he held "in utter abhorrence."

He saw from afar the plots of southern politicians, plots for extending the area of slavery, for narrowing the area of freedom, and exposed those plots. You all remember the tumult it excited when he rose in his place holding a petition from slaves; that the American Congress was thrown into long and dis-

* Mr. Van Buren.

graceful confusion. You cannot have forgotten the uproar which followed his presenting a petition to dissolve the Union!* I know few speeches more noble and manly than his on the right of petition,—occasioned by that celebrated attempt to stifle debate, and on the annexation of Texas. Some proposed to censure him, some clamored, "expel him," some cried out, "burn the petitions!" and "him with them," screamed yet others. Some threatened to have him indicted by the grand jury of the district, "or be made amenable to *another tribunal*," hoping to see "an incendiary brought to condign punishment." "My life on it," said a southern legislator, "if he presents that petition from slaves, we shall yet see him within the walls of the penitentiary." Some in secret threatened to assassinate him in the streets. They mistook their man; with justice on his side he did "not fear all the grand juries in the universe." He would not curl nor cringe, but snorted his defiance in their very face. In front of ridicule, of desertion, obloquy, rage, and brutal threats, stood up that old man, bald and audacious, and the chafed

---

* See the *Debates of the House*, January 23d and following, 1837; or Mr. Adams's own account of the matter in his *Letters to his Constituents*, etc. (Boston, 1837.) See, too, his *Series of Speeches on the Right of Petition and the Annexation of Texas*, January 14th and following, 1838. (Printed in a pamphlet. Washington, 1838.)

rock of Cohasset stands not firmer mid the yesty waves, nor more triumphant spurns back into the ocean's face the broken billows of the storm. That New England knee bent only before his God. That unpretending man — the whole power of the nation could not move him from his post.

Men threatened to increase the slave power. Said one of the champions of slavery with prophetic speech, but fatal as Cassandra's in the classic tale, Americans "would come up in thousands to plant the lone star of the Texan banner on the Mexican capital. . . . The boundless wealth of captured towns and rifled churches, and a lazy, vicious, and luxurious priesthood, would soon enable Texas to pay her soldiery and redeem her State debt, and push her victorious arms to the very shores of the Pacific. And would not all this extend the bounds of slavery? Yes, the result would be, that before another quarter of a century the extension of slavery would not stop short of the Western ocean." Against this danger Mr. Adams armed himself, and fought in the holiest cause — the cause of human rights.

I know few things in modern times so grand as that old man standing there in the House of Representatives, the compeer of Washington, a man who had borne himself proudly in kings' courts, early doing service in high places, where honor may be won; a man who had filled the highest office in any nation's gift; a President's son, himself a President, standing there the champion of the neediest of the oppressed: the conquering cause pleased others; him only, the cause of the conquered. Had he once been servile to the hands that wielded power? No thunderbolt can scare him now! Did he once make a treaty and bind Mexico to bewray the wandering fugitive who took his life in his hand and fled from the talons of the American eagle? Now he would go to the stake sooner than tolerate such a deed! When he went to the Supreme Court, after an absence of thirty years, and arose to defend a body of friendless negroes torn from their home and most unjustly held in thrall; when he asked the judges to excuse him at once both for the trembling faults of age and the inexperience of youth, the man having labored so long elsewhere that he had forgotten the rules of court; when he summed up the conclusion of the whole matter, and brought before those judicial but yet moistening eyes the great men whom he had once met there — Chase, Cushing, Martin, Livingston, and Marshall himself; and while he remembered them that were "gone, gone, all gone," remembered also the Eternal Justice that is never gone, — why the sight was sublime. It was not an old patrician of Rome who had been consul, dictator, coming out of his honored retirement at the Senate's call, to stand in the forum to levy new armies, marshal them to victory afresh, and gain thereby new laurels for his brow; — but it was a plain citizen of America, who had held an office far greater than that of consul, king, or dictator, his hand reddened by no man's blood, expecting no honors, but coming in the name of Justice to plead for the slave, for the poor barbarian negro of Africa, for Cinque and Grabbo, for their deeds comparing them to Harmodius and Aristogeiton, whose classic memory made each bosom thrill. That was worth all his honors, — it was worth while to live fourscore years for that.

When he stood in the House of Representatives, the champion of the rights of a minority, of the rights of man, he stood colossal. Frederick the Great seems doubly so, when, single-handed, "that son of the Dukes of Brandenburg" contended against Austria, France, England, Russia, kept them all at bay, divided by his skill, and conquered by his might. Surely he seems great, when measured merely by his deeds. But, in comparison, Frederick the Great seems Frederick the little: for Adams fought not for a kingdom, nor for fame, but for Justice and the Eternal Right; fought, too, with weapons tempered in a heavenly stream! *

---

* "Acer et indomitus, quo spes, quoque ira vocasset,
Ferre manum, et nunquam temerando parcere ferro;
Successus urgere suos; instare favori
Numinis; impellens quicquid sibi summa petenti
Obstaret, gaudensque viam fecisse ruina."

He had his reward. Who ever missed it? From mythological Cain, who slew his brother, down to Judas Iscariot, and Aaron Burr; from Jesus of Nazareth, down to the least man that dies or lives — who ever lost his reward? None. No; not one. Within the wicked heart there dwells the avenger, with unseen hands, to adjust the cord, to poison the fatal bowl. In the impenetrable citadel of a good man's consciousness, unseen by mortal eyes, there stands the palladium of justice, radiant with celestial light; mortal hands may make and mar, — this they can mar not, no more than they can make. Things about the man can others build up or destroy; but no foe, no tyrant, no assassin, can ever steal the man out of the man. Who would not have the consciousness of being right, even of trying to be right, though affronted by a whole world, rather than conscious of being wrong, and hollow, and false, have all the honors of a nation on his head? Of late years, no party stood up for Mr. Adams, "The madman of Massachusetts," as they called him, on the floor of Congress; but he knew that he had, and in his old age, done one work, — he had contended for the unalienable rights of man, done it faithfully. The government of God is invisible, His justice the more certain, — and by that Mr. Adams had his abundant reward.

But he had his poorer and outward rewards, negative and positive. For his zeal in behalf of freedom he was called "a monarchist in disguise," "an alien to the true interests of his country," "a traitor." A slaveholder from Kentucky published to his constituents that he "was sincerely desirous to check that man, for if he could be removed from the councils of the nation, or silenced upon the exasperating subject to which he had devoted himself, none other, I believe, could be found hardy enough or bad enough to fill his place." It was worth something to have an enemy speak such praise as that: but the slaveholder was wrong in his conjecture; the North has yet other sons not less hardy, not more likely to be silenced. Still more praise of a similar sort: — at a fourth of July dinner at Walterborough, in South Carolina, this sentiment was proposed and responded to with nine cheers: "May we never want a democrat to trip up the heels of a federalist, or a hangman to prepare a halter for John Quincy Adams." Considering what he had done and whence those rewards proceeded, that was honor enough for a yet greater man.

Let me turn to things more grateful. Mr. Adams, through lack of genial qualities, had few personal friends, yet from good men throughout the North there went up a hearty thanksgiving for his manly independence, and prayers for his success. Brave men forgot their old prejudices, forgot the "Embargo," forgot the "Hartford Convention," forgot all the hard things which he had ever said, forgot his words in the Senate, forgot their disappointments, and said — "For this our hearts shall honor thee, thou brave old man!" In 1843, when, for the first time, he visited the West, to assist at the foundation of a scientific institution, all the West rose up to do him reverence. He did not go out to seek honors, they came to seek him. It was the movement of a noble people, feeling a noble presence about them no less than within. When Cicero, the only great man whom Rome never feared, returned from his exile, all Italy rose up and went out to meet him; so did the North and the West welcome this champion of freedom, this venerable old man. They came not to honor one who had been a President, but one who was a man. That alone, said Mr. Adams, with tears of joy and grief filling his eyes, was reward enough for all that he had done, suffered, or undertaken. Yes, it was too much; too much for one man as the reward of one life!

You all remember the last time he was at any public meeting in this city. A man had been kidnapped in Boston, kidnapped at noon-day, "on the high road between Faneuil Hall and old Quincy," and carried off to be a slave! New England hands had seized their brother, sold him into bondage for ever, and his children after him. In the presence of slavery, as of arms, the laws are silent, — not always men. Then it appears who are men, who not! A meeting was called to talk the matter over, in a plain way, and look in one another's faces. Who was fit to preside in such a case? That old man sat in the chair in Faneuil Hall; above him was the image of his father, and his own; around him were Hancock and the other Adams, — Washington, greatest of all; before him were the men and women of Boston, met to consider the wrongs done to a miserable negro slave; the roof of the old Cradle of Liberty spanned over them all. Forty years before, a young man and a Senator, he had taken the chair at a meeting called to consult on the wrong done to American seamen, violently impressed by the British from an American ship of war, the unlucky Chesapeake; some of you remember that event. Now, an old man, clothed with half a century of honors, he sits in the same hall, to preside over a meeting to consider the outrage done to a single slave; a greater outrage — alas, not done by a hostile, not by an alien hand! One was the first meeting of citizens he ever presided over, the other was the last; both for the same object — the defence of the Eternal Right.

But I would not weary you. His death was noble; fit ending for such a life. He was an old man, the last that had held a diplomatic office under Washington. He had uttered his oracles; had done his work. The highest honors of the nation he had worthily worn; but, as his townsmen tell us, — caring little for the President, and much for the man, —

that was very little in comparison with his character. The good and ill of the human cup he had tasted, and plentifully, too, as son, husband, father. He had borne his testimony for freedom and the rights of mankind; he had stood in Congress almost alone; with a few gallant men had gone down to the battle-field, and if victory escaped him, it was because night came on.

He saw others enter the field in good heart, to stand in the imminent deadly breach; he lived long enough for his own welfare, for his own ambition; long enough to see the seal broken, — and then, this aged Simeon, joyful in the consolation, bowed his head and went home in peace. His feet were not hurt with fetters; he died with his armor on; died like a Senator in the capitol of the nation; died like an American, in the service of his country; died like a Christian, full of immortality; died like a man, fearless and free!

You will ask, What was the secret of his strength? Whence did he gain such power to stand erect where others so often cringed and crouched low to the ground? It is plain to see: he looked beyond time, beyond men; looked to the eternal God, and fearing Him forgot all other fear. Some of his failings he knew to be such, and struggled with them though he did not overcome. A man, not over-modest, once asked him what he most of all lamented in his life, and he replied, "My impetuous temper and vituperative speech; that I have not always returned good for evil, but in the madness of my blood have said things that I am ashamed of before my God!" As the world goes, it needed some greatness to say that.

When he was a boy, his mother, a still woman, and capable, deep-hearted, and pious, took great pains with his culture; most of all with his religious culture. When, at the age of ten, he was about to leave home for years of absence in another land, she took him aside to warn him of temptations which he could not then understand. She bade him remember religion and his God—his secret, silent prayer. Often in his day there came the earthquake of party strife; the fire, the storm, and the whirlwind of passion; he listened—and God was not there; but there came, too, the remembrance of his mother's whispered words; God came in that memory, and earthquake and storm, the fire and the whirlwind were powerless, at last, before that still small voice. Beautifully did she write to her boy of ten, "Great learning and superior abilities will be of little value . . . unless virtue, honor, truth, and integrity, are added to them. Remember that you are accountable to your Maker for all your words and your actions." "Dear as you are to me," says this more than Spartan, this Christian mother, "Dear as you are to me, I would much rather you should have found your grave in the ocean you have crossed, or that any untimely death cross you in your infant years, than see you an immoral, profligate, or graceless child. Let your observations and comparisons produce in your mind an abhorrence of domination and power — the parents of slavery, ignorance, and barbarism. May you be led to an imitation of that disinterested patriotism and that noble love of your country, which will teach you to despise wealth, titles, pomp, and equipage, as mere external advantages, which cannot add to the internal excellence of your mind, or compensate for the want of integrity and virtue." She tells him in a letter, that her father, a plain New England clergyman, of Braintree, who had just died, "left you a legacy more valuable than gold or silver; he left you his blessing, and his prayers that you might become a useful citizen, a guardian of the laws, liberty, and religion of your country. . . . . Lay this bequest up in your memory and practise upon it; believe me, you will find it a treasure that neither moth nor rust can destroy."

If a child have such a mother, there is no wonder why he stood fearless, and bore a charmed life which no opposition could tame down. I wonder more that one so born and by such a mother bred, could ever once bend a servile knee; could ever indulge that fierce and dreadful hate; could ever stoop to sully those hands which hers had joined in prayer. It ill accords with teachings like her own. I wonder that he could ever have refused to "deliberate."

Religion is a quality that makes a man independent; disappointment will not render such an one sour, nor oppression drive him mad, nor elevation bewilder; power will not dazzle, nor gold corrupt; no threat can silence and no fear subdue.

There are men enough born with greater abilities than Mr. Adams, men enough in New England, in all the walks of man. But how many are there in political life who use their gifts so diligently, with such conscience, such fearless deference to God? — nay, tell us one. I have not spared his faults; I am no eulogist, to paint a man with undiscriminating praise. Let his follies warn us, while his virtues guide. But look on all his faults, and then compare him with our famous men of the North or the South; with the great whigs or the great democrats. Ask which was the purest man, the most patriotic, the most honest; which did his nation the smallest harm and the greatest good; which for his country and his kind denied himself the most. Shall I examine their lives, public and private, strip them bare and lay them down beside his life, and ask which, after all, has the least of blemish and the most of beauty? Nay, that is not for me to do or to attempt.

In one thing he surpassed most men, — he grew more liberal the more he grew old, ripening and mellowing, too, with age. After he was seventy years old, he welcomed new ideas, kept his mind vigorous, and never fell into that crabbed admiration of past times and buried institutions, which is the palsy of so many a man, and which makes old age nothing but a pity, and gray hairs provocative of tears. This is the more remarkable in a man of his habitual reverence for the past, in one who judged oftener by the history than by the nature of man.

Times will come when men shall look to that vacant seat. But the thunder is silent, the lightning gone; other men must take his place and fill it as they can. Let us not mourn that he has gone from us; let us remember what was evil in him, but only to be warned of ambition, of party strife, to love more that large charity which forgives an enemy, and, through good and ill, contends for mankind. Let us be thankful for the good he has said and done, be guided by it and blessed. There is a certain affluence of intellectual power granted to some men, which provokes admiration for a time, let the man of myriad gifts use his talent as he may. Such merely cubic greatness of mind is matter of astonishment rather than a fit subject for esteem and praise. Of that, Mr. Adams had little, as so many of his contemporaries had more. In him what most commands respect is, his independence, his love of justice, of his country and his kind. No son of New England has been ever so distinguished in political life. But it is no great thing to be President of the United States; some men it only makes ridiculous.

A worm on a steeple's top is nothing but a worm, no more able to fly than while creeping in congenial mud; a mountain needs no steeple to lift its head and show the world what is great and high. The world obeys its great men, stand where they may.

After all, this must be the greatest praise of Mr. Adams: In private he corrupted no man nor woman; as a politician he never debauched the public morals of his country, nor used public power for any private end; in public and private he lived clean and above board; he taught a fearless love of truth and the right, both by word and deed. I wish I could add, that was a small praise. But as the times go, as our famous men are, it is a very great fame, and there are few competitors for such renown; I must leave him alone in that glory. Doubtless, as he looked back on his long career, his whole life, motives as well as actions, must have seemed covered with imperfections. I will seek no further to disclose his merits, or "draw his frailties from their dead abode."

He has passed on, where superior gifts and opportunities avail not, nor his long life, nor his high station, nor his wide spread fame; where enemies cease from troubling, and the flattering tongue also is still. Wealth, honor, fame, forsake him at the grave's mouth. It is only the living soul, sullied or clean, which the last angel bears off in his arms to that world where many that seem first shall be last, and the last first; but where justice shall be lovingly done to the great man full of power and wisdom who rules the State, and the feeblest slave whom oppression chains down in ignorance and vice — done by the all-seeing Father of both President and slave, who loves both with equal love. The venerable man is gone home. He shall have his praise. But who shall speak it worthily? Mean men and little, who shrank from him in life, who never shared what was manliest in the man, but mocked at his living nobleness, shall they come forward and with mealy mouths, to sing his requiem, forgetting that his eulogy is their own ban? Some will rejoice at his death; there is one man the less to fear, and they who trembled at his life may well be glad when the earth has covered up the son she bore. Strange men will meet with mutual solace at his tomb, wondering that their common foe is dead, and they are met! The Herods and Pilates of contending parties may be made friends above his grave, and clasping hands may fancy that their union is safer than before; but there will come a day after to-day! Let us leave him to his rest.

The slave has lost a champion who gained new ardor and new strength the longer he fought; America has lost a man who loved her with his heart; Religion has lost a supporter; Freedom an unfailing friend, and Mankind a noble vindicator of our unalienable rights.

It is not long since he was here in our own streets; three winter months have scantly flown: he set out for his toil — but went home to his rest. His labors are over. No man now threatens to assassinate; none to expel; none even to censure. The theatrical thunder of Congress, noisy but harmless, has ended as it ought, in honest tears. South Carolina need ask no more a halter for that one northern neck she could not bend nor break. The tears of his country are dropped upon his urn; the muse of history shall write thereon, in letters not to be effaced, THE ONE GREAT MAN SINCE WASHINGTON, WHOM AMERICA HAD NO CAUSE TO FEAR.

To-day that venerable form lies in the Capitol, — the disenchanted dust. All is silent. But his undying soul, could we deem it still hovering o'er its native soil, bound to take leave yet lingering still, and loath to part, that would bid us love our country, love man, love justice, freedom, right, and above all, love God. To-morrow that venerable dust starts once more to join the dear presence of father and mother, to mingle his ashes with their ashes, as their lives once mingled, and their souls again. Let his native State communicate her last sad sacrament, and give him now, it is all she can, a little earth for charity.

But what shall we say as the dust returns?

"Where slavery's minions cower
Before the servile power,
He bore their ban;
And like the aged oak,
That braved the lightning's stroke,
When thunders round it broke,
Stood up a man.

"Nay, when they stormed aloud,
And round him like a cloud,
Came thick and black, —
He single-handed strove,
And like Olympian Jove,
With his own thunder drove
The phalanx back.

"Not from the bloody field,
Borne on his battered shield,
By foes o'ercome; —
But from a sterner fight,
In the defence of Right,
Clothed with a conqueror's might,
We hail him home.

"His life in labors spent,
That 'Old man eloquent'
Now rests for aye; —
His dust the tomb may claim; —
His spirit's quenchless flame,
His 'venerable name,' *
Pass not away." †

---

* *Clarum et venerabile nomen.*

† The above lines are from the pen of the Rev. John Pierpont.

VII.

SPEECH AT A MEETING OF THE AMERICAN ANTI-SLAVERY SOCIETY, TO CELEBRATE THE ABOLITION OF SLAVERY BY THE FRENCH REPUBLIC, APRIL 6, 1848.

MR. CHAIRMAN, — The Gentleman before me* has made an allusion to Rome. Let me also turn to that same city. Underneath the Rome of the Emperors, there was another Rome; not seen by the sun, known only to a few men. Above, in the sunlight, stood Rome of the Cæsars, with her markets and her armies, her theatres, her temples, and her palaces, glorious and of marble. A million men went through her brazen gates. The imperial city, she stood there, beautiful and admired, the queen of nations. But underneath all that, in caverns of the earth, in the tombs of dead men, in quarries whence the upper city had been slowly hewn, there was another population, another Rome, with other

* Mr. Wendell Phillips.

thoughts; yes, a devout body of men, who swore not by the public altars; men whose prayers were forbidden; their worship disallowed, their ideas prohibited, their very lives illegal. Time passed on; and gradually Rome of the Pagans disappeared, and Rome of the Christians sat there in her place, on the Seven Hills, and stretched out her sceptre over the nations.

So underneath the laws and the institutions of each modern nation, underneath the monarchy and the republic, there is another and unseen State, with sentiments not yet become popular, and with ideas not yet confirmed in actions, not organized into institutions, ideas scarcely legal, certainly not respectable. Slowly from its depths comes up this ideal State, the State of the Future; and slowly to the eternal deep sinks down the actual State, the State of the Present. But sometimes an earthquake of the nations degrades of a sudden the actual; and speedily starts up the ideal Kingdom of the Future. Such a thing has just come to pass. In France, within five-and-forty days, a new State has arisen from underneath the old. Men, whose words were suppressed, and their ideas reckoned illegal but two months ago, now hold the sceptre of five-and-thirty millions of grateful citizens, hold it in clean and powerful hands. A great revolution has taken place; one which will produce effects that we cannot foresee. It is itself the greatest act of this century.

God only knows what it will lead to. We are here to express the sympathy of republicans for a new republic. We are here to rejoice over the rising hopes of a new State, not to exult over the fallen fortunes of the Bourbons. Louis Philippe has done much which we may thank him for. He has kept mainly at peace the fiercest nation of the world; has kept the peace of Europe for seventeen years. Let us thank him for that. He has consolidated the French nation, helped to give them a new unity of thought and unity of action, which they had not before. Perhaps he did not intend all this. Since he has brought it about, let us thank him for it, even if his conduct transcended his intention. But, most of all, I would thank this "Citizen King" for another thing. His greatest lesson is his last. He has shown that five-and-thirty millions of Frenchmen, in this nineteenth century, are only to be ruled by Justice and the Eternal Law of Right. We have seen this crafty king, often wise and always cunning, driven from his throne. He was the richest man in Europe, and the embodiment of the idea of modern wealth. He had an army the best disciplined, probably, in the world, and, as he thought, completely in his power. He had a Chamber of Peers of his own appointment; a Chamber of Deputies almost of his own election. He ruled a nation that contained three hundred thousand office-holders, appointed by himself, and only two hundred and forty thousand voters! Who sat so safe as the citizen king on his throne, surrounded by republican institutions! So confident was he, as the journals tell, that he bade a friend stop a day or two, "and see how I will put down the people!" For once, this shrewd calculator reckoned without his host.

Well, we have seen this man, this citizen monarch, who married his children only to kings, rush from his place; his peers and his deputies were unavailing; his office-holders could not sustain him; his army "fraternized with the people;" and he, forgetful of his own children, ignominiously is hustled out of the kingdom, in a street cab, with nothing but a five-franc piece in his pocket. For the lesson thus taught, let us thank him most of all.

Men tell us it is too soon to rejoice: "Perhaps the Revolution will not hold;" "it will not last;" "the kings of Europe will put it down." When a sound, healthy child is born, the friends of the family congratulate the parents then; they do not wait till the child has grown up, and got a beard. Now this is a live child; it is well born in both senses, come of good parentage, and gives signs of a good constitution. Let us rejoice at its birth, and not wait to see if it will grow up. Let us now baptize it in the crystal fountain of our own Hope.

In a great revolution, there are always two things to be looked at, namely, the actions, and the ideas which produce the actions. The actions I will say little of; you have all read of them in the newspapers. Some of the actions were bad. It is not true that all at once the French have become angels. There are low and base men, who swarm in the lanes and alleys of Paris; for that great city also is like all capitals, girt about with a belt of misery, of vice and of crime, eating into her painful loins. It was a bad thing to sack the Tuileries; to burn bridges, and chateaux, and railroad stations. Property is under the insurance of mankind, and the human race must pay in public for private depredations. It was a bad thing to kill men; the human race cannot make up that loss; only suffer and be penitent. I am sorry for these bad actions; but I am not surprised at them. You cannot burn down the poor dwelling of a widow in Boston, but some miserable man will steal pot or pan, in the confusion of the fire. How much more should we expect pillage and violence in the earthquake which throws down a king!

I have said enough of the actions; but there was one deed too symbolical to be passed by. In the garden of the Tuileries, before the great gate of the palace, there stands a statue of Spartacus, a colossal bronze, his broken chain in the left hand, his Roman sword in the right. Spartacus was a Roman gladiator. He broke his chains; gathered about him other gladiators, fugitive slaves, and assembled an army. He and his comrades fought for freedom; they cut off four consular armies sent against them; at last the hero fell amid a heap of men, slain by his own well-practised hand. When the people took the old and emblematic French throne, and burned it solemnly with emblematic fire, they stripped off some of the crimson trappings of the royal seat, made a tiara thereof, and bound it on the gladiator's brazen head! But red is the color of revolution, the color of blood; the unconscious gladiator was an image too savage for new France. So they hid the Roman sword in his hand, and wreathed it all over with a chaplet of flowers!

Let us say a word of the ideas. Three ideas filled the mind of the nation: the idea of Liberty, Equality and Fraternity. Three noble words. Liberty meant liberty of all. So, at one word, they set free the slaves, and, if my friend's ciphers are correct, at once three hundred thousand souls rise up from the ground disenthralled, free men. That is a great act. A population as large as the whole family of our sober sister Connecticut, all at once find their chains drop off, and they are free: not beasts, but men. This may not hold. Our Declaration of Independence was not the Confederation of '78 — still less was it the Constitution of '87. The French may be as false as the Americans to their idea of liberty. At any rate, it is a good beginning. Let us rejoice at that.

Equality means that all are equal before the law;

equal in rights, however unequal in mights. So all titles of nobility come at once to the ground. The royal family is like the family of our Presidents. The Chamber of Peers is abolished. Universal suffrage is decreed; all men over twenty-one are voters. Men here in America say, "The French are not ready for that." No doubt the king thought so. At any rate, he was not ready for it. But it is not a thing altogether unknown in France. It has been tried several times before. The French Constitution was accepted by the whole people in 1800; Napoleon was made Consul by the whole people; made Emperor by the whole people. Even in 1815, the "acte additionelle" to the "Charte" was accepted by the whole people. To decree universal suffrage was the most natural thing in the world. Those two ideas, liberty and equality, have long been American ideas; they were never American facts. America sought liberty only for the whites. Our fathers thought not of universal suffrage.

But France has not only attempted to make our ideas into facts; she has advanced an idea not hinted at in the American Declaration; the idea of Fraternity. By this she means human brotherhood. This points not merely to a political, but to a social revolution. It is not easy for us to understand how a government can effect this. Here, all comes from the people, and the people have to take care of the government, meaning thereby the men in official power; have to furnish them with ideas, and tell them what application to make thereof. There all comes from the government. So the new provisional government of France must be one that can lead the nation; have ideas in advance of the nation. Accordingly, it proposes many plans which with us could never have come from any party in power. Here, the government is only the servant of the people. There, it aims to be the father and teacher thereof; a patriarchal government with Christian thoughts and feelings. But as an eloquent man is to come after me, whose special aim is to develop the idea of human brotherhood into social institutions, I will not dwell on this, save to mention an act of the provisional authorities. They have abolished the punishment of death for all political offences. You remember the guillotine, the massacres of September, the drowning in the Loire and the Seine, the dreadful butchery in the name of the law.

Put this new decree side by side with the old, and you see why Spartacus, though crowned by a revolution, bears peaceful blossoms in his hand.

But let us hasten on; time would fail me to speak of the cause or point out the effect of this movement of the people. Only a word concerning the objections made to it. Some say, "It is only an extempore affair. Men drunk with new power are telling their fancies, and trying in their heat to make laws thereof." It is not so. The ideas I have hinted at have been long known and deeply cherished by the best minds in France. Last autumn, M. Lamartine, in his own newspaper, for the deputy for Macon is an editor, published the "Programme and confession of his political faith." *

Others say, "The whole thing seems rash." Well, so it does; so does any good thing seem rash to all except the man who does it, and such as would do it if he did not. What is rash to one is not to another. It is dangerous for an old man to run, fatal for him to leap, while his grandson jumps over wall and ditch without hurt. The American Revolution was a rash act; the English Revolution a rash act; the Protestant Reformation was a rash act. Was it safe to withstand the Revolution? Did the king of the French find it so? Yet others say, "The leaders are unknown," "Lamartine, you might as well put any man in the street at the head of the nation." But when the American Revolution begun, who, in England, had ever heard of John Hancock, President of the Congress? To the men who knew him, John Hancock was a country trader, the richest man in a town of ten thousand inhabitants: That did not sound very great at London. Samuel Adams, and

---

* See the *Courier des Etats Unis*, for Nov. 24, 1847, which contains passages from M. Lamartine's programme, which set forth all the schemes that the provisional government had afterwards tried to carry out.

John Adams, and Thomas Jefferson, and all the other men, what did the world know of them? Only that they had been christened with Hebrew names. Why, George Washington was only, as Gen. Braddock called him, "A young Buckskin." But the world heard of these men afterwards. Let us leave the French statesmen to make to the future what report of themselves they can! Let me tell a story of Dupont de l'Eure, the head of the government at this moment. He was one of the movers of the Revolution of 1830. He dined with the citizen king, once, in some council. At the table, he and the king differed; the king affirmed, and Dupont denied. Said the king, "Do you tell me I lie?" Said Dupont, "When the king says yes, and Dupont de l'Eure replies no, France will know which to believe!" The king said, "Yes, we will put the people down;" Dupont said, "No, you shall not put the people down;" and now France knows which to believe.

Again, say others yet, "War may come; royalty may come back, despotism may come back. Other kings will interpose, and put down a republic." Other kings interpose to put down the French! Perhaps they will. They tried it in 1793, but did not like the experiment very well. They will be well off if they do not find it necessary to put down a republic a little nearer at hand; their anti-revolutionary work may begin at home. War followed the American Revolution. It cost money, it cost men. But if we calculate the value of American ideas, they are worth what they cost. Even the French Revolution, with all its carnage, robbery and butchery, is worth what it cost. But it is possible that war will not come. From a foreign war, France has little to fear. There seems little danger that it will come at all. What monarchy will dare fight republican France? Internal trouble may indeed come. It is to be expected that the new republic will make many a misstep. But is it likely that all the old tragedies will be enacted again? Surely not; the burnt child dreads the fire. Besides, the France of '48 is not the France of '89. There is no triple despotism weighing on the nation's neck, a trinity of despotic powers — the throne, the nobility, the church. The king has fled; the nobles have ceased to be; the church seems republican. There is no hatred between class and class, as before. The men of '89 sought freedom for the middle class, not for all classes, neither for the high, nor for the low. Religion pervades the church and the people, as never before. Better ideas prevail. It is not the gospel of Jean Jaques, and the scoffing negations of Voltaire, that are now proclaimed to the people; but the broad maxims of Christian men; the words of human brotherhood. The men of terror knew no weapon but the sword; the provisional government casts the sword from its hands, and will not shed blood for political crimes.

Still, troubles may come; war may come from without, and, worse still, from within; the republic may end. But if it lasts only a day, let us rejoice in that day. Suppose it is only the dream of the nation; it is worth while to dream of liberty, of equality, of fraternity; and to dream that we are awake, and trying to make them all into institutions and common life. What is only a dream now, will be a fact at last.

Next Sunday is the election day of France; six millions of voters are to choose nine hundred representatives! Shall not the prayers of all Christian hearts go up with them on that day, a great deep prayer for their success? The other day, the birthday of Washington, the calm, noiseless spirit of death came to release the soul of the patriarch of American statesmen. While his sun was slowly sinking in the western sky, the life-star of a new nation was visibly rising there, far off in the east. A pagan might be pardoned for the thought, that the intrepid soul of that old man foresaw the peril, and, slowly quitting its hold of the worn-out body, went thither to kindle anew the flames of liberty he fanned so often here. That is but a pagan thought. This is a Christian thought: The same God who formed the world for man's abode, presides also in the movements of mankind, and directs their voluntary march. See how this earth has been brought to her present firm and settled state. By storm and earthquake, continent has been rent from continent; oceans have swept over the mountains, and the scars of ancient war still mark our parent's venerable face. So is it in the growth of human Society: it is the child of pain; revolutions have rocked its cradle, war and violence rudely nursed it into hardy life. Good institutions, how painfully, how slowly have they come!

> "Slowly as spreads the green of earth
> O'er the receding ocean's bed,
> Dim as the distant stars come forth,
> Uncertain as a vision slow,
> Has been the old world's toiling pace,
> Ere she can give fair freedom place."

Let us welcome the green spot, when it begins to spread; let us shout as the sterile sea of barbarism goes back; let us rejoice in the vision of good things to come; let us welcome the distant and rising orb, for it is the Bethlehem star of a great nation, and they who behold it may well say — "Peace on earth, and good-will to men."

VIII.

SPEECH AT FANEUIL HALL, BEFORE THE NEW ENGLAND ANTI-SLAVERY CONVENTION, MAY 31, 1848.

THE design of the Abolitionists is this, — to remove and destroy the institution of slavery. To accomplish this well, two things are needed, ideas and actions. Of the ideas first, and then a word of the actions.

What is the idea of the abolitionists? Only this, That all men are created free, endowed with unalienable rights; and in respect of those rights, that all men are equal. This is the idea of Christianity, of human nature. Of course, then, no man has a right to take away another's rights; of course, no man may use me for his good, and not my own good also; of course, there can be no ownership of man by man; of course, no slavery in any form. Such is the idea, and some of the most obvious doctrines that follow from it.

Now, the abolitionists aim to put this idea into

the minds of the people, knowing that if it be there, actions will follow fast enough.

It seems a very easy matter to get it there. The idea is nothing new; all the world knows it. Talk with men, democrats and whigs, they will say they like freedom in the abstract, they hate slavery in the abstract. But you find that somehow they like slavery in the concrete, and dislike abolitionism when it tries to set free the slave. Slavery is the affair of the whole people; not Congress, but the nation, made slavery; made it national, constitutional. Not Congress, but the voters, must unmake slavery; make it un-constitutional, un-national. They say Congress cannot do it. Well, perhaps it is so; but they that make can break. If the people made slavery, they can unmake it.

You talk with the people; the idea of freedom is there. They tell you they believe the Declaration of Independence — that all men are created equal. But somehow they contrive to believe that negroes now in bondage are an exception to the rule, and so they tell us that slavery must not be meddled with, that we must respect the compromises of the Constitution. So we see that respect for the Constitution overrides respect for the inalienable rights of three millions of negro men.

Now, to move men, it is necessary to know two things — first, What they think, and next, Why they think it. Let us look a little at both.

In New England, men over twenty-one years old may be divided into two classes. First, the men that vote, and secondly, the men that choose the Governor. The voters in Massachusetts are some hundred and twenty thousand; the men that choose the Governor, who tell the people how to vote, whom to vote for, what laws to make, what to forbid, what policy to pursue — they are not very numerous. You may take one hundred men out of Boston, and fifty men from the other large towns in the State — and if you could get them to be silent till next December, and give no counsel on political affairs, the people would not know what to do. The democrats would not know what to do, nor the whigs. We are a very democratic people, and suffrage is almost universal; but it is a very few men who tell us how to vote, who make all the most important laws. Do I err in estimating the number at one hundred and fifty? I do not like to exaggerate — suppose there are six hundred men, three hundred in each party; that six hundred manage the political action of the State, in ordinary times.

I need not stop to ask what the rest of the people think about freedom and slavery. What do the men who control our politics think thereof? I answer, They are not opposed to slavery; to the slavery of three millions of men. They may not like slavery in the abstract, or they may like it, I do not pretend to judge; but slavery in the concrete, at the South, they do like; opposition to that slavery, in the mildest form, or the sternest, they do hate.

That is a serious charge to bring against the prominent rulers of the State. Let me call your attention to a few facts which prove it. Look at the men we send to Congress. There are thirty-one New England men in Congress. By the most liberal construction you can only make out five anti-slavery men in the whole number. Who ever heard of an anti-slavery Governor of Massachusetts in this century? Men know what they are about when they select candidates for election. Do the voters always know what they are about when they choose them?

Then these men always are in favor of a pro-slavery President. The President must be a slaveholder. There have been fifteen presidential elections. Men from the free States have filled the chair twelve years, or three terms; men from the slave States forty-four years, or eleven terms. During one term, the chair was filled by an amphibious presidency, by General Harrison, who was nothing but a concrete availability, and John Tyler, who was—John Tyler. They called him an accident; but there are no accidents in politics. A slaveholder presides over the United States forty-eight years out of sixty! Do those men who control the politics of New England not like it? It is no such thing. They love to have it so. We have just seen the democratic party, or their leaders, nominate General Cass for their candidate — and General Cass is a northern man; but on that account is he any the less a pro-slavery man? He did oppose the South once, but it was in pressing a war with England. Everybody knows General Cass, and I need say no more about him. But the northern whigs have their leaders — are they anti-slavery men? Not a whit more. Next week you will see them nominate, not the great Eastern whig, though he is no opponent of slavery, only an Expounder and Defender of the Constitution; not the great Western whig, the Compromiser, though steeped to the lips in slavery; no, they will nominate General Taylor, a man who lives a little further south, and is at this moment dyed a little more scarlet with the sin of slavery.

But go a step further as to the proof. Those men who control the politics of Massachusetts, or New England, or the whole North, they have never opposed the aggressive movements of the slave power. The annexation of Texas, did they oppose that? No, they were glad of it. True, some earnest men came up here in Faneuil Hall, and passed resolutions, which did no good whatever, because it was well known that the real controllers of our politics thought the other way. Then followed the Mexican war. It was a war for slavery, and they knew it; they like it now — that is, if a man's likings can be found out by his doings, not his occasional and exceptional deeds, but his regular and constant actions. They knew that there would be a war against the currency, a war against the tariff, or a war against Mexico. They chose the latter. They knew what they were about.

The same thing is shown by the character of the Press. No "respectable" paper is opposed to slavery; no whig paper, no democratic paper. You would as soon expect a Catholic newspaper to oppose the Pope and his church, for the slave power is the Pope of America, though not exactly a pious Pope. The churches show the same thing; they also are in the main pro-slavery, at least not anti-slavery. There are some forty denominations or sects in New England. Mr. President, is one of these anti-slavery? Not one! The land is full of ministers, respectable men, educated men — are they opposed to slavery? I do not know a single man, eminent in any sect, who is also eminent in his opposition to slavery. There was one such man, Dr. Channing; but just as he became eminent in the cause of freedom, he lost power in his own church, lost caste in his own little sect; and though men are now glad to make sectarian capital out of his reputation after he is dead, when he lived, they cursed him by their gods! Then, too, all the most prominent men of New England fraternize with slavery. Massachusetts received such an insult from South Carolina as no State ever before received from another State in this Union; an affront which no nation would dare offer another, without grinding its sword first. And what does Massachusetts do? She does — nothing. But her foremost man goes off there, "The schoolmaster that gives no lessons,"* to accept the hospitality of the South, to take the chivalry of South Carolina by the hand; the Defender of the Constitution fraternizes with the State which violates the Constitution, and imprisons his own constituents on account of the color of their skin.

Put all these things together, and they show that the men who control the politics of Massachusetts, of all New England, do not oppose or dislike slavery.

So much for what they think; and now for the Why they think so.

First, there is the general indifference to what is absolutely right. Men think little of it. The Anglo-Saxon race, on both sides of the water, have always felt the instinct of freedom, and often contended stoutly enough for their own rights. But they never cared much for the rights of other men. The slaves are at a distance from us, and so the wrong of this institution is not brought home to men's feelings as if it were our own wrong.

* This was a sentiment offered at a public dinner given by the citizens of Charleston, S. C., to Hon. Daniel Webster.

Then the pecuniary interests of the North are supposed to be connected with slavery, so that the North would lose dollars if the South lost slaves. No doubt this is a mistake; still, it is an opinion currently held. The North wants a market for its fabrics, freight for its ships. The South affords it; and, as men think, better than if she had manufactures and ships of her own, both of which she could have, were there no slaves. All this seems to be a mistake. Freedom, I think, can be shown to be the interest of both North and South.

Yet another reason is found in devotion to the interests of a party. Tell a whig he could make whig capital out of anti-slavery, he would turn abolitionist in a moment, if he believed you. Tell a democrat that he can make capital out of abolition, and he also will come over to your side. But the fact is, each party knows it would gain nothing for its political purposes by standing out for the rights of man. The time will come, and sooner too than some men think, when it will be for the interest of a party to favor abolition; but that time is not yet. It does seem strange, that while you can find men who will practise a good deal of self-denial for their sect or their party, lending, and hoping nothing in return, you so rarely find a man who will compromise even his popularity for the sake of mankind.

Then again, there is the fear of change. Men

who control our politics seem to have little confidence in man, little in truth, little in justice, and the eternal right. Therefore, while it is never out of season to do something for the tariff, for the moneyed interests of men, they think it is never in time to do much for the great work of elevating mankind itself. They have no confidence in the people, and take little pains to make the people worthy of confidence. So any change which gives a more liberal government to a people, which gives freedom to the slave, they look on with distrust, if not alarm. In 1830, when the French expelled the despotic king who encumbered their throne, what said Massachusetts, what said New England, in honor of the deed? Nothing. Your old men? Nothing. Your young men? Not a word. What did they care for the freedom of thirty millions of men? They were looking at their imports and exports. In 1838, when England set free eight hundred thousand men in a day, what did Massachusetts say about that? What had New England to say? Not a word in its favor from these political leaders of the land. Nay, they thought the experiment was dangerous, and ever since that it is with great reluctance you can get them to confess that the scheme works well. In 1848, when France again expels her king, and all the royalty in the kingdom is carted off in a one-horse cab — when the broadest principles of human government are laid down, and a great nation sets about the difficult task of moving out of her old political house, and into a new one, without tearing down the old, without butchering men in the process of removal, — why, what has Boston to say to that? What have the political leaders of Massachusetts, of New England, to say? They have nothing to say for liberty; they are sorry the experiment was made; they are afraid the French will not want so much cotton; they have no confidence in man, and fear every change.

Such are their opinions, to judge by what they do; such the reasons thereof, judging by what they say.

But now how can we change this, and get the idea of freedom into men's minds? Something can be done by the gradual elevation of men, by schools and churches, by the press. The churches and colleges of New England have not directly aided us in the work of abolishing slavery. No doubt by their direct action they have retarded that work, and that a good deal. But indirectly they have done much to hasten the work. They have helped educate men; helped make men moral, in a general way; and now this moral power can be turned to this special business, though the churches say, "No, you shall not." I see before me a good and an earnest man,* who, not opening his mouth in public against

* Rev. Cyrus Pierce, Teacher of the Normal School at Newton.

slavery, has yet done a great service in this way: he has educated the teachers of the Commonwealth, has taught them to love freedom, to love justice, to love man and God. That is what I call sowing the seeds of anti-slavery. The honored and excellent Secretary of Education,* who has just gone to stand in the place of a famous man, and I hope to fill it nobly, has done much in this way. I wish in his reports on education he had exposed the wrong which is done here in Boston, by putting all the colored children in one school, by shutting them out of the Latin School and the English High School. I wish he had done that duty, which plainly belongs to him to do. But without touching that, he has yet done, indirectly, a great work towards the abolition of slavery. He has sown the seeds of education wide spread over the State. One day these seeds will come up; come up men, men that will both vote and choose the Governor; men that will love right and justice; will see the iniquity of American slavery, and sweep it off the continent, cost what it may cost, spite of all compromises of the Constitution, and all compromisers. I look on that as certain. But that is slow work, this waiting for a general morality to do a special act. It is going without dinner till the wheat is grown for your bread.

So we want direct and immediate action upon the

* Hon. Horace Mann.

people themselves. The idea must be set directly before them, with all its sanctions displayed, and its obligations made known. This can be done in part by the pulpit. Dr. Channing shows how much one man can do, standing on that eminence. You all know how much he did do. I am sorry that he came so late, sorry that he did not do more, but thankful for what he did do. However, you cannot rely on the pulpit to do much. The pulpit represents the average goodness and piety; not eminent goodness and piety. It is unfair to call ordinary men to do extraordinary works. I do not concur in all the hard things that are said about the clergy, perhaps it is because I am one of them; but I do not expect a great deal from them. It is hard to call a class of men all at once to rise above all other classes of men, and teach a degree of virtue which they do not understand. But you may call them to be true to their own consciences.

So the pulpit is not to be relied on for much aid. If all the ministers of New England were abolitionists, with the same zeal that they are Protestants, Universalists, Methodists, Calvinists, or Unitarians, no doubt the whole State would soon be an anti-slavery State, and the day of emancipation would be wonderfully hastened. But that we are not to look for.

Much can be done by lecturers, who shall go to the people and address them, not as whigs or democrats, not as sectarians, but as men, and in the name of man and God present the actual condition of the slaves, and show the duty of the North and the South, of the nation, in regard to this matter. For this business, we want money and men, the two sinews of war; money to pay the men, men to earn the money. They must appeal to the people in their primary capacity, simply as men.

Much also may be done by the press. How much may be done by these two means, and that in a few years, these men* can tell; all the North and South can tell. Men of the most diverse modes of thought can work together in this cause. Here on my right is Mr. Phillips, an old-fashioned Calvinist, who believes all the five points of Calvinism. I am rather a new-fashioned Unitarian, and believe only one of the five points, the one Mr. Phillips has proved — the perseverance of the saints; but we get along without any quarrel by the way.

Some men will try political action. The action of the people, of the nation, must be political action. It may be constitutional, it may be unconstitutional. I see not why men need quarrel about that. Let not him that voteth, condemn him that voteth not; nor let not him that voteth not, condemn him that voteth, but let every man be faithful to his own convictions.

---

* Messrs. Garrison, Phillips and Quincy.

It is said, the abolitionists waste time and wind in denunciation. It is partly true. I make no doubt it inspires the slaveholder's heart to see division amongst his foes. I ought to say his friends, for such we are. He thinks the day of justice is deferred, while the ministers thereof contend. I do not believe a revolution is to be baptized with rose-water. I do not believe a great work is to be done without great passions. It is not to be supposed that the Leviathan of American Slavery will allow himself to be drawn out of the mire in which he has made his nest, and grown fat and strong, without some violence and floundering. When we have caught him fairly, he will put his feet into the mud to hold on by; he will reach out and catch hold of every thing that will hold him. He has caught hold of Mr. Clay and Mr. Webster. He will catch hold of General Cass and General Taylor. He will die, though slowly, and die hard. Still it is a pity that men who essay to pull him out, should waste their strength in bickerings with one another, or in needless denunciation of the leviathan's friends. Call slaveholding, slaveholding; let us tell all the evils which arise from it, if we can find language terrible enough; let us show up the duplicity of the nation, the folly of our wise men, the littleness of our great men, the baseness of our honorable men, if need be; but all that with no unkind feelings toward any one. Virtue never appears so lovely as when destroying sin, she loves the sinner, and seeks to save him. Absence of love is absence of the strongest power. See how much Mr. Adams lost of his influence, how much he wasted of his strength, by the violence with which he pursued persons. I am glad to acknowledge the great services he performed. He wished to have every man stand on the right side of the anti-slavery line; but I believe there were some men whom he would like to have put there with a pitchfork. On the other hand, Dr. Channing never lost a moment by attacking a personal foe; and see what he gained by it! However, I must say this, that no great revolution of opinion and practice was ever brought about before with so little violence, waste of force, and denunciation. Consider the greatness of the work: it is to restore three millions to liberty; a work, in comparison with which the American Revolution was a little thing. Yet consider the violence, the denunciation, the persecution, and the long years of war, which that Revolution cost. I do not wonder that abolitionists are sometimes violent; I only deplore it. Remembering the provocation, I wonder they are not more so and more often. The prize is to be run for, "not without dust and heat."

Working in this way, we are sure to succeed. The idea is an eternal truth. It will find its way into the public mind, for there is that sympathy between man and the truth, that he cannot live without it and be blessed. What allies we have on our side! True, the cupidity, the tyranny, the fear and the atheism of the land are against us. But all the nobleness, all the honor, all the morality, all the religion, are on our side. I was sorry to hear it said, that the religion of the land opposed us. It is not true. Religion never opposed any good work. I know what my friend meant, and I wish he had said it, calling things by their right names. It is the irreligion of the land that favors slavery; it is the idolatry of gold; it is our atheism. Of speculative atheism there is not much; you see how much of the practical!

We are certain of success; the spirit of the age is on our side. See how the old nations shake their tyrants out of the land. See how every steamer brings us good tidings of good things; and do you believe America can keep her slaves? It is idle to think so. So all we want is time. On our side are Truth, Justice, and the Eternal Right. Yes, on our side is religion, the religion of Christ; on our side are the hopes of mankind, and the great power of God.

IX.

SOME THOUGHTS ON THE FREE SOIL PARTY AND THE ELECTION OF GENERAL TAYLOR. DECEMBER, 1848.

THE people of the United States have just chosen an officer, who, for the next four years, will have more power than any monarch of Europe; yet three years ago he was scarcely known out of the army in Florida, and even now has appeared only in the character of a successful general. His supporters at the North intend, by means of his election, to change the entire commercial policy of the country, and perhaps, also, its financial policy; they contemplate, or profess to contemplate, a great change. Yet the election has been effected without tumult or noise; not a soldier has drawn his bayonet; scarcely has a constable needed his official rod to keep order withal. In Europe, at the same time, the beginning of a change in the national dynasty or the national policy is only attempted by violence, by soldiers with arms ready for fight, by battle and murder. One day or another, men will be wise enough to see the cause of this difference, and insular statesmen in England, who now sneer at the new government in America, may learn that democracy has at least one quality—that of respecting law and order, and may live to see ours the oldest government in the whole Caucasian race.

Since the election is now over, it is worth while to look a moment at the politics and political parties of the country, that we may gain wisdom for the future, and perhaps hope; at any rate, may see the actual condition of things. Each political party is based on an Idea, which corresponds to a Truth, or an Interest. It commonly happens that the idea is represented as an interest, and the interest as an idea, before either becomes the foundation of a large party. Now when a new idea is introduced to any party, or applied to any institution, if it be only auxiliary to the old doctrines incarnated therein, a regular growth and new development take place; but when the new idea is hostile to the old, the development takes place under the form of a revolution, and that will be greater or less in proportion to the difference between the new idea and the old doctrine; in proportion to their relative strength and value. As Aristotle said of seditions, a revolution comes on slight occasions, but not of slight causes;* the occa-

* *Γίγνονται μὲν οὖν αἱ στάσεις οὐ περὶ μικρῶν ἀλλ' ἐκ μικρῶν, στασιάζουσι δὲ περὶ μεγάλων.*—Aristotle's *Polit.*, Lib. V. Chap. 4, § 1.

sion may be obvious and obviously trivial, but the cause obscure and great. The occasion of the French Revolution of 1848 was afforded by the attempt of the king to prevent a certain public dinner: he had a legal right to prevent it. The cause of the Revolution was a little different; but some men in America and England, at first, scarcely looked beyond the occasion, and, taking that for the cause, thought the Frenchmen fools to make so much ado about a trifle, and that they had better eat their *soupe maigre* at home, and let their victuals stop their mouths. The occasion of the American Revolution may be found in the Stamp-Act, or the Sugar-Act, the Writs of Assistance, or the Boston Port-Bill; some men, even now, see no further, and logically conclude the colonists made a mistake, because for a dozen years they were far worse off than before the "Rebellion," and have never been so lightly taxed since. Such men do not see the cause of the Revolution, which was not an unwillingness to pay taxes, but a determination to govern themselves.

At the present day it is plain that a revolution, neither slow nor silent, is taking place in the political parties of America. The occasion thereof is the nomination of a man for the presidency who has no political or civil experience, but who has three qualities that are important in the eyes of the leading men who have supported and pushed him forward: one is, that he is an eminent slaveholder, whose interests and accordingly whose ideas are identical with those of the slaveholders; the next, that he is not hostile to the doctrines of northern manufacturers respecting a protective tariff; and the third, that he is an eminent and very successful military commander. The last is an accidental quality, and it is not to be supposed that the intelligent and influential men at the North and South who have promoted his election, value him any more on that account, or think that mere military success fits him for his high office, and enables him to settle the complicated difficulties of a modern State. They must know better; but they must have known that many men of little intelligence are so taken with military glory that they will ask for no more in their hero; it was foreseen, also, that honest and intelligent men of all parties would give him their vote because he had never been mixed up with the intrigues of political life. Thus "far-sighted" politicians of the North and South saw that he might be fairly elected, and then might serve the purposes of the slaveholder, or the manufacturer of the North. The military success of General Taylor, an accidental merit, was only the occasion of his nomination by the whigs; his substantial merit was found in the fact, that he was supposed, or known, to be favorable to the "peculiar institution" of the South, and the protective policy of the manufacturers at the North: this was the cause of his formal nomination by the Whig

Convention of Philadelphia, and his real nomination by members of the whig party at Washington. The men of property at the South wanted an extension of slavery; the men of property at the North, a high protective tariff; and it was thought General Taylor could serve both purposes, and promote the interests of the North and South.

Such is the occasion of the revolution in political parties: the cause is the introduction of a new idea into these parties entirely hostile to some of their former doctrines. In the electioneering contest, the new idea was represented by the words "Free Soil." For present practice it takes a negative form: "No more Slave States, no more Slave Territory," is the motto. But these words and this motto do not adequately represent the idea, only so much thereof as has been needful in the present crisis.

Before now there has been much in the political history of America to provoke the resentment of the North. England has been ruled by various dynasties; the American chair has been chiefly occupied by the Southern House, the Dynasty of Slaveholders: now and then a member of the Northern House has sat on that seat, but commonly it has been a "Northern man with Southern principles," never a man with mind to see the great idea of America, and will to carry it out in action. Still the spirit of liberty has not died out of the North; the attempt to put an eighth slaveholder in the chair of "The model republic," gave occasion for that spirit to act again.

The new idea is not hostile to the distinctive doctrine of either political party; neither to free trade, nor to protection; so it makes no revolution in respect to them: it is neutral, and leaves both as it found them. It is not hostile to the general theory of the American State, so it makes no revolution there; this idea is assumed as self-evident, in the Declaration of Independence. It is not inimical to the theory of the Constitution of the United States, as set forth in the preamble thereto, where the design of the Constitution is declared to be "To form a more perfect union, establish justice, insure domestic tranquillity, provide for the common defence, promote the general welfare, and secure the blessings of liberty to ourselves and our posterity."

There are clauses in the Constitution, which are exceptions to this theory, and hostile to the design mentioned above; to such, this idea will one day prove itself utterly at variance, as it is now plainly hostile to one part of the practice of the American government, and that of both the parties.

We have had several political parties since the Revolution: the federalists, and anti-federalists,—the latter shading off into republicans, democrats, and loco focos; the former tapering into modern whigs, in which guise some of their fathers would scarcely recognize the family type. We have had a protective party and an anti-protective party; once there was a free-trade party, which no longer appears in politics. There has been a National Bank party, which seems to have gone to the realm of things lost on earth. In the rise and fall of these parties, several dramas, tragic and comic, have been performed on the American boards, where "One man in his time plays many parts," and stout representatives of the Hartford Convention find themselves on the same side with worshippers of the Gerrymander, and shouting the same cry. It is kindly ordered that memory should be so short, and brass so common. None of the old parties is likely to return; the living have buried the dead. "We are all federalists," said Mr. Jefferson, "we are all democrats," and truly, so far as old questions are concerned. It is well known that the present representatives of the old federal party, have abjured the commercial theory of their predecessors; and the men who were "Jacobins" at the beginning of the century, curse the new French Revolution by their gods. At the presidential election of 1840, there were but two parties in the field — democrats and whigs. As they both survive, it is well to see what interests or what ideas they represent.

They differ accidentally in the possession and the desire of power; in the fact that the former took the initiative, in annexing Texas, and in making the Mexican war, while the latter only pretended to oppose either, but zealously and continually coöperated in both. Then, again, the democratic party sustains the sub-treasury system, insisting that the government shall not interfere with banking, shall keep its own deposits, and give and take only specie in its business with the people. The whig party, if we understand it, has not of late developed any distinctive doctrine, on the subject of money and financial operations, but only complained of the action of the sub-treasury; yet, as it sustained the late Bank of the United States, and appropriately followed as chief mourner at the funeral thereof, uttering dreadful lamentations and prophecies which time has not seen fit to accomplish, it still keeps up a show of differing from the democrats on this matter. These are only accidental or historical differences, which do not practically affect the politics of the nation to any great degree.

The substantial difference between the two is this: The whigs desire a tariff of duties which shall directly and intentionally protect American industry, or, as we understand it, shall directly and intentionally protect manufacturing industry, while the commercial and agricultural interests are to be protected indirectly, not as if they were valuable in themselves, but were a collateral security to the manufacturing interest: a special protection is desired for the great manufactures, which are usually conducted by large capitalists — such as the manufacture of wool, iron, and cotton. On the other hand, the democrats disclaim all direct protection of any special interest, but, by raising the national revenue from the imports of the nation, actually afford a protection to the articles of domestic origin to the extent of the national revenue, and much more. That is the substantial difference between the two parties — one which has been much insisted on at the late election, especially at the North.

Is this difference of any practical importance at the present moment? There are two methods of raising the revenue of a country: first, by direct taxation, — a direct tax on the person, a direct tax on the property; second, by indirect taxation. To a simple-minded man direct taxation seems the only just and equal mode of collecting the public revenue: thereby, the rich man pays in proportion to his much, the poor to his little. This is so just and obvious, that it is the only method resorted to, in towns of the North, for raising their revenue. But while it requires very little common sense and virtue to appreciate this plan in a town, it seems to require a good deal to endure it in a nation. The four direct taxes levied by the American government since 1787 have been imperfectly collected, and only with great difficulty and long delay. To avoid this difficulty, the government resorts to various indirect modes of taxation, and collects the greater part of its revenue from the imports which reach our shores.

In this way a man's national tax is not directly in proportion to his wealth, but directly in proportion to his consumption of imported goods, or directly to that of domestic goods, whose price is enhanced by the duties laid on the foreign article. So it may happen that an Irish laborer, with a dozen children, pays a larger national tax than a millionnaire who sees fit to live in a miserly style. Besides, no one knows when he pays or what. At first it seems as if the indirect mode of taxation made the burden light, but in the end it does not always prove so. The remote effect thereof is sometimes remarkable. The tax of one per cent. levied in Massachusetts on articles sold by auction, has produced some results not at all anticipated.

Now since neither party ventures to suggest direct taxation, the actual question between the two is not between free trade and protection, but only between a protective and a revenue tariff. So the real and practical question between them is this: Shall there be a high tariff or a low one? At first sight a man not in favor of free trade might think the present tariff gave sufficient protection to those great manufactures of wool, cotton, and iron, and as much as was reasonable. But the present duty is perhaps scarcely adequate to meet the expenses of the nation, for with new territory new expenses must come; there is a large debt to be discharged, its interest to be paid; large sums will be demanded as pensions for the soldiers. Since these things are so, it is but reasonable to conclude that, under the administration of the whigs or democrats, a pretty high tariff of duties will continue for some years to come. So the great and substantial difference between the two parties ceases to be of any great and substantial importance.

In the mean time another party rises up, representing neither of these interests; without developing any peculiar views relative to trade or finance, it proclaims the doctrine that there must be no more slave territory, and no more slave States. This doctrine is of great practical importance, and one in which the free soil party differs substantially from both the other parties. The idea on which the party rests is not new; it does not appear that the men who framed the Constitution, or the people who accepted it, ever contemplated the extension of slavery beyond the limits of the United States at that time; had such a proposition been then made, it would have been indignantly rejected by both. The principle of the Wilmot Proviso boasts the same origin as the Declaration of Independence. The state of feeling at the North occasioned by the Missouri Compromise is well known, but after that there was no political party opposed to slavery. No President has been hostile to it; no Cabinet; no Congress. In 1805, Mr. Pickering, a Senator from Massachusetts, brought forward his bill for amending the Constitution, so that slaves should not form part of the basis of representation; but it fell to the ground, not to be lifted up by his successors for years to come. The refusal of John Quincy Adams, while President, to recognize the independence of Hayti, and his efforts to favor the slave power, excited no remark. In 1844, for the first time the anti-slavery votes began seriously to affect the presidential election. At that time the whigs had nominated Mr. Clay as their candidate, a man of great powers, of popular manners, the friend of northern industry, but still more the friend of southern slavery, and more directly identified with that than any man in so high a latitude. The result of the anti-slavery votes is well known. The bitterest reproaches have been heaped on the men who voted against him as the incarnation of the slave power; the annexation of Texas, though accomplished by a whig senate, and the Mexican war, though only sixteen members of Congress voted against it, have both been laid to their charge; and some have even affected to wonder that men conscientiously opposed to slavery could not forget their principle for the sake of their party, and put a most decided slaveholder, who had treated not only them but their cause with scorn and contempt, in the highest place of power.

The whig party renewed its attempt to place a slaveholder in the President's chair, at a time when all Europe was rising to end for ever the tyranny of man. General Taylor was particularly obnoxious to the anti-slavery men. He is a slaveholder, holding one or two hundred men in bondage, and enlarging that number by recent purchases; he employs them in the worst kind of slave labor, the manufacture of sugar; he leaves them to the mercy of overseers, the dregs and refuse of mankind; he has just returned from a war undertaken for the extension of slavery; he is a southern man with southern interests, and opinions favorable to slavery, and is uniformly represented by his supporters at the South, as decidedly opposed to the Wilmot Proviso, and in favor of the extension of slavery. We know this has been denied at the North; but the testimony of the South settles the question. The convention of democrats in South Carolina, when they also nominated him, said well, "His interests are our interests: . . . . we know that on this great, paramount, and leading question of the rights of the South [to extend slavery over the new territory], he is for us and he is with us." Said a newspaper in his own State, "General Taylor is from birth, association, and conviction, identified with the South and her institutions, being one of the most extensive slaveholders in Louisiana, and supported by the slaveholding interest; is opposed to the Wilmot Proviso, and in favor of procuring the privilege to the owners of slaves to remove with them to newly acquired territory."

The southerners evidently thought the crisis an important one. The following is from the distinguished whig senator, Mr. Berrien.

"I consider it the most important Presidential election, especially to southern men, which has occurred since the foundation of the government.

"We have great and important interests at stake. If we fail to sustain them now, we may be forced too soon to decide whether we will remain in the Union, at the mercy of a band of fanatics or political jugglers, or reluctantly retire from it for the preservation of our domestic institutions, and all our rights as freemen. If we are united, we can sustain them; if we divide on the old party issues, we must be victims.

"With a heart devoted to their interests on this great question, and without respect to party, I implore my fellow-citizens of Georgia, whig and democratic, to forget for the time their party divisions: to know each other only as southern men: to act upon the truism uttered by Mr. Calhoun, that on this vital question, — the preservation of our domestic institutions, — the southern man who is furthest from us, is nearer to us than any northern man can be; that General Taylor is identified with us, in feeling and interest, was born in a slaveholding State, educated in a slaveholding State, is himself a slaveholder; that his slave property constitutes the means of support to himself and family; that he cannot desert us without sacrificing his interest, his principle, the habits and feelings of his life; and that with him, therefore, our institutions are safe. I beseech them, therefore, from the love which they bear to our noble State, to rally under the banner of Zachary Taylor, and, with one united voice, to send him by acclamation to the executive chair."

All this has been carefully kept from the sight of the people at the North.

There have always been men in America, who were opposed to the extension and the very existence of slavery. In 1787, the best and the most celebrated statesmen were publicly active on the side of freedom. Some thought slavery a sin, others a mistake, but nearly all in the Convention thought it an error. South Carolina and Georgia were the only States thoroughly devoted to slavery at that time. They threatened to withdraw from the Union, if it were not sufficiently respected in the new Constitution. If the other States had said, "You may go, soon as you like, for hitherto you have been only a curse to us, and done little but brag," it would have been better for us all. However, partly for the sake of keeping the peace, and still more for the purpose of making money by certain concessions of the South, the North granted the southern demands. After the adoption of the Constitution, the anti-slavery spirit cooled down; other matters occupied the public mind. The long disasters of Europe; the alarm of the English party, who feared their sons should be "conscripts in the armies of Napoleon," and the violence of the French party, who were ready to compromise the dignity of the nation, and add new elements to the confusion in Europe; the subsequent conflict with England, and then the efforts to restore the national character, and improve our material condition, — these occupied the thought of the nation, till the Missouri Compromise again disturbed the public mind. But that was soon forgotten; little was said about slavery. In the eighteenth century, it was discussed in the colleges and newspapers, even in the pulpits of the North; but, in the first quarter of the nineteenth, little was heard of it. Manufactures got established at the North, and protected by duties; at the South, cotton was cultivated with profit, and a heavy duty protected the slave-grown sugar of Louisiana. The pecuniary interests of North and South became closely connected, and both seemed dependent on the peaceable continuance of slavery. Little was said against it, little thought, and nothing done. Southern masters voluntarily brought their slaves to New England, and took them back, no one offering the African the conventional shelter of the law, not to speak of the natural shelter of justice. We well remember the complaint made somewhat later, when a Judge decided that a slave, brought here by his master's consent, became, from that moment, free!

But where sin abounded, grace doth much more abound. There rose up one man who would not compromise, nor be silent,—who would be heard.* He spoke of the evil, spoke of the sin—for all true reforms are bottomed on religion, and while they seem adverse to many interests, yet represent the idea of the Eternal. He found a few others, a very

* William Lloyd Garrison.

few, and began the anti-slavery movement. The "platform" of the new party was not an interest, but an idea — that "All men are created equal, and endowed by their Creator with certain unalienable rights." Every truth is also a fact; this was a fact of human consciousness, and a truth of necessity.

The time has not come to write the history of the abolitionists, — other deeds must come before words; but we cannot forbear quoting the testimony of one witness, as to the state of anti-slavery feeling in New England in 1831. It is the late Hon. Harrison Gray Otis, a former mayor of Boston, who speaks in his recent letter.

> "The first information received by me, of a disposition to agitate this subject in our State, was from the Governors of Virginia and Georgia, severally remonstrating against an incendiary newspaper, published in Boston, and, as they alleged, thrown broadcast among their plantations, inciting to insurrection and its horrid results. It appeared, on inquiry, that no member of the city government [of Boston] had ever heard of the publication. Some time afterwards it was reported to me by the city officers, that they had ferreted out the paper and its editor; that his office was an obscure hole, his only visible auxiliary a negro boy, and his supporters a very few insignificant persons of all colors. This information . . . . I communicated to the above-named governors, with an assurance of my belief that the new fanaticism had not made, nor was likely to make, proselytes among the respectable classes of our people."

Such was the state of things in 1831. Anti-slavery had "an obscure hole" for its head-quarters; the one agitator, who had filled the two doughty Governors of Virginia and Georgia with uncomfortable forebodings, had a "negro boy" "for his only visible auxiliary," and none of the respectable men of Boston had heard of the hole, of the agitator, of the negro boy, or even of the agitation. One thing must be true: either the man and the boy were pretty vigorous, or else there was a great truth in that obscure hole; for, in spite of the governors and the mayors, spite of the many able men in the South and the North, spite, also, of the wealth and respectability of the whole land, it is a plain case that the abolitionists have shaken the nation, and their idea is the idea of the time; and the party which shall warmly welcome that is destined before long to override all the other parties.

One thing must be said of the leaders of the anti-slavery movement. They asked for nothing but justice; not justice for themselves — they were not Socratic enough to ask that, — but only justice for the slave; and to obtain that, they forsook all that human hearts most love. It is rather a cheap courage that fought at Monterey and Palo Alto, a bravery that can be bought for eight dollars a month; the patriotism which hurras for "our side," which makes speeches at Faneuil Hall, nay, which carries torch-lights in a procession, is not the very loftiest kind of patriotism; even the man who stands up at the stake, and in one brief hour of agony anticipates the long torment of disease, does not endure the hardest, but only the most obvious kind of martyrdom. But when a man, for conscience' sake, leaves a calling that would insure him bread and respectability; when he abjures the opinions which give him the esteem of honorable men; when, for the sake of truth and justice, he devotes himself to liberating the most abused and despised class of men, solely because they are men and brothers; when he thus steps forth in front of the world, and encounters poverty and neglect, the scorn, the loathing, and the contempt of mankind — why, there is something not very common in that. There was once a Man who had not where to lay his head, who was born in "an obscure hole," and had not even a negro boy for his "auxiliary;" who all his life lived with most obscure persons — eating and drinking with publicans and sinners; who found no favor with mayors or governors, and yet has had some influence on the history of the world. When intelligent men mock at small beginnings, it is surprising they cannot remember that the greatest institutions have had their times which tried men's souls, and that they who have done all the noblest and best work of mankind, sometimes forgot self-interest in looking at a great truth; and though they had not always even a negro boy to help them, or an obscure hole to lay their heads in, yet found the might of the universe was on the side of right, and themselves workers with God!

The abolitionists did not aim to found a political party; they set forth an idea. If they had set up the interest of the whigs or the democrats, the manufacturers or the merchants, they might have formed a party and had a high place in it, with money, ease, social rank and a great name in the party—newspapers. Some of them had political talents, ideas more than enough, the power of organizing men, the skill to manage them, and a genius for eloquence. With such talents, it demands not a little manliness to keep out of politics and in the truth.

To found a political party there is no need of a great moral idea: the whig party has had none such this long time; the democratic party pretends to none and acts on none; each represents an interest which can be estimated in dollars; neither seems to see that behind questions of political economy there is a question of political morality, and the welfare of the nation depends on the answer we shall give! So long as the abolitionists had nothing but an idea, and but few men had that, there was no inducement for the common run of politicians to join them; they could make nothing by it, so nothing of it. The guardians of education, the trustees of the popular religion, did not like to invest in such funds. But still the idea went on, spite of the most entire, the most bitter, the most heartless and unrelenting opposition ever known in America. No men were ever hated as the abolitionists; political parties have joined to despise, and sectarian churches to curse them. Yet the idea has gone on, till now all that is most pious in the sects, most patriotic in the parties, all that is most Christian in modern philanthropy, is on its side. It has some representative in almost every family, save here and there one whose God is mammon alone, where the parents are antediluvian and the children born old and conservative, with no faculty but memory to bind them to mankind. It has its spokemen in the House and the Senate. The tide rises and swells, and the compact wall of the whig party, the tall ramparts of the democrats, are beginning to "cave in."

As the idea has gained ground, men have begun to see that an interest is connected with it, and begun to look after that. One thing the North knows well — the art of calculation, and of ciphering. So it begins to ask questions as to the positive and comparative influence of the slave power on the country. Who fought the Revolution? Why the North, furnishing the money and the men, Massachusetts alone sending fourteen thousand soldiers more than all the present slave States. Who pays the national taxes? The North, for the slaves pay but a trifle. Who owns the greater part of the property, the mills, the shops, the ships? The North.

Who writes the books — the histories, poems, philosophies, works of science, even the sermons and commentaries on the Bible? Still the North. Who sends their children to school and college? The North. Who builds the churches, who founds the Bible societies, Education societies, Missionary societies, the thousand-and-one institutions for making men better and better off? Why the North. In a word, who is it that in seventy years has made the nation great, rich, and famous for her ideas and their success all over the world? The answer is, still the North, the North.

Well, says the calculator, but who has the offices of the nation? The South. Who has filled the Presidential chair forty-eight years out of sixty? Nobody but slaveholders. Who has held the chief posts of honor? The South. Who occupy the chief offices in the army and navy? The South. Who increases the cost of the post-office and pays so little of its expense?* The South. Who is most blustering and disposed to quarrel? The

---

* The following table shows the facts of the case: —

Cost of post-office in slave States for the year ending July 1st, 1847,	$1,318,541	Cost of post-office in free States for the year ending July 1st, 1847,	$1,038,219
Receipts from post-office,	624,380	Receipts from post-office,	1,459,631

So the Southern post-office cost the nation $694,161, and the Northern post-office paid the nation $421,412, making a difference of $1,115,573 against the South.

South. Who made the Mexican war? The South. Who sets at nought the Constitution? The South. Who would bring the greatest peril in case of war with a strong enemy? Why the South, the South. But what is the South most noted for abroad? For her three million slaves; and the North? for her wealth, freedom, education, religion!

Then the calculator begins to remember past times — opens the account-books and turns back to old charges: five slaves count the same as three freemen, and the three million slaves, which at home are nothing but property, entitle their owners to as many representatives in Congress as are now sent by all the one million eight hundred thousand freemen who make the entire population of Maine, New Hampshire, Vermont, Rhode Island, and Massachusetts, and have created a vast amount of property worth more than all the slave States put together! Then the North must deliver up the fugitive slaves, and Ohio must play the traitor, the kidnapper, the bloodhound, for Kentucky! The South wanted to make two slave States out of Florida, and will out of Texas; she makes slavery perpetual in both; she is always bragging as if she made the Revolution, while she only laid the Embargo, and began the late war with England, — but that is going further back than is needful. The South imprisons our colored sailors in her ports, contrary to justice, and even contrary to the Constitution. She drove our commissioners out of South Carolina and Louisiana, when they were sent to look into the matter and legally seek for redress. She affronts the world with a most odious despotism, and tried to make the English return her runaway slaves, making the nation a reproach before the world; she insists on kidnapping men even in Boston; she declares that we shall not abolish slavery in the capital of the Union; that she will extend it in spite of us from sea to sea. She annexed Texas for a slave-pasture, and then made the Mexican war to enlarge that pasture, but the North must pay for it; she treads the Constitution under her feet, the North under her feet, justice and the unalienable rights of man under her feet.

The North has charged all these items and many more; now they are brought up for settlement, and, if not cancelled, will not be forgot till the Muse of History gives up the ghost; some Northern men have the American sentiment, and the American idea, put the man before the dollar, counting man the substance, property the accident. The sentiment and idea of liberty are bottomed on Christianity, as that on human nature; they are quite sure to prevail; the spirit of the nation is on their side — the spirit of the age and the everlasting right.

It is instructive to see how the political parties have hitherto kept clear of anti-slavery. It is "no part of the whig doctrine;" the democrats abhor it. Mr. Webster, it is true, once claimed the Wilmot

Proviso as his thunder, but he cannot wield it, and so it slips out of his hands, and runs round to the chair of his brother senator from New Hampshire.* No leading politician in America has ever been a leader against slavery. Even Mr. Adams only went as he was pushed. True, among the whigs there are Giddings, Palfrey, Tuck, Mann, Root, and Julian; among the democrats there is Hale — and a few others; but what are they among so many? The members of the family of Truth are unpopular, they make excellent servants but hard masters, while the members of the family of Interest are all respectable, and are the best company in the world; their livery is attractive; their motto, "The almighty dollar," is a passport everywhere. Now it happens that some of the more advanced members of the family of Truth fight their way into "good society," and make matrimonial alliances with some of the poor relations of the family of Interest. Straightway they become respectable; the church publishes the banns; the marriage is solemnized in the most Christian form; the attorney declares it legal. So the gospel and law are satisfied, Truth and Interest made one, and many persons after this alliance may be seen in the company of Truth who before knew not of her existence.

The free soil party has grown out of the anti-

* Mr. John P. Hale.

slavery movement. It will have no more slave territory, but does not touch slavery in the States, or between them, and says nothing against the compromises of the Constitution; the time has not come for that. The party has been organized in haste, and is composed, as are all parties, of most discordant materials, some of its members seeming hardly familiar with the idea; some are not yet emancipated from old prejudices, old methods of action, and old interests; but the greater part seem hostile to slavery in all its forms. The immediate triumph of this new party is not to be looked for; not desirable. In Massachusetts they have gained large numbers in a very short period, and under every disadvantage. What their future history is to be, we will not now attempt to conjecture; but this is plain, that they cannot remain long in their present position; either they will go back, and, after due penance, receive political absolution from the church of the whigs, or the democrats, — and this seems impossible, — or else they must go forward where the idea of justice impels them. One day the motto "No more slave territory" will give place to this, "No slavery in America." The revolution in ideas is not over till that is done, nor the corresponding revolution in deeds while a single slave remains in America. A man who studies the great movements of mankind feels sure that that day is not far off; that no combination of northern and southern interest, no declamation, no violence, no love of money, no party zeal, no fraud and no lies, no compromise, can long put off the time. Bad passions will ere long league with the holiest love of right, and that wickedness may be put down with the strong hand which might easily be ended at little cost and without any violence, even of speech. One day the democratic party of the North will remember the grievances which they have suffered from the South, and, if they embrace the idea of freedom, no constitutional scruple will long hold them from destroying the "peculiar institution." What slavery is in the middle of the nineteenth century is quite plain; what it will be at the beginning of the twentieth it is not difficult to foresee. The slave power has gained a great victory: one more such will cost its life. South Carolina did not forget her usual craft in voting for a northern man that was devoted to slavery.

Let us now speak briefly of the conduct of the election. It has been attended, at least in New England, with more intellectual action than any election that I remember, and with less violence, denunciation, and vulgar appeals to low passions and sordid interest. Massachusetts has shown herself worthy of her best days; the free soil vote may be looked on with pride, by men who conscientiously cast their ballot the other way. Men of ability and integrity have been active on both sides, and able speeches have been made, while the vulgarity that marked the "Harrison campaign" has not been repeated.

In this contest the democratic party made a good confession, and "owned up" to the full extent of their conduct. They stated the question at issue, fairly, clearly, and entirely; the point could not be mistaken. The Baltimore Convention dealt honestly in declaring the political opinions of the party; the opinions of their candidate on the great party questions, and the subject of slavery, were made known with exemplary clearness and fidelity. The party did not fight in the dark; they had no dislike to holding slaves, and they pretended none. In all parts of the land they went before the people with the same doctrines and the same arguments; everywhere they "repudiated" the Wilmot Proviso. This gave them an advantage over a party with a different policy. They had a platform of doctrines; they knew what it was; the party stood on the platform; the candidate stood on it.

The whig party have conducted differently; they did not publish their confession of faith. We know what was the whig platform in 1840 and in 1844. But what is it in 1848? Particular men may publish their opinions, but the doctrines of the party are "not communicated to the public." For once in the history of America there was a whig convention which passed no "Resolutions;" it was the Convention at Philadelphia. But on one point, of the greatest importance too, it expressed the opinions of the whigs: it rejected the Wilmot Proviso, and Mr. Webster's thunder, which had fallen harmless and without lightning from his hands, was "kicked out of the meeting!" As the party had no platform, so their candidate had no political opinions. "What!" says one, "Choose a President who does not declare his opinions, — then it must be because they are perfectly well known!" Not at all: General Taylor is raw in politics, and has not taken his first "drill!" "Then he must be a man of such great political and moral ability, that his will may take the place of reason!" Not at all: he is known only as a successful soldier, and his reputation is scarcely three years old. Mr. Webster declared his nomination "not fit to be made," and nobody has any authentic statement of his political opinions; perhaps not even General Taylor himself.

In the electioneering campaign there has been a certain duplicity in the supporters of General Taylor: at the North it was maintained that he was not opposed to the Wilmot Proviso, while at the South quite uniformly the opposite was maintained. This duplicity had the appearance of dishonesty. In New England the whigs did not meet the facts and arguments of the free soil party; in the beginning of the campaign the attempt was made, but was afterwards comparatively abandoned; the matter of slavery was left out of the case, and the old question of the sub-treasury and the tariff was brought up again, and a stranger would have thought, from some whig newspapers, that that was the only question of any importance. Few men were prepared to see a man of the ability and experience of Mr. Webster in his electioneering speeches pass wholly over the subject of slavery. The nation is presently to decide whether slavery is to extend over the new territory or not; even in a commercial and financial point of view, this is far more important than the question of banks and tariffs; but when its importance is estimated by its relation to freedom, right, human welfare in general, — we beg the pardon of American politicians for speaking of such things, — one is amazed to find the whig party of the opinion that it is more important to restore the tariff of 1842 than to prohibit slavery in a country as large as the thirteen States which fought the Revolution! It might have been expected of little, ephemeral men — minute politicians, who are the pest of the State, — but when at such a crisis a great man rises,* amid a sea of upturned faces, to instruct the lesser men, and forgets right, forgets freedom, forgets man, and forgets God, talking only of the tariff and of banks, why a stranger is amazed, till he remembers the

* Hon. Daniel Webster.

peculiar relation of the great man to the moneyed men, — that he is their attorney, retained, paid, and pensioned to do the work of men whose interest it is to keep the question of slavery out of sight. If General Cavaignac had received a pension from the manufacturers of Lyons and of Lisle, to the amount of half a million of francs, should we be surprised if he forgot the needy millions of the land? Nay, only if he did not forget them!

It was a little hardy to ask the anti-slavery men to vote for General Taylor; it was like asking the members of a temperance society to choose an eminent distiller for president of their association. Still, we know that honest anti-slavery men did honestly vote for him. We know nothing to impeach the political integrity of General Taylor; the simple fact that he is a slaveholder, seems reason enough why he should not be President of a nation who believe that "All men are created equal, and endowed by their Creator with certain unalienable rights." Men will be astonished in the next century to learn that the "model republic," had such an affection for slaveholders. Here is a remarkable document, which we think should be preserved:

DEED OF SALE.

"John Hagard, Sr. To Zachariah Taylor.

"*Received for Record*, 18*th Feb.*, 1843.

"*This Indenture*, made this twenty-first day of April, eighteen hundred and forty-two, between John Hagard, Sr., of the City of

New Orleans, State of Louisiana, of one part, and Zachariah Taylor, of the other part, *Witnesseth*, that the said John Hagard, Sr., for and in consideration of the sum of *Ninety-Five Thousand Dollars* to him in hand paid, and secured to be paid, as hereafter stated by the said Zachariah Taylor, at and before the sealing and delivering of these presents, has this day bargained, sold, and delivered, conveyed, and confirmed, and by these Presents does bargain, sell, deliver, and confirm unto the said Zachariah Taylor, his heirs and assigns, forever, all that plantation and tract of land: . . . .

"Also, all the following Slaves — Nelson, Milley, Peldea, Mason, Willis, Rachel, Caroline, Lucinda, Ramdall, Wirman, Carson, Little Ann, Winna, Jane, Tom, Sally, Gracia, Big Jane, Louisa, Maria, Charles, Barnard, Mira, Sally, Carson, Paul, Sansford, Mansfield, Harry Oden, Harry Horley, Carter, Henrietta, Ben, Charlotte, Wood, Dick, Harrietta, Clarissa, Ben, Anthony, Jacob, Hamby, Jim, Gabriel, Emeline, Armstead, George, Wilson, Cherry, Peggy, Walker, Jane, Wallace, Bartlett, Martha, Letitia, Barbara, Matilda, Lucy, John, Sarah, Bigg Ann, Allen, Tom, George, John, Dick, Fielding, Nelson, or Isom, Winna, Shellod, Lidney, Little Cherry, Puck, Sam, Hannah or Anna, Mary, Ellen, Henrietta, and two small children: — Also, all the Horses, Mules, Cattle, Hogs, Farming Utensils, and Tools, now on said Plantation — together with all and singular, the hereditaments, appurtenances, privileges, and advantages unto the said Land and Slaves belonging or appertaining. *To have and to hold* the said Plantation and tract of Land and Slaves, and other property above described, unto the said Zachariah Taylor, his heirs and assigns, for ever, and to his and to their only proper use, benefits, and behoof, for ever. And the said John Hagard, Sr., for himself, his heirs, executors, and administrators, does covenant, promise, and agree to and with said Zachariah Taylor, his heirs and assigns, that the aforesaid Plantation and tract of Land and Slaves, and other property, with the appurtenances, unto the said Zachariah Taylor, his heirs, and assigns against the claim or claims of all persons whomsoever claiming or to claim the same, or any part or parcel thereof, shall and will warrant, and by these Presents for ever defend.

"*In Testimony Whereof*, the said John Hagard, Sr., has hereunto set his hand and seal, the day and year first above written."

If this document had been discovered among some Egyptian papyri, with the date 1848 before Christ, it would have been remarkable as a sign of the times. In a republic, nearly four thousand years later, it has a meaning which some future historian will appreciate.

The free soil party have been plain and explicit as the democrats; they published their creed in the celebrated Buffalo platform. The questions of sub-treasury and tariff are set aside; "No more slave territory" is the watchword. In part they represent an interest, for slavery is an injury to the North in many ways, and to a certain extent puts the North into the hands of the South; but chiefly an idea. Nobody thought they would elect their candidate, whosoever he might be; they could only arrest public attention and call men to the great questions at issue, and so, perhaps, prevent the evil which the South was bent on accomplishing. This they have done, and done well. The result has been highly gratifying. It was pleasant and encouraging to see men ready to sacrifice their old party attachments and their private interests, oftentimes, for the sake of a moral principle. I do not mean to say that there was no moral principle in the other parties — I know better. But it seems to me that the free soilers committed a great error in selecting Mr. Van Buren as their candidate. True, he is a man of ability, who has held the highest offices and acquitted himself honorably in all; but he had been the "Northern man, with Southern principles;" had shown a degree of subserviency to the South, which was remarkable, if not singular or strange: his promise, made and repeated in the most solemn manner, to veto any act of Congress, abolishing slavery in the capital, was an insult to the country, and a disgrace to himself. He had a general reputation for instability, and want of political firmness. It is true, he had opposed the annexation of Texas, and lost his nomination in 1844 by that act; but it is also true that he advised his party to vote for Mr. Polk, who was notoriously in favor of annexation. His nomination, I must confess, was unfortunate; the Buffalo Convention seems to have looked at his availability more than his fitness, and, in their contest for a principle, began by making a compromise of that very principle itself. It was thought he could "carry" the State of New York; and so a man who was not a fair representative of the idea, was set up. It was a bad beginning. It is better to be defeated a thousand times, rather than seem to succeed by a compromise of the principle contended for. Still, enough has been done, to show the nation that the dollar is not almighty; that the South is not always to insult the North, and rule the land, annexing, plundering, and making slaves when she will; that the North has men who will not abandon the great sentiment of freedom, which is the boast of the nation and the age.

General Taylor is elected by a large popular vote; some voted for him on account of his splendid military success; some because he is a slaveholder, and true to the interests of the slave power; some because he is a "Good whig," and wants a high tariff of duties. But we think there are men who gave him their support, because he has never been concerned in the intrigues of a party, is indebted to none for past favors, is pledged to none, bribed by none, and intimidated by none; because he seems to be an honest man, with a certain rustic intelligence; a plain blunt man, that loves his country and mankind. We hope this was a large class. If he is such a man, he will enter upon his office under favorable auspices, and with the best wishes of all good men.

But what shall the free soil party do next? they cannot go back, — conscience waves behind them her glittering wings and bids them on; they cannot stand still, for as yet their measures and their watchword do not fully represent their idea. They must go forward, as the early abolitionists went, with this for their motto: "No slavery in America." "He that would lead men, must walk but one step before them;" says somebody. Well, but he must think many steps before them, or they will presently tread him under their feet. The present success of the idea is doubtful; the interests of the South will demand the extension of slavery;* the interests of the

---

* The following extract, from the *Charleston Mercury*, shows the feeling of the South. "Pursuant to a call, a meeting of the citizens of Orangeburg District was held to-day, 6th November, in the court-house, which was well filled on the occasion. . . . . Gen. D. F. Jamison then rose, and moved the appointment of a committee of twenty-five, to take into consideration the continued agitation by Congress of the question of slavery; . . . . the committee, through their chairman, Gen. Jamison, made the following report:—

"The time has arrived when the slaveholding States of the confederacy must take decided action upon the continued attacks of the North against their domestic institutions, or submit in silence to that humiliating position in the opinions of mankind, that longer acquiescence must inevitably reduce them to. . . . . The agitation of the subject of slavery commenced in the fanatical murmurings of a few scattered abolitionists, to whom it was a long time confined; but now it has swelled into a torrent of popular opinion at the North; it has invaded the fireside and the church, the press and the halls of legislation; it has seized upon the deliberations of Congress, and at this moment is sapping the foundations, and about to overthrow the fairest political structure that the ingenuity of man has ever devised.

"The overt efforts of abolitionism were confined for a long period to annoying applications to Congress, under color of the pretended

party now coming into power, will demand their peculiar boon. So another compromise is to be feared,

---

right of petition; it has since directed the whole weight of its malign influence against the annexation of Texas, and had well-nigh cost to the country the loss of that important province; but emboldened by success and the inaction of the South, in an unjust and selfish spirit of national agrarianism it would now appropriate the whole public domain. It might well have been supposed that the undisturbed possession of the whole of Oregon Territory would have satisfied the non-slaveholding States. This they now hold, by the incorporation of the ordinance of 1787 into the bill of the last session for establishing a territorial government for Oregon. That provision, however, was not sustained by them from any apprehension that the territory could ever be settled from the States of the South, but it was intended as a gratuitous insult to the southern people, and a malignant and unjustifiable attack upon the institution of slavery.

"We are called upon to give up the whole public domain to the fanatical cravings of abolitionism, and the unholy lust of political power. A territory, acquired by the whole country for the use of all, where treasure has been squandered like chaff, and southern blood poured out like water, is sought to be appropriated by one section, because the other chooses to adhere to an institution held not only under the guaranties that brought this confederacy into existence, but under the highest sanction of Heaven. Should we quietly fold our hands under this assumption on the part of the non-slaveholding States, the fate of the South is sealed, the institution of slavery is gone, and its existence is but a question of time. . . . . Your committee are unwilling to anticipate what will be the result of the combined wisdom and joint action of the southern portion of the confederacy on this question; but as an initiatory step to a concert of action on the part of the peo-

and the extension of slavery yet further West. But the ultimate triumph of the genius of freedom is cer-

---

ple of South Carolina, they respectfully recommend, for the adoption of this meeting, the following resolutions: —

"*Resolved*, That the continued agitation of the question of slavery, by the people of the non-slaveholding States, by their legislatures, and by their representatives in Congress, exhibits not only a want of national courtesy, which should always exist between kindred States, but is a palpable violation of good faith towards the slaveholding States, who adopted the present Constitution 'in order to form a more perfect union.'

"*Resolved*, That while we acquiesce in adopting the boundary between the slaveholding and non-slaveholding States, known as the Missouri Compromise line, we will not submit to any further restriction upon the rights of any southern man to carry his property and his institutions into territory acquired by southern treasure and by southern blood.

"*Resolved*, That should the Wilmot Proviso, or any other restriction, be applied by Congress to the territories of the United States, south of 36 deg. 30 min. north latitude, we recommend to our representative in Congress, as the decided opinion of this portion of his district, to leave his seat in that body, and return home.

"*Resolved*, That we respectfully suggest to both houses of the legislature of South Carolina, to adopt a similar recommendation as to our senators in Congress from this State.

"*Resolved*, That upon the return home of our senators and representatives in Congress, the legislature of South Carolina should be forthwith assembled to adopt such measures as the exigency may demand.

"The resolutions were then submitted, *seriatim*, and, together with the report, were unanimously adopted."

tain. In Europe, it shakes the earth with mighty tread; thrones fall before its conquering feet. While in the eastern continent, kings, armies, emperors, are impotent before that power, shall a hundred thousand slaveholders stay it here with a bit of parchment?

www.ingramcontent.com/pod-product-compliance
Lightning Source LLC
LaVergne TN
LVHW020109110826
845151LV00001B/115

* 9 7 8 1 4 2 5 5 4 3 8 7 7 *